# SO MUCH SADNESS
# SO MUCH FUN

## RAF Ibsley 1941 – 1952

Compiled by Vera Smith
of
The RAF Ibsley Historical Group

Published by
The R.A.F. Ibsley Historical Group
Norden
Mockbeggar Lane
Ibsley
Ringwood
BH24 3PR

Copyright © 2002

All rights reserved. No part of this publication may be reproduced, stored in a retrieval system, or transmitted in any form or by any means, electronic, mechanical, photocopying, recording or otherwise, without prior permission in writing from R.A.F. Ibsley Historical Group.

First published 1997
Revised and updated 2002

ISBN 0 9530931 1 5

Produced by
The Short Run Book Company Ltd
St Stephen's House
Arthur Road
Windsor
Berkshire
SL4 1RY

Foreword
by
Wing Commander Christopher 'Bunny' F. Currant,
D.S.O., D.F.C. and Bar, Croix de Guerre.

Vera Smith of the R.A.F. Ibsley Historical Group is to be congratulated for the amount of research she has put into compiling this revised edition of "So Much Sadness, So Much Fun", R.A.F. Ibsley 1941-1952. Five years after it was first published it contains an even more wonderful miscellany of history and personal stories. The crowded details of the World War II airfield at Ibsley, just outside of Ringwood in Hampshire, which is my favourite County, and was my favourite Fighter Airfield. Although it had a very short life, what a life it has to tell as both an R.A.F. Fighter Station and United States Army Air Force Fighter base, then for several years, post-war, an accommodation base for personnel working at R.A.F. Sopley. What a magnificent contribution Ibsley made to the defence of England in those turbulent wartime days. One of the many busy, busy, never stop defence posts of Fighter Command and the U.S.A.A.F. Fighter Groups. So many historical details and fascinating stories in this book to keep one reading late into the night. A compilation of astounding detail and exciting, sad, and funny events of those incredible years. I am lost for words. Readers, this is a book not to be missed.

C.F. Currant
Wg Cdr (Retd)

30th April, 2002.

*Wing-Commander C.F.Currant, D.S.O., D.F.C. and Bar,
Croix de Guerre, Station Commander, R.A.F. Ibsley, 1942, pictured in 1940 as a Flt. Lt.*
Photo: W/Cdr. Currant

Born in December, 1911, Christopher 'Bunny' Currant, entered the Royal Air Force in 1936. On completion of training he joined No. 46 Squadron as a Sgt Pilot. This was followed by moves to No. 151 and then 605 Squadrons. He was commissioned in 1940. Awarded the D.F.C. in October, 1940 and a Bar to this in November. Early in 1941 was posted to No. 52 Officer Training Unit at Debden where, in July, he became Chief Flying Instructor. In August 'Bunny' Currant took command of No. 501 Squadon at Ibsley. In 1942 was promoted to Station Commander at Ibsley, and on July 7th awarded the D.S.O. He left Ibsley in August 1942, moving to Zeals to form and command 122 Wing, which he led in June 1944 during D-Day. Was awarded the Belgian Croix de Guerre. After a four month lecture tour, in the United States went to Control Centre, 84 Group, in Holland. After various post-war appointments Wing Commander C. F. Currant, D.S.O., D.F.C. and Bar, C. de G., retired from the Royal Air Force in January 1959. Of those five and a half years of war, he says:. "They have worn a groove in me which has never really gone. That period ate up so much of my energy. So much emotion. Tense concern and anxiety. So much hope, fear, excitement every day. In those years I was swamped with emotions which never let up. I find it incredible, almost, awe inspiring, that I survived it all and am still here. I survived seven events:

1  August 1939. Oxygen total loss 26,000 feet. Woke up at 4,000 feet in dive over Chelmsford. Slap above city centre.
2. April 1940. Collision North Scotland, 2 Hurricanes. My colleague killed, I survived.
3. May 1940. Dunkirk period over Northern France. Crash landed. Broken nose. Hitched to Calais.
4. Battle of Britain, 1940. Five months. Not a scratch.
5. 1941. Over France, in fog. Survived loss of controls.
6. 1942. Over France. Bullet in skull. Somersault on landing in England.
7. Normandy. Shelled one day, mortared the next. Not a scratch.

No wonder gratitude and incredulous amazement swamps me, even now."

The R.A.F. Ibsley Historical Group
dedicate this book to all those
(named and unnamed within its pages)
who lost their lives whilst
serving or, or based at
R.A.F. Ibsley, 1941 to 1952
also to
Peter Smith, founder member and Secretary of the Group
who passed away in March 2002.

"So Much Sadness, So Much Fun" has been compiled from personal stories and diary extracts contributed by those who were at Ibsley, also information given by relatives of others who served at the Station during its operational years, various book sources, and newspaper cuttings of events at the time they happened and public records. Whilst some historical details are listed, the stories contained in this book give only a glimpse of life at this busy Fighter Station. Also included are some of the boyhood memories of the late Peter Smith, Group Secretary, for nearly ten years until the time of his death, who lived in the village of Ibsley all his life, and whose boyhood wartime home was situated just yards from the end of one of the Ibsley Airfield runways.

The R.A.F. Ibsley Historical Group, which was formed in 1992, has members worldwide. Among its aims are the putting in touch again after many years, comrades who served at Ibsley, and also relatives of those who served and lost their lives in the service of their country.

The title for this book came from a W.A.A.F. Ambulance Driver stationed at Ibsley, Hazel Sims (maiden name Sheppard) who said those wartime days were ones of "So Much Sadness, So Much Fun".

Whilst every effort has been made to verify historical details please accept our apologies for any errors made.

## Contents

| | |
|---|---|
| 1940-1941, Airfield Construction – Operations Begin | 9 |
| 1942, Backs to the wall | 59 |
| 1943, A busy year, many comings and goings | 123 |
| 1944, Generous Americans at Ibsley | 164 |
| 1945, Dakotas, Gliders and Victory | 185 |
| 1946-1952, End of an Era | 195 |
| Summer-Lug Gen | 229 |
| Bits and Pieces | 237 |
| Hints for Pilots | 242 |
| The Formation of an R.A.F. Fighter Squadron | 246 |
| Operational Code Names | 247 |
| Memories | 248 |
| Roll of Honour | 249 |
| Appendix | 260 |
| Acknowledgements | 268 |
| Bibliography | 271 |

Front cover picture from an original painting by Don Williams. Spitfire of No. 118 Squadron coming in to land over Ibsley Church and Spitfires of No. 501 Squadron.

Back cover: R.A.F. Ibsley Commemorative Plaque at Cross Lanes, Mockbeggar, (North East corner of wartime airfield).

# 1940/41
## *Airfield Construction – Operations Begin*

In Southern England, midway between Ringwood and Fordingbridge, on the Western Edge of the New Forest, in Hampshire, alongside the River Avon, once famous for its salmon fishing, lies the village of Ibsley, with its pretty thatched cottages overlooking the river and water meadows of Harbridge to the West. The village, although mentioned in Domesday Book, as Tibbeslei, was not, before the Second World War, steeped in history. The little red brick Church of St. Martin's, re-built in 1852, on the site of an earlier church, was declared redundant in 1990, and is now used as an art gallery. It houses a curious monument to Sir John Constable, Knight, and his wife, who was the sister-in-law of the essayist Francis Bacon, (1627). The monument, from the earlier church, embodies the heads of their five children, also shields and arms intertwined with vine.

However, the tranquil life of Ibsley and the nearby hamlets of Mockbeggar, Rockford, South Gorley, North Gorley, and Ellingham changed dramatically in 1940 with the construction of an airfield, which for the remainder of the Second World War became a busy Royal Air Force and United States Army Air Force station. The farm fields which were taken over for the purpose, formed part of the Earl of Normanton's Somerley Estate, and were, at that time, farmed mainly by tenant farmers, Mr. Harold Bennett of Mockbeggar Farm and Mr. William Sampson of Ellingham Farm, and in a small part by Mr. James Sampson from Evans Farm, South Gorley, now known as Hucklesbrook Farm. The main contractors were Mowlems, a firm still in existence, but there were also a number of other sub-contractors.

To-day, many motorists travelling along the main A338 from Ringwood to Fordingbridge, and vice versa, will be unaware that between Ibsley and Ellingham, their journey is taking them along a road which was the Western boundary of such a busy wartime Fighter aerodrome.

Peter Smith was a six year old boy in the early days of the War, and his first memory of hostilities was when local villagers began digging air-raid shelters in their gardens. He recalled how his father, Fred, got together with a neighbour, Sid Gould, a veteran of the Battle of Jutland in the First World War, and dug a six foot deep shelter, with steps leading down into it. Galvanised iron sheets with earth piled on top formed the roof. On the first day the shelter was found to be full of water, so proved useless. Concerned that they might become trapped if their home was bombed, Peter's mother, Dorothy, decided that they should push their large dining table up against the fireplace opening of the chimney breast so that they could at least get some air via the flue if such a situation arose. Enough non-perishable food to last for a week was stored under the table. Peter remembers how the air raid warning siren sounded, they all got under the table, and during that first night ate all the food. They didn't bother any more after that, just took things as they came.

Early in 1940 evacuees started coming into Ibsley and the surrounding villages from both Portsmouth and Southampton, to be billeted with local families.

Ibsley airfield was originally bounded by Mockbeggar Lane to the North, Gorley Road (also known as Birch Lane) to the East, Ellingham Drove to the South and the A338 road to the West, but after a year the main North-South runway of 1,600 yards was extended from Ellingham Drove, which entailed a road diversion, further southward to Ivy Lane at Blashford, the total length then was recorded as being 3,600 yards, while the South East-North West runway was 1,700 yards and the South West-North East 1,500 yards, all were 50 yards wide. Construction of the airfield started in the Autumn of 1940, but it was not completed however, until long after it had become operational. Most of the preparatory work consisted of removing hedges and trees from two small woods, namely Game Copse and Pigot Piece. The surrounding villages and hamlets were then rocked by explosions when the roots of the larger trees which had been felled were blasted out by dynamite. These were then hauled by the lorries of Hines Bros., of Blashford, to two old gravel pits on Ibsley Common, to the East of the airfield, just beyond the property then known as Mockbeggar Slade. A small stream which

## 1940-1941

ran from Mockbeggar Lane across to Ellingham Drove had to be piped and covered. This stream was formed from ditches carrying water from Newtown and Ibsley Common.

Much of the hardcore for the foundations of the main runways and perimeter track at Ibsley was rubble from bomb damaged buildings in Southampton.

There were eight sites constructed, six of which were quarters sites and two communal. The quarters sites were at Gorley, Cuckoo Hill, Ibsley Drove, Newlands Plantation, Newtown Hill and South Gorley.

The Communal sites were at Gorley and South Gorley, the latter being the biggest, and containing: 'The N.A.A.F.I.' (where Ibsley's Village Hall now stands), Gymnasium, Tailor's shop, Barber's shop, Shoemaker's shop, Post Office, Officer's Mess, Sergeant's Mess and Airmen's Mess.

There were numerous other buildings including emergency water tanks and shelters. Several of the sites were connected to a hastily built sewerage system, the sewer beds for which were situated between Ibsley and Hucklesbrook. After treatment the purified water (crystal clear) was discharged into the River Avon. Today, over fifty years on, the residents of Ibsley have to rely on their own septic tanks for drainage. So much for progress!

The Station Headquarters was situated in Moyles Court House, the ancient manor house which was the ancestral home of the Lisle family. Dame Alicia was the widow of Colonel John Lisle, one of the judges of Charles I and M.P., for Winchester in 1640. At the Restoration of the Monarchy he fled to the Continent and was murdered in Switzerland. On the night of July 28th, 1685, after the Sedgemoor battle and flight of Monmouth, Dame Alicia, then seventy years old, and a loyalist, as was also her son, who was in the army, gave shelter and food to two fugitives from the rebel camp – a dissenting minister and a lawyer. King's troops entered Moyles Court House and arrested the rebels and the poor lady. She was arraigned before Judge Jeffreys, who had just opened his Bloody Assize at Winchester. Twice did a jury respect her age and Christian kindness and acquit her, but Jeffreys bullied another jury to condemn her. Jeffreys gave direction that Alice Lisle should be burned alive, but this was later commuted from burning to beheading. She was put to death on a scaffold in the market-place of

## So Much Sadness, So Much Fun

*Eastwood House, Mockbeggar Lane, used as Watch Office and Officer's Quarters, 1941/42*
Photo: M. Lambert

*Station Headquarters, 1941-1946, Moyles Court House,
the outbuildings of which were used as the M.T. Sections*
Photo: The Moyles Court Old Pupils Association

## 1940-1941

Winchester. The tomb of Dame Alice Lisle is near the South door of Ellingham Church.

The yards and outbuildings of Moyles Court were used as the station's M.T. Sections.

Mockbeggar Slade (was re-named Crossley Towers, after the first Commanding Officer at Ibsley, Squadron Leader Michael Crossley, D.S.O., D.F.C., of No. 32 Squadron, a name it carries to this day). Lying at the foot of Ibsley Common it was requisitioned as an Officers' Mess, and later as W.A.A.F. quarters. It was a beautiful country retreat into which the owners, Mr. and Mrs. Bostock, had put much loving care in the layout of their garden which had been built up on reclaimed moorland. Streams, ponds with goldfish, rockeries and many rare plants and trees provided a scene of beauty and tranquillity. One could not help feeling sorry for the owners, who after years of toil in India had returned to the peace of England only to be uprooted in the cause of military necessity. The late Audrey Warner, a W.A.A.F. at Ibsley recalled being bitten by a rat when billeted at Crossley Towers.

Beacon Cottage, just down the lane from Mockbeggar Slade, was another pretty little house, with an equally pretty garden with rockeries, to be requisitioned, as was Cuckoo Hill House at South Gorley which belonged to the well known local Antiquary and artist Heywood Sumner, F.S.A. The latter was a comparatively modern house built in the early Edwardian style with a pleasantly set out sloping garden, a vegetable plot and apple orchard. Chatley Wood, a charming thatched cottage at Rockford, again with well laid out gardens, was also requisitioned for use as an Officers' Mess.

Early on, before the airfield Control Tower was built, another property was requisitioned and used to control the aircraft, Eastwood House in Mockbeggar Lane. A mobile caravan was also used, while a small single storey Watch Office was built, on the airfield, to a 17658/40 specification.

The Control Tower, or Watch Office to use R.A.F. terminology, (which still stands today), was positioned on the inside corner of Cherry Orchard, and can still be seen from the Mockbeggar to Moyles Court road. This Control Tower was based on a drawing, No. 518/40, a Watch Office with Meteorological Section, and was for a brick and timber building. A further drawing, No. 8936/40 called for only the floor above the watch office room and balcony to be in

13

timber, the remaining floor area, roof and staircase to be in pre-cast concrete slabwork. This was achieved by replacing the internal 4.5 inch walls with load-bearing 9 inch walls to support the heavier floor. At Ibsley timber was replaced altogether at first floor level by concrete, and this was one of the few Control Towers constructed with a concrete balcony. It is believed that the Ibsley Control Tower is unique, in that it was the only one constructed to the modified drawing, with the use of concrete in the balcony, first floor and stairways. This is probably the reason it is still standing, and the only known example still in reasonably good condition. The walls are believed to be structurally sound but it is minus windows and has a very leaky roof.

Aviation fuel installations were situated near to the Control Tower, halfway down Ellingham Drove, and behind what, in those War days was Rockford School (now the Alice Lisle Public House). There was an M.T. Fuel installation at the Moyles Court end of Ellingham Drove, and also at Moyles Court itself, the concrete pillar on which it stood still being there to this day.

Two large Bellman Hangars were erected at Ibsley, one was situated to the East of the airfield, off the Gorley Road, and the other off Ellingham Drove. Records show twelve blister hangars were to be situated around the airfield, although it is believed only nine were constructed. The number of hard standings were listed as thirty six, Tarmac (circular and pen type).

The station armoury and workshops were situated in the small copse known as Cherry Orchard, on the East side of the airfield, to the North of Moyles Court, while the Fire Station sheds were opposite the property Keepers Cottage (now called Forelock Farm). Keepers Cottage itself, across the road from the main gate, was used as the Fire Headquarters, and John Laverie who served with the Fire Section at Ibsley in 1941, recalled how three of them slept in a bell tent on the front lawn. Their food was supplied by the Army and they very often had to chase the free roaming New Forest ponies off the airfield in the morning.

At North Gorley, some two miles North of the Airfield, the 'As You Like it Motel', alongside the main A338 road, which has seen many name changes over the years, but is presently known as 'The Open Country', was initially used as a Mess, but later converted into the Station Hospital and Dentistry.

## 1940-1941

L.A.C. Maurice Barrett who served with No. 32 Squadron was billeted there in 1941. Maurice recalled some of the many variety artistes who performed in shows at Ibsley, including Len and Bill Lowe, and Johnny Lockwood who has appeared in the present day soap 'Neighbours'. It is also widely believed that singer Al Bowley performed at Ibsley.

Ibsley's village Church, St. Martin's, sadly closed in 1990, was used by the Station, and Church records (now in the Hampshire Record Office at Winchester), show that regular Sunday morning R.A.F. Church Parades were held there. The services were conducted, mainly, by the Station Chaplain, Reverend Catley.

There was a large site of Nissen Huts in what is known as Newlands Wood and these were used by the American Negroes when Ibsley was occupied by the U.S.A.A.F., in 1942 and 1944. They were, however, well segregated and also had different meal-times and their own officers.

Daisy Porter who was with the N.A.A.F.I. at Ibsley recalled how she would get cakes from Bickham's Bakery in Ringwood High Street and others and slab-cake from the N.A.A.F.I. Daisy operated the N.A.A.F.I. van on the airfield and said the young coloured lads didn't dare come up to it until all the white Americans had been served. "I was really disliked when it was found out I was keeping some cakes hidden for those coloured lads", said Daisy.

Gun Pits (mainly Bofors) were situated on the main A338 road at Ellingham, on Ibsley Common, near Bridge Farm at Ibsley, and North of Mockbeggar Lane, not far from Cross Lanes Chapel. There was a Rifle Range off the Linwood Road, the wall of which was approximately 55 feet long and 15 inches wide, with a sandbank on one side into which bullets were fired, from across the stream known as Dockens Water. In front of the target area there was an iron trolley, on rails, which was pulled backwards and forwards with a very long rope. This provided a moving target. The wall and sandbank are still there to-day, but the iron rails have gone and it is understood that shortly after the war the trolley itself was pushed into Dockens Water by a group of local lads, but what became of it after that is not known.

The Battle Headquarters at Ibsley was built deep into the hillside of Newlands, off the Moyles Court – Gorley road, behind Keepers Cottage. That too, is still there to-day. It has two Observation Post blocks which again is considered to be unique. It has been suggested the reason for this is, probably, that the first was originally intended to cover the old airfield, but when the runway was extended Southward to Ivy Lane the field of vision had to be increased, hence the second Observation Post block.

An interesting method of airfield defence was provided at Ibsley by the Parachute and Cable Unit (P.A.C. Unit). They were equipped with rocket batteries situated around the airfield. Each rocket was attached to a large diameter steel cable, and was also fitted with a parachute to hold the cable in position once airborne. Then in the event of an enemy aircraft attacking the airfield, these rockets would be fired to create a barrage of wires in its path, with the intent of either the cables fouling the propellers or the wings, or just deterring the aircraft from flying too low. Whether it was ever used is open to doubt.

However, Sid Watson, a Royal Canadian Air Force Pilot, who served at Ibsley in 1942, first with No. 234 Squadron, then No. 118 Squadron, gave us the following story. In his own words Sid said: "What interested me for a time was the sight of a bod wearing a leather jerkin and a steel helmet, sitting in a hole in the ground, not far from our dispersal hut. There were a number of these people sitting in these little holes all around the perimeter of the airfield. Curiosity getting the better of me, I ambled over to the nearest one, and probably breaking the 'Official Secrets Act' enquired what the hell he was doing down there day after day. As he was bored to death, he was only too eager to disregard the 'OSA' and divulge his purpose in life and how he may in some small way shorten the war!

(I'll bet you can't wait to become privy to this innermost secret). In the hole, attached to a little control panel was a little "Red" button. If the airfield was attacked by enemy aircraft this chap, after all those hours, all those days, sitting down there in that miserable little hole can finally do something useful and press that "little red button".

Had he ever had occasion to press the button? Well, no he hadn't but he had thought about it, you know just for the hell-of-it. He had been told what a responsible job it was. One little 'press' on that button and look out! A rocket will leave the launching pad at tremendous velocity carrying a wire cable to a height of 1,000 feet where a parachute will deploy, suspending the cable as the parachute slowly sinks to earth. This will take place all around the perimeter of the airfield. "Death to the invader"!!

A week or so later all flying was cancelled because a group of very high officials had arrived for a demonstration. The count-down is commenced. Everyone takes cover! Three-two-one, Zero! There is a fair amount of smoke, and we have lift off! The rockets zoom up to about 50 feet and we have *"fizzle"*, then a crash back to earth. There is a great deal of coiled wire all over the perimeter of the airfield. The 'brass hats' are climbing into their cars. Soon the little holes will all be filled in and the men that were in those little holes will, no doubt, be assigned to some other secret project!"

Also, in 1941, with the threat of invasion, anti-glider obstacles, in the shape of large poles were set into the ground over Ibsley Common, to the North and East of Whitefield Plantation.

Ibsley, R.A.F. Station No. 134, opened on Saturday, 15th February, 1941, as a Fighter Command Station, although it was clearly incomplete at that time, and a local resident recalls seeing two Hurricanes land on the airfield that day. When it was realised that there was a desperate need for another forward airfield it was put into use in an incomplete condition. It was a forward airfield in the Middle Wallop Sector, 10 Group, the headquarters of which were at Rudloe Manor, Box, Wiltshire.

The first Squadron to arrive, on Monday 17th February, 1941, was No. 32, under the Command of Squadron Leader Mike Crossley, D.S.O., D.F.C., with Hurricane Mk I's, code letters GZ. This Squadron, which was formed on 11th October, 1915, had been engaged in the Battle of Britain, flying from Biggin Hill in Kent. They had later moved to Acklington. The Squadron Badge is "A hunting horn 'stringed' and the Motto: "Adeste comites" ("Rally round comrades"). The hunting horn signifies the squadron's ability to hunt the enemy".

On 21st February, just four days after arriving at Ibsley, No. 32 Squadron lost Sergeant Pilot Vaclav Skřivanék, a 22 year old Czechoslovakian, in a tragic accident. Three Hurricanes were giving a demonstration over Bournemouth when Skřivanék failed to pull out of a roll, the pilot being killed when the plane crashed on to properties, Nos. 36 and 38 St. Clements Road. No one on the ground was injured, although the occupant of No. 38 had to be rescued by firemen from the rubble. The decision at the inquest into the crash decided that it was caused by an error of judgement while the plane was flying upside down. Sergeant Pilot Skřivanék is buried in the War Graves section of Ringwood Cemetery.

Shortly after this tragedy, on Sunday 9th March, another Czechoslovakian pilot, of No. 32 Squadron, was killed in an accident only a few hundred yards from Ibsley airfield. During low level aerobatics Sergeant Vladamir Kyselo's Hurricane spun into the ground, alongside the A338, at Blashford. Sergeant Kyselo is buried alongside Vaclav Skřivanék in Ringwood Cemetery.

The Luftwaffe soon found out about the new airfield at Ibsley and promptly bombed it at 23.10 hours on Thursday, 13th March, when about thirty-one light bombs were dropped. Nine fell on one runway, but luckily only one Hurricane was damaged.

Norman Jenkins of Hightown, Ringwood, remembers William Joyce, "Lord Haw Haw", who in the mid-thirties lived alone (except for two Alsatian dogs), in "Lensmere Cottage" at Hightown, just off the lane, known to locals as "Mucky Down".

As a young boy Norman remembers seeing Joyce driving his brown Austin Seven of 1934 vintage with one of his dogs.

Norman's father worked as one of the gardeners at the large house "Lensmere", and he often spoke of the Alsatians playing with baby rabbits on the green outside. No one was ever allowed to enter the grounds of the cottage, and a box on the fence was where the tradesmen and postmen left their deliveries. Norman says he cannot recall William Joyce having any friends at Hightown and he left in about 1937. That was the year he married 26 year old Margaret White.

In August, 1939, Joyce accompanied by his wife, went to Germany from where, in 1940, as "Lord Haw Haw", Joyce, originally an American citizen who had become a naturalised German citizen that year, re-appeared on a German Radio Station, with his slogan "Germany calling, Germany calling". His wife, as "Lady Haw Haw", made her first broadcast on November 10th, 1940 from Berlin. Her weekly talks dealt, in the main, with "women's economic problems" and contrasted, unfavourably, the British social system with that of Germany.

Obviously Joyce "Lord Haw Haw" had spies in this area, for Peter Smith remembers his father Fred recalling, many times, that one

## 1940-1941

Wednesday evening, he heard Joyce broadcasting over the radio the prices which cattle and other goods, sold in Ringwood market earlier in the day, were fetching.

William Joyce, and his wife Margaret, were arrested, in Germany, at different times on May 28th, 1945, and in January, 1946, Joyce was executed in London, after being found guilty of treason. However, Margaret, who was born in Manchester, was spared not only the gallows, but any punishment at all because there was a notable lack of evidence that she too had taken German citizenship. Prior to her husband's execution she was brought to London to be near him, and held in Holloway prison. She was deported to Germany after her husband's execution where she was interned as a security suspect. Eventually she returned to Britain, where she died in 1972.

Although Ibsley was seldom attacked, a stick of bombs was dropped early in the war, probably jettisoned by a bomber being chased. Thirteen bombs in all fell, in a line from Evans Farm (now Hucklesbrook Farm) to the Linwood road. The second of these dropped straight down the well at New Farm, South Gorley, the home of Mr. and Mrs. Jack Thomas and their young daughter Elaine, who were in residence at the time. It blew the heavy iron hand pump, situated not far from their back door, on to the top of the thatched roof of the farmhouse, while a whet-stone finished up on a shed roof. Luckily no one was injured.

The third bomb dropped in farmer Harold Bennett's field, and when carter Fred Smith went to bring in the cart-horses, Jolly and Violet, for work the following morning, he found that his bay coloured charges had turned white with sweat and lather, they were so frightened.

A Fitter 2E with No. 32 Hurricane Squadron, L. W. Rea recalls that being the first squadron to be stationed at Ibsley, everything seemed very basic. He was a member of the Maintenance Flight. All was open air work, wind and weather no obstacle. He remembers an extremely busy period of inspections, repairs, refuelling and re-arming during long days of readiness. Double summertime then with dusk stand-down around 11 p.m. and later.

Rea also remembers that there was no control tower at Ibsley at that time, just the mobile unit, and also that Eastwood House in Mockbeggar Lane was used as the Watch Office. A field kitchen was within walking distance of the maintenance area, and he has recollections of open air early morning breakfasts, huge bully-beef sandwiches for lunch and cocoa late evening. One night he returned from leave to find his Nissen hut empty and on his bed several pieces of shrapnel. This must have been after the raid on March 13th. At the time there was a feeling of apprehension in the air as rumours of invasion were rife. He says one always kept an ear open for the ringing of church bells!! which would have been the signal for invasion.

Roy Warrell also served with No. 32 Squadron and recalls being billeted in an unlined and unpainted wooden hut with feather edged boarding which did not fit at all well and allowed the winds to blow in one side and out the other. In fact it was so strong they had to put rocks on top of their great coats on the beds to stop them being blown off. He also remembers sprinting slowly and reluctantly round the perimeter track at first light for a wash and shave at the water bowser.

Another who came to Ibsley with No. 32 Squadron was Mr. S. T. Curtis, who, because his normal job was not required, was given the post of barman at the Officers' Mess at Crossley Towers, Mockbeggar. For a time Curtis was billeted with Jack and Lily Sharman and their family at Rose Villa, a semi-detached cottage at the bottom of the lane leading to the Mess. If, while walking back to his billet, after closing the bar for the night, he heard enemy aircraft overhead he would dive into the hedge alongside the lane, for fear they would be dropping their bomb load.

In 1941, at the age of fourteen, the late Morris Thompson left school in nearby Ringwood and went to the Labour Office in the town looking for a job. He was told to report to a man at Ibsley, and to paint the airfield. He jumped on his bike, the only transport in those days, met the boss there who told him "there will be three of you boys and the job is to make the airfield look like a farm from the air". They were given a map and each section was done according to the map. Sometimes they would spray around the edges to make it look like a grass paddock and then put a few blobs here and there; that would be the trees, and then some small blobs to look like cattle. In some paddocks they would paint long, thin black lines, that was a ploughed paddock.

In the summer they would work from 7 a.m. to 6 p.m. six days a week. The work was all done by hand, two on the pump and one spraying. The paint was in 44 gallon drums, which were loaded on to a trailer, three or four drums at a time, and pushed and pulled to where they were working. They used to talk to the pilots of the Spitfires while they were sitting in their deck chairs waiting to scramble. When asked "what does the airfield look like from the air"? one pilot replied "You're doing a good job. When we come back its hard to find the bloody place".

At this time there were huge amounts of rabbits inhabiting the airfield, especially in Cherry Orchard, and Mr. Fred Smith, who worked at Mockbeggar Farm was issued with a pass from the Station Warrant Officer to enter restricted area to ferret and net these. They were a very valuable addition to the meagre food rations which were beginning to come into force. Fortunately, Dorothy his wife was a good cook and found many ways of making rabbit appetising.

During its operational years a number of units were based at Ibsley to defend the airfield, carry out aircraft maintenance and provide numerous other services. These included the Dorset Regiment, Royal West Kents, Duke of Cornwall's Light Infantry, 70th Battalion Dorset Regiment Young Soldiers, Royal Hampshire Regiment, Irish Guards, 439 Light Anti-Aircraft Battery, then when formed in 1942, 2763 Squadron of the R.A.F. Regiment.

Daisy Porter recalled how one day a "Panic Stations" situation occurred while she was in a stationary N.A.A.F.I. van on the airfield. Suddenly the R.A.F. Regiment boys were rushing past to surround the airfield. As they passed one shouted out "Don't worry Mrs. Porter, we'll look after you", and the following one said "Well, we would if we had any b..... ammunition. Thank goodness it turned out to be a false alarm.

Maurice Annison was at Ibsley during 1941-1943 on Airfield Defence. He recalled that one day, whilst shooting on the rifle range off the Linwood road, a stray bullet from a Browning gun hit the glycol tank on a Spitfire. The pilot's Perspex canopy was splattered with glycol and the aircraft had to make a hasty landing.

Also at Ibsley were 3042 Servicing Echelon, 44 Works Flight, 49 Maintenance Unit, R.A.F. Police and the Women's Land Army.

Ibsley also had its own Home Guard who met outside the property known as Thatched Eaves, alongside the main A338 road. The late Tom Sampson of Harbridge Farm recalled that their armoury was situated in the end room of the property which is now The Old Beams public house.

Les Holmes was an R.A.F. Ground Gunner at Ibsley, in 1941, and transferred to the R.A.F. Regiment on its formation in February, 1942. He was employed mostly on the Bofors Guns, arrayed round the airfield, but they also had Lewis and Vickers guns at their disposal as well as a two-pounder field gun.

The vehicles which they used were a seven ton Scout car and a Beaverette with a crew of three, namely a Car Commander, Machine Gunner and a driver. They also had a Whippet tank. Les remembers that the Irish Guards were well equipped while at Ibsley, having a Medium Crusader Tank and a Bren-Gun Carrier.

Early in April Squadron Leader Humphrey Russell replaced Squadron Leader Mike Crossley, who was sent to the U.S.A. as a test pilot. No. 32 Squadron remained at Ibsley until April 17th, 1941, having been engaged mainly on shipping convoy patrols in the Channel.

The following day, April 18th, the Spitfires of No. 118 Squadron, which had been re-formed at Filton on 20th February, 1941, under the Command of Squadron Leader Frank Howell, D.F.C., flew in to Ibsley. No 118 Squadron had first been formed at Catterick in January 1918 as a night bomber unit and moved to Bicester as a training unit to receive Handley Page 0/40G's. It was disbanded, in November 1918, before becoming operational. The re-formed No. 118 Squadron came to Ibsley after brief spells at Colerne and Warmwell, where it had become operational on 11th April, flying Spitfire Mk II's. Their Unit identification letters were NK. Theirs was to prove a long and eventful stay. Squadron Leader Frank Howell, D.F.M. had been with No. 609 Squadron during the Battle of Britain, being credited with nine victories.

In April, 1941, Pilot Officer Grenville LeMesurier was posted from Fighter Command to No. 118 Squadron as Intelligence Officer, a position he held throughout 118's time at Ibsley, and beyond. A married man with three children, it is understood that Grenville LeMesurier, who for more than eighteen years had been involved in tea planting in India, had on his appointment as Squadron I.O., described himself as being fair, fat and forty. In fact he did not reach this milestone in his life until a few months into his service at Ibsley, and this was celebrated with a party at Cuckoo Hill, by then 118

## 1940-1941

Squadron's Officers' Mess. During his time at Ibsley Grenville LeMesurier, nicknamed "Misery", was promoted to the rank of Flying Officer.

Tom Smart joined No. 118 Squadron at Filton, and was a flight armourer in 'A' Flight. He told of how he identified strongly with the Squadron and had its plaque prominently displayed on his study wall. The badge depicts a burning, masted ship with the motto 'Occido Redoque' – 'I kill and then I go back'. It is believed that the design of the 'galleon' on the badge was selected, from several others, by Pilot Officer Stanley Jones, D.F.M., of No. 118 Squadron.

Of Frank Howell, the Commanding Officer, Tom Smart said:. "A man greatly admired; and rightly so. A good confident pilot and a natural leader, a man capable of getting the best out of people without very much effort. A traditional, real fighter 'type', and so very human. One evening, after we had been stood down, he came across to his 'Spit' and asked me to hold a small parcel. He got in, strapped up, and when I handed him the parcel he said, "I bet you are wondering what it is"; and I said I was. "It's for my girl friend. It's a box of chocolates. I've got a date", and off he flew. Officially of course on Service business. Rumour had it that she was a W.A.A.F at H.Q. Middle Wallop. Tom said he felt honoured, as a flight armourer, to service Squadron Leader Howell's machine.

Tom Smart's first impression of Ibsley was that although as a Squadron they were ready, the Station wasn't. There was a runway, a few huts, Headquarters at Moyles Court, but little else. No airmen's Mess room or marquee, no ablutions, no running water on the billet sites, no N.A.A.F.I., and certainly little or no time off. Tom said; "We sat with our backs to trees to eat our meals, which at that time varied from mediocre to incredibly poor, and we washed in cold water from the bowser. We made no complaints then, and I make none now. Compared with action units in other Services we were not badly off."

"After a while though", Tom recalled "they were getting distinctly scruffy, and possibly smelly too". "Because there were no baths or showers, at least not to start with" said Tom, "we were taken down to Bournemouth periodically to have a shower and swim, in that order in the Public Baths by the town pier. Three quarters of the blokes though used to skive off immediately into the nearby Pavilion Bar and, no doubt remained smelly."

## So Much Sadness, So Much Fun

Tom also remembered that on the Squadron there were a number of airmen who had no particular trade, and were listed as general duties men. Some of them were in their late twenties. They had originally volunteered for air-crew, but often for some trivial reason, had been taken off the courses. In 'A' Flight they had about half a dozen of them. In civvy street some had attained high positions at an early age. One had been Manager of the Times Furnishing Company in Hackney, another of the German (Deutsch) Shipping Company in Newcastle, and another Head of the Sales Department of a well known cigarette company.

They were given quite menial jobs to do. One of them had given up a highly paid job as head camouflage designer for the Medway area of Kent. He drove the tractors for the water and petrol bowsers. Some of them became Armourers' Mates. They were excellent fellows. Never outwardly resentful they were well known and well liked. They earned less than 20p per day in modern money. One who had lost quids playing solo before the war was upset one night when we took 1/6d off him, and then he laughed at his change of circumstances.

Bob Wise was a flight mechanic (rigger) with No. 118 Squadron at Ibsley for four months in 1941, and recalls being billeted in huts in a very old, un-used orchard, where the trees were diseased, cankered, there was long grass and stinging nettles.

He recalled the time a ferry pilot was bringing in a new kite and forgot to put the wheels down, belly landed, and out stepped a woman, all in white.

Roy Gould, also a mechanic with No. 118 Squadron remembers two Spitfires being flown in to Ibsley by The Air Transport Auxilliary Ferry Pilots. One pilot was a one-armed man and the other a woman.

Bob Wise said that during his stay at Ibsley a notice was put on the pole holding up the servicing tent which read "aircrew all trades wanted", so he put his name down. No. 118 Squadron had a yellow "Maggy" (Miles Magister) and pilots took us up to see what we were good enough at, etc. Bob says he remembers diving over Bournemouth Pier as if it was yesterday.

Of Ibsley Bob said,. "there was nothing to do on evenings off but walk or thumb a lift to Ringwood for a pint in the "Red Lion". Sometimes Fordingbridge, and on one occasion Salisbury".

## 1940-1941

Another time Bob recalled how he walked through the night from Brockenhurst Station, the little train for Ringwood didn't wait for the one from London. He had got as far as Burley, which he remembered only too well, when a voice yelled, "Halt, who goes there?". An Army camp gave him a nights rest, and then took him into Ringwood in a Bren-gun carrier, believe it or not, next morning.

He also remembered only too well the day when he was going back to his hut from the dining hall when a voice said "Hello airman", and an elderly lady asked if I would like a drink. She held a stone bottle and a glass, home made wine, it was lovely.

On Monday, 4th May, 1941, a strange incident occurred involving two Ibsley pilots. Pilot Officer Roderick 'Mac' MacKenzie and Pilot Officer John 'Robbie' Robson were engaged in mortal combat with an empty Whitley. The Whitley, which was improperly marked and did not answer challenges, was shot to pieces and fell into the sea, P/O MacKenzie being the successful pilot. Several other squadrons also claimed to have shot down this machine, until it was discovered that it really was one of our own aircraft. Apparently the Whitley, from No. 78 Squadron had been returning to its base at Middleton St. George, near Darlington, after bombing Cologne, but due to damage to the communication system lost direction, so the five man crew, Hatcher, Chandos, Butteell, Moodie and Hall, abandoned the aircraft near Leominster and baled out safely. The Whitley continued to fly on, *empty*, and was eventually destroyed 30 miles out to sea South of Portland at 0625 hours.

The first night landing at Ibsley was made on 6th May, 1941, when the flare path was lit for the first time. The pilot to have the honour of making the first night landing was Flying Officer David Fulford, of No. 118 Squadron.

Royal Canadian Air Force pilot Douglas 'Duke' Warren, D.F.C., one of twin pilots at Ibsley in 1943 with No. 165 Squadron, says in his book 'Gemini Flight' that "Spitfires were designed as day fighters, and never really intended to fly at night. They might take off at dawn, or land at dusk, but "dark of the moon" was out. The aircraft had no exhaust dampers, and this was a serious fault.". He goes on to say: "We would sit around in the crew room wearing dark goggles to give our eyes night vision, climb in the cockpit, take the goggles off, taxi out and open the throttle, and there went any night vision one might have had as the exhaust flames shot back into your night vision. Once at height and throttled back to cruise speed, it

*So Much Sadness, So Much Fun*

Pilots and Officers, No. 118 Squadron, in front of Spitfire IIa P8088, NK-K, Ibsley, May 1941
Front. L-R. F/O H. Mallory, F/L M. Boddington, D.F.C., S/Ldr. F. Howell, D.F.C. F/L. V. Simmonds, F/O J. Gibson (Adjutant)
Middle L-R ?, F/O E. Badcoe, Sgt. Jones, P/O A. Lumsden, F/O J. Fulford, F/O J. Robson, F/O R. McKenzie, ?, P/O J. Booth, F/O G. LeMesurier
Back L-R. ?, ?, ?, Sgt. M. Beatty, ?, Sgt. R. Birtles, D.F.M., ?, ?.
Photo: A.S.C. Lumsden

26

*1940-1941*

Spitfire "Borough of Lambeth", No. 118 Squadron, 1941. Cross Lanes Chapel, at Mockbeggar visible in background.
Photo: A.S.C. Lumsden

## So Much Sadness, So Much Fun

*Pilot Officer McKenzie and Flight Lieutenant Robson take it easy in the garden at Heather Cottage*
Photo: Mrs. S-A. Salm

was not bad, but then when landing as you throttled back on round-out, the flames blinded you again. Definitely not made for night flying."

He also said "that shortly after starting night flying, a highly qualified night fighter pilot was sent to brief the squadron on what night fighting was all about. His first step was to fly a Spitfire at night, something he had never done before. Like us, he sat in the crew room with goggles on, went out to his aircraft and took off. About 45 minutes later he was back, came in the crew room sat down and wrote an eight page report as to why the Spitfire was unsuitable for night fighting. We already knew that, but what impressed us was the Squadron Leader's (for that was his rank) ability to write an eight page report. Our administrative talents at that time in our careers were very limited."

Some of the W.A.A.F.'s and N.A.A.F.I. girls at Ibsley kept autograph books and collected signatures of many of the pilots. "Ginger" Lacey, and six foot seven and a half inch Flight Lieutenant Bob Dafforn, who it is said, because of his height, it took three men and nearly five minutes to get him in or out of the cockpit of a Spitfire, were among those who signed Daisy Porter's. Dafforn was

*1940-1941*

only at Ibsley, with No. 501 Squadron, for a short while before being posted. Tragically, on 9th September, 1943, then as a Squadron Leader and holder of the D.F.C., he was killed in an accident while flying a Spitfire, from Eastchurch, Kent. Hazel Sims, maiden name Sheppard in 1941/42 when she served as a W.A.A.F. ambulance driver, still treasures her book which has many autographs collected at Ibsley, including the paw print of 'Butch' the dog of Pilot Officer Dickie Newbery of No. 118 Squadron.

*Flight Lieutenants John Robson, No. 118 Squadron, and Bob Dafforn, No. 501 Squadron, Ibsley, August, 1941*
*Photo courtesy J. S. Robson*
*Inset autograph from D. Porter's autograph book*

## So Much Sadness, So Much Fun

Daisy Porter whose home was in Ringwood cycled to Ibsley to serve in the N.A.A.F.I., and had to have a pass to show to the guard. There was some delay in her pass being issued, and although she had been allowed past the guard on several occasions, one morning as she went to cycle past, she was ordered to 'Halt', and she still had no pass. The guard dropped his bayonet in front of Daisy who told him that as he saw her nearly every morning, he should let her go by or she would be late for the men's tea break. At this point their was the sound of rustling in the hedge and a "brass hat" emerged with foliage on his hat. He said to let me go on. In the evening when I went to cycle home I found that a high wire fence had been erected across the road, and I had the same performance to get out. I was told to get my pass as soon as I could. She became the first to drive the mobile canteen van on to the airfield in 1941/42.

Daisy also recalled an incident one evening, when it was getting dark, and she was on the airfield in the mobile N.A.A.F.I. van, and two Spitfires came back in very late. It was thought they would not return. Daisy said "Suddenly I noticed two black objects coming across the grass of the airfield and could see that I was going to be right in their path on the perimeter track. I very hastily turned right and drove down between them with virtually no room to spare. When I got back on to the perimeter again they had both parked in their dispersal bays and ran to my van (pilots weren't supposed to) and said to me, "Just in time for supper". I poured some tea out for them and one said "Gosh, was it you that came between us". I said "Yes", and what did you think you were doing coming across the grass like that. I think they were just so thankful that they had managed to get back again, safely.

Cyril Risbridger, M.B.E., recalls that there were three Flashing Beacon sties used at Ibsley during 1941/42, and the Beacons were used to assist pilots to locate their base at night.

"The sites were used in a random fashion, sometimes for a single night, the Beacon then moving to another site, perhaps for only a few days. The Beacon only operated whilst Ibsley aircraft were flying, and in most circumstances only for short duration. They were crewed by three Airmen, a Fitter Driver, Electrician and General Duties Airman. The Ibsley Beacon flashed for the first time on Tuesday, 17th June.

The Beacon flashed out a two letter code which was changed daily, as authorised by the Station Headquarters Intelligence Officer.

## 1940-1941

The accommodation at each Beacon site was pretty basic, i.e. a Bell Tent (later replaced by a small Hut), a slit trench and the Beacon and Generator Set that was mounted on a three ton, four wheeled trailer, and towed into position by a three ton lorry.

The Beacon sites, as Cyril Risbridger remembers them, were at Three Legged Cross, Dorset, on Lower Common. Here the Travellers Rest Public House was within a kilometre, and very convenient on a dirty rainy night when flying was not possible; Verwood, Dorset, which was a remote site, the nearest Public House being the Railway Hotel, that is what Cyril believes it was called, next to Verwood Station; and Hyde Common, near Fordingbridge, not far from the Practice Bombing Range at Ashley Walk, which was fenced in during the war. This site was also very close to Ogdens Farm, where they were able to get black market dairy produce.

The only other directional aid at the Beacon site was an arrow shaped appliance, which Cyril says they made up from a 4 metre length of timber with arrow heads 1.5 metres festooned with a large number of 12 volt 20 watt lamps. This arrowhead was positioned approximately fifty metres away from the Beacon and pointed in the direction of the airfield. It was only used if they considered that the aircraft was lost and friendly. Contact was made with the pilot via an Aldis lamp, and providing he gave the correct Airfield recognition letters, by flashing his lights, the arrow was illuminated until we were sure that the aircraft was on course with base.

Cyril also recalls that he personally was involved in quite a lot of duty of this nature, perhaps over a hundred operations, so they got to know the locals quite well, although at first they were a bit apprehensive of having a Flashing Beacon so close to their villages. Duty of this type did involve risk, and they were often buzzed by unidentified aircraft. This story of the Beacon sites gives an insight into some of the more mundane jobs that were necessary to operations at a Wartime Airfield.

It was not long before No. 118 squadron damaged a Junkers 88 in combat, and in May it went over to the offensive, escorting Beauforts attacking ships off Cherbourg. It also flew patrols to reinforce Tangmere.

On 30th June Sergeant Pilots Chris Bland and John Gilbert when practising a head on attack, near Fordingbridge, collided, both planes crashing close to Breamore village and bursting into flames. The pilots baled out, Sergeant Pilot Bland landed, uninjured in a

## So Much Sadness, So Much Fun

F/O LeMesurier, Intelligence Officer, debriefing pilots of No. 118 Squadron, 1941
Photo: Mrs J.J.Dexter

F/Lt. Peter Howard-Williams, D.F.C. alongside cannon-shell hole inflicted by Me109F on 2nd February 1942, during attack on distillery at Eroudville. He had himself already destroyed one and damaged two of his attackers during this operation.
Photo: P. Howard-Williams

## 1940-1941

duck pond, but Sergeant Pilot Gilbert was not quite so fortunate, receiving numerous superficial injuries which required hospital treatment. In the circumstances both pilots had lucky escapes.

On most days training and test flights also took place from Ibsley. These included cloud flying, formation flights, practice attacks and dog fights, dusk and night landings, air to sea firing practice, altitude tests, weather tests, smoke trail tests, cannon and engine tests, cloud firing, and camera gun practice, etc. All very necessary activities to keep a squadron up to scratch for operational flying.

The first 'kill' by an Ibsley unit occurred on 7/8 July, when Squadron Leader Frank Howell, D.F.M., Flight Lieutenant Michael Boddington, D.F.M., Flying Officer Peter Howard-Williams and Pilot Officer David Fulford were up on a fighter vigil the first Fighter night at Ibsley, and also in No. 118 Squadron's history; and what a night!! At 0240 hours the Commanding Officer contacted a Heinkel III over Southampton, which he attacked, but after overshooting several times, owing to the slowness of the enemy aircraft, he put in a burst, in reply to an opening burst by the enemy aircrafts' lower gunner. Following a second burst there was the mother and father of an explosion on the Heinkel, which Commanding Officer Frank Howell expected to fall to bits. Instead, however, although its port engine was on fire, the enemy aircraft continued to fly. It turned South over Bognor, and dived rapidly away. It was last seen emitting quantities of white smoke from both engines eight miles out to sea South of Worthing. The occupants of the machine were rescued from the Channel and taken Prisoners of War.

Four days later a telegram was received from the Air Officer Commanding (A.O.C.) confirming the victim.

The Summer of 1941 was gloriously hot, and Tom Smart can remember only one occasion when the Squadron was stood down because of bad weather. In fact it was so hot at times that the armourers working on the 'Spits' had to cover the main-planes with blankets to save burning their bottoms. Incidentally, said Tom, "we never said "Spitfire", it was always 'Spit'. Never 'Aircraft', always 'Kite'."

"Between leaves and the precious but rare 48 hour passes we hardly ever had a day off. Sundays lost their identities. We only knew it was Sunday because we paid a penny more for the newspapers."

"A two-day programme for us would be: Arrive at the airfield at 8.00 a.m., be on duty until 10.00 p.m., then occasionally be on guard all night, back to work at 8.00 a.m., and then off at 5.00 p.m. By this time we were so tired that very often we just lay around in our scruff instead of smartening up and going out".

Of morale, Tom said "although it was fashionable to moan, with airmen going through the graded processes of being 'browned', 'cheesed' and finally 'brassed' off, morale was generally high. Even though conditions were somewhat primitive, and the nature of life necessarily restrictive, there was a good deal of camaraderie, a lot of humour, and fun, and a strong sense of belonging. It was rare for an airman to overstay his leave"

Tom also recalled that Ibsley was an open Station. Had any organisations or individuals been so minded they could have come in the night and destroyed a lot of aircraft. There was no security fence and at that time no main gate with a guardroom. For a while though an Army detachment of young soldiers did night duty, but they were so curious about the machines, and apt to interfere with them, that we had to do guard duty to protect the aircraft from them

He also told of how, during earlier square-bashing and training periods discipline had been firm – to put it mildly. However, once on an operational station it all changed. The only parades they had at Ibsley were pay parades. They worked in overalls, and looked more like greased monkeys than R.A.F. personnel. They didn't shave if they didn't feel like it and often walked about causally with fags in their mouths, except when near aircraft. There was an unacceptable limit, as Tom personally found out. One afternoon he was sauntering along the lane leading from South Gorley to Moyles Court when he was picked up by the Station Adjutant and Warrant Officer. He was whipped into the Station Wing Commander's Office, had his forage cap removed, and was then charged by the Warrant Officer. He was on a 'Fizzer for his slovenly appearance. In giving evidence the W.O. said that Tom was unshaven, had his respirator on the wrong shoulder, was wearing a roll-neck comforts fund sweater instead of the regulation collar and tie, and that he had a cigarette in the corner of his mouth. Fairly normal, really, but those two didn't think so.

Tom was told by Wing Commander Norman Benge, "Smart, you appear to be a decent sort of chap, but you know this isn't good enough. We have enough on our plates here without having to put up with pinpricks like this. You are very much to blame, but you can go. Smarten yourself up, and for goodness sake think". When Tom got outside the Adjutant and Warrant Officer were livid. Tom says: "Put me on a 'Fizzer' for being scruffy was so much at odds with the real me."

More successes quickly followed that of the C.O. Frank Howell in July, and with the completion of the airfield in the Summer of 1941, Ibsley became a two squadron station when No. 501 (County of Gloucester) Auxiliary Squadron arrived from Chilbolton on August 4th, flying Spitfire Mk II's, code letters SD. They had been led by Squadron Leader Adrian Boyd, D.F.C., but he was promoted to Wing Commander early in August and posted to Middle Wallop as Wing Leader. His successor, who took command on 14th August, 1941, was Squadron Leader Christopher "Bunny" Currant, D.S.O., D.F.C., whose flying career started in December 1936 as a Sergeant Pilot, first with No. 151 Squadron and then No. 46 Squadron. "Bunny" Currant was flying Hurricanes with No. 605 Squadron at the start of the Battle of Britain, and had shot down or shared in the destruction of nineteen enemy aircraft between April and December, 1940.

A pre-war Auxiliary Squadron, No. 501 were formed on 14th June, 1929, their motto being 'Nil Time' – Fear Nothing, and the squadron badge, A boar's head couped, taken from the Gloucester coat of arms. This squadron had slugged out the Battle of Britain from Middle Wallop, Gravesend and Kenley, and had lost nineteen pilots in the battle, more than any other squadron. Together No. 118 and 501 squadrons carried out many fighter sweeps, in the course of which several enemy aircraft were destroyed.

On 4th August No. 118 lost Sergeant Pilot Cyril Smith, who, on returning from a convoy patrol, got lost in cloud and crashed into a hillside at Owermoigne near Warmwell, the aircraft bursting into flames immediately.

No. 501 were not very fortunate on their first Sweep from Ibsley, on 5th August, for they lost Sergeant Pilot Alan Beacham in mysterious circumstances. On the return journey they saw an enemy balloon and shot it up. Sergeant Beacham was not seen again and it was presumed that in doing a steep turn he hit the water and went into the sea.

Pilot Officer James H. "Ginger" Lacey, D.F.C., who had been with No. 501 Squadron for two years, departed from Ibsley on 18th August. A Yorkshireman, he had joined No. 501 as an NCO pilot, and during his time with the squadron had destroyed no less than twenty six aircraft and four probables, with a further seven damaged. Ginger left Ibsley for a tour of instruction at Hawarden, near Chester, but was to return to Ibsley as a duty Flight Controller after the War, when it became an accommodation base for R.A.F. Sopley.

Flight Sergeant R. Opie was at Ibsley in 1941, and remembers the two McLauchlin brothers there at that time, one of whom had only one arm, but was still able to fly aircraft. Flight Sergeant Opie also recalls that he was billeted with two aged ladies, Miss Linder and Miss Phillips, at "Pemba", Mockbeggar (now Whispering Hills), but when Miss Phillips was taken ill he moved in with Mr. and Mrs. Newman at their bungalow home in what was then called Downing Street, but is now New Road.

Air Commodore David Roberts was Sector Commander of Royal Air Force Middle Wallop, in those days a station in No. 10 Group Fighter Command, of which Ibsley was part, and home for two Squadrons of the Middle Wallop Wing, Nos. 118 and 501. He remembers how he frequently flew down to Ibsley to visit the squadrons and conduct briefings before they took off on offensive action, low level beat ups on targets in the Cherbourg peninsular, made on several occasions, by Whirlwind equipped fighter squadrons who were on short detachment from another Sector in 10 Group.

No. 118 and 501 squadrons also carried out a number of "Rhubarbs", these were low-level strike operations mounted in cloudy conditions against enemy targets in occupied countries; "Ramrods", bomber raids escorted by fighters aimed at the destruction of a particular target in daylight; and "Roadsteads", fighter operations against shipping, as well as the inevitable convoy patrols.

Numerous squadrons used Ibsley for operations in the late summer of 1941, including a detachment of six Whirlwinds of No. 263 Squadron who arrived on 17th August, followed by further detachments from several other squadrons who used Ibsley as an advanced base for operations over France. These included the Mark IIa Spitfires of No. 302 (Poznan Polish) Squadron, code letters WX, from Warmwell, although they did not stay long before moving on to Harrowbeer. During August and September No. 118 and No. 501 squadrons converted to Spitfire Vb's and Vc's.

As they still do to-day, the New Forest ponies and cattle wandered freely around the area in those wartime days, but the

## 1940-1941

provision of cattle grids some years ago now prevents them from getting on to the busy main A338 road. It is understood that three Sergeant Pilots, returning from a night out in Bournemouth ran into and killed one of the ponies. They were unhurt but their car suffered. The Officers of No. 118 Squadron at Cuckoo Hill were convinced that the following day they were served with what, they said, was the toughest New Forest pony, with Yorkshire pudding thrown in to put them off the scent!!!

Tom Smart also remembers some of the sport which personnel managed to get in. Football was played against sides from neighbouring Army Camps, a bit of hockey cricket and rugby, the C.O. Frank Howell being a good player whenever he could spare the time. Howell was a keen golfer too, and persuaded an armourer Jack Wroe, a low handicap player to bring his clubs with him when he came back from leave. Then one evening 'A' Flight took on 'B' Flight at rugger, and there was a singles knock-out tennis tournament. A lot of darts was played, and we made our own local rules, recalled Tom. For instance, if your dart hit a wire and bounced back you could have it again as long as you could reach it without putting your feet in front of the line. Chess was also a favourite with pilots waiting in dispersals.

"People may be surprised to learn that so much sport took place", said Tom, "but we found time. Once the aircraft had been serviced and the famous Form 700 signed, there was not so very much for ground staff to do. Even when we were on stand-by, and that could last for hours, there was still a strange air of calm."

It is also understood that No. 118 Squadron had some makeshift cricket nets at their dispersals. At 'A' Flight the pitch was said to be of plain hard-baked mud, while 'B' Flight's was described as being of long coarse grass.

The Summer of 1941 also saw the making of the film "The First of the Few" at Ibsley. Leslie Howard's Company with David Niven and Rosamund John came to Ibsley to produce a film about the life of Reginald J. Mitchell, designer of the Spitfire. The Battle of Britain was to be a feature in the picture with a number of the leading aces in No. 501 and No. 118 Squadrons re-enacting some of the scenes in which they had figured in the Summer of 1940. Leslie Howard, the director and producer, starred as R. J. Mitchell and David Niven as Crisp the Test Pilot.

## So Much Sadness, So Much Fun

During the afternoon of 1st September, Pilot Officers Peter Anderson and David Fulford went on a shipping reconnaissance off Point de Barfleur and reported on a convoy. Nos. 118 and 501 Squadrons went over to attack and discovered that two of the ships were destroyers. Tremendous flak was experienced and unfortunately Pilot Officer Anderson was hit, his aircraft blew up and he plunged into the sea. "Andy" was only 19 years old and described as a capable and fearless pilot, the type the Squadron and Royal Air Force could ill afford to lose.

Members of the Women's Land Army were also working on the airfield at this time, and Kitty Smith (maiden name Heane), remembers grass seeding the areas alongside the tarmac runways after they were laid. The Land Army girls worked under the auspices of the Hampshire War Ag. (Ag. as it was called being short for Agriculture). There were also German and Italian Prisoners of War from the hostel at Stuckton working for them. The local Headquarters of the War Ag. were at East Mills Garage, in Fordingbridge, where Percy Webb undertook maintenance work on the agricultural machinery which was used.

It was whilst at Ibsley that Kitty met Richard 'Dick' Smith, who she later married. From September, 1941, till February, 1942, Dick was the Intelligence Officer of No. 501 Squadron. He held the rank of Flying Officer and worked from Eastwood House, the Watch Office at that time.

Dusk landings were practiced along the flare path at Ibsley, and one evening Pilot Officer John Heap, of No. 118 Squadron, landed on the runway at a tremendous speed, touching down half way along, and piling up (true to his name) in a heap, in a pile of earth at the end of the runway. The Spitfire was a nice new one, but became a very sorry sight. Pilot Officer Heap was dazed, but unhurt, and became the hero of the hour, for having crashed his Spitfire, he found that it had been pounced upon by the film company, Leslie Howard Productions, to play a leading role. Squadron Leader Frank Howell played the part of the wounded Squadron Leader who crashed on landing. The 118 Squadron Spitfire, bearing the code letters NK was hastily re-painted with the code letters of No. 501 Squadron, SD, for its part in the film.

The airfield rapidly took on the appearance of a miniature Hollywood, even though operational, and was over-run by a generous collection of camera men, make-up merchants, technicians, engineers and various hangers on, many of whom had no business at all on the airfield!!

On 30th September, 1941, the 'Baby of the R.A.F.' Sergeant Pilot Geoffrey Arthur Painting, the youngest pilot in the Royal Air Force, flying as No. 2 to Flight Lieutenant Peter Howard-Williams, was lost. Whilst attacking shipping his plane was hit by pom pom fire and he was shot down into the sea and undoubtedly killed immediately. This happened just two days before his 18th birthday. Of Painting, Peter Howard-Williams said: "Geoffrey was only 17 years old – God knows how he managed to get through training and onto a squadron at that age, but he was one of the better pilots. As Flight Commander, I used to pick my No. 2 very carefully, and the squadron lost a good man that day."

It is understood that Painting's mother, Eva, had notified the War Department that her son was only seventeen years old. He should *not* have been flying operationally and Ibsley were instructed to take him off such duties. As he was already on a mission this was to have been done immediately on his return to base, but sadly it was too late.

A newspaper report published in the Daily Mirror at the time quoted his father, Albert, as saying: "Geoffrey was always keen to get into the Army, but when war broke out like many of his schools old boys, he joined the R.A.F. We did not want him to go but he was too set on it for us to stop him. I know now that he gave his age as eighteen and a half. Actually he was barely seventeen and a half. He went through his training with flying colours, and was posted to his first squadron two weeks before his last flight. Geoffrey told us he would be home on leave for his birthday, but it was not to be."

Tom Smart remembers how Peter Howard-Williams was know to some of them as 'Hairy Willy', not because he was particularly hirsute, but because his initials seemed to invite that variation. "He was a good pilot, very much an individual and his own man. It was believed, and I am sure no one would have split on him," recalls Tom, "that he got the odd spot of petrol for his car out of the 100 Octane aircraft petrol bowser. Maybe he didn't.". But Tom says he will never forget the time Howard-Williams gave him a lift into Bournemouth. It was in an open-top sports car, and the experience was hair-raising and possibly car raising. "He obviously liked being in the air, even when he was in a car!"

*So Much Sadness, So Much Fun*

*Above: Spitfires of No. 501 Squadron during filming. Eastwood House, Mockbeggar Lane in Background.
Photo: P. Howard-Williams*

*Left: L. to R. David Niven, Leslie Howard, S/Ldr. Frank Howell, D.F.C.
Photo: R. Smith*

*1940-1941*

Leslie Howard directing with S/Ldr. Frank Howell, D.F.C.
Photo: P. Howard-Williams

Spitfire of No. 118 Squadron which P/O John Heap crash-landed. Re-painted SD-E for filming
Photo: W/Cdr. C. Currant

## So Much Sadness, So Much Fun

*Heinkel III used in filming "The First of the Few", parked on Ibsley Airfield late summer, 1941. Ibsley Common and Whitefield Plantation in background.*
*Photo: Mrs. S-A. Salm*

A Sergeant Pilot of No. 118 Squadron at Ibsley was not so fortunate, however, for he was unlucky enough to be caught with 100 octane in his car by the Special Air Force Police. The outcome of his Court Martial was that he should be reduced to the rank of L.A.C. He was then grounded, but a few weeks later was restored to full operational privileges. 'We Want More Petrol' is what a Sunday Express report said about it then:

> "Instead of bothering our heads about kindness to Germans and a happy life in the sweet by-and-by, I suggest we might see if we can give a little more consideration to some of our own men in the war.
> THE FIGHTER PILOTS FOR INSTANCE. I AM WORRIED ABOUT THE GRAND BOYS SINCE THE DAYLIGHT SWEEPS ON FRANCE BEGAN, IT SEEMS TO ME THAT TOO MANY ARE BEING DRIVEN TOO HARD.
> They are at it day after day, often without respite. You can see the effects of the strain on them. I see many of them being in a state of complete exhaustion.
> 
> **GIVE THEM A BREAK**
> 
> They have no time to get the tension relaxed before they are up again. I do not think this is either good or wise. And I do not think it is necessary.

Before this year is ended we shall need all these boys. Let us therefore take care that we do not waste them needlessly now. War puts a tremendous strain on them. It is our responsibility to ease that strain as much as we can. They need change and fun, and all the brightness we can put into their lives.

Yet what do we do? We plant on them the same stupid austerity rules we plan on the war profiteer.

When the basic petrol ration goes next month these pilots will not be able to get petrol.

We owe more to these boys than we can ever repay with a few hundred gallons of petrol. But petrol at least would be a gesture. I would rather see it go to the fighting boys than to the office wallahs of Whitehall, who seem to swim in it. I am told that one department of State now has 3,000 cars to run its ants about."

"Bunny" Currant recalls that the aerial shots for "The First of the Few" were flown by pilots of both No. 118 and No. 501 Squadrons, but using the Spitfires of No. 501 for the flying sequences, in order to portray the earlier Marks of the Spitfire in action. The Mark II still being used by No. 501 carried an armament of eight machine guns. In fact, No. 501 squadron were in the process of converting to Mark Vb's as filming was about to start, the first machine arriving at Ibsley on 15th September.

Filming of 'The First of the Few' was in full swing during late September 1941, and there was added interest in October when Flight Lieutenant Peter Howard-Williams and Pilot Officer Wally Milne flew to Duxford to escort a Heinkel!! to Ibsley, which was to be used on the set. The ground staff then had to paint on the German markings.

One day, Tom Smart remembers seeing two planes with German marking, (they were a Heinkel and a Messerschmitt), on the airfield when returning from leave, and thinking they had been invaded took as much cover as he could until he saw that the airfield was still full of our own aircraft. He made his way to the armourers' hut where everybody was excited and anxious to tell him about the film being made, and that they were to be used as extras. The next day a few of them were chosen, including Tom, to simulate some of the drills such as re-arming the machines on their return, re-fuelling and generally servicing them.

The aircraft used by the film crew as camera aircraft was a Mark IV Blenheim. Peter Howard-Williams said that it still had both its chin

## So Much Sadness, So Much Fun

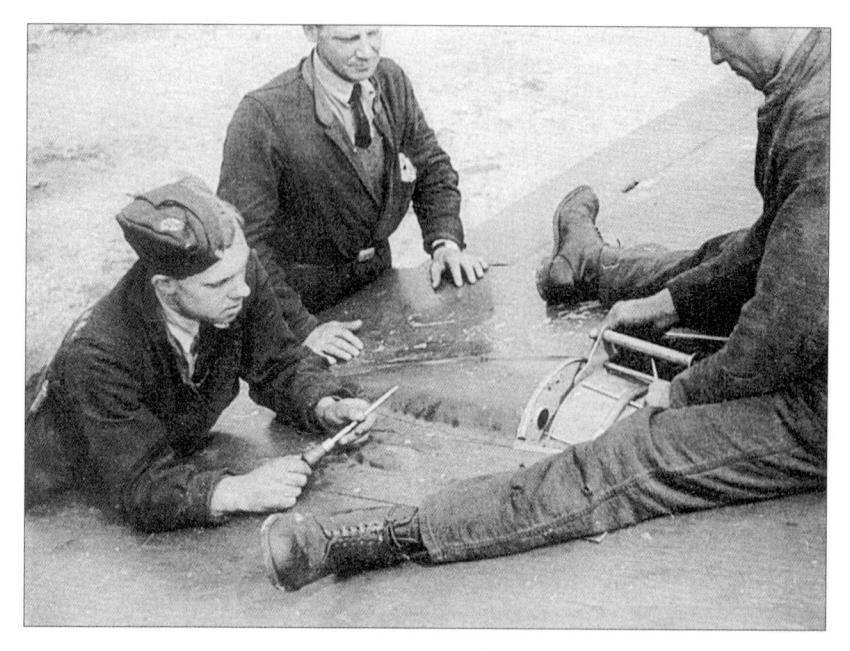

*"Keep trying! It will fit!"*
Armourers fitting cannon magazine (holds 60 rounds of 20mm) into aircraft wing housing, at Ibsley.
Photo: S. Watson, D.F.C., Nos. 234 and 118 Squadron, Ibsley

and dorsel turrets, so he imagined they must have put the camera, instead of the gun, in the top turret.

After a days filming for 'The First of the Few' some of the pilots and others who had taken part would go to the Regal Cinema in Ringwood during the evening to see "shots" ("rushes") which had been taken.

In October No.118 Squadron pilots, Jock Gillam, Peter Howard-Williams, David Fulford and John "Robbie" Robson, also "Bunny" Currant and several of the No. 501 Squadron pilots who had taken part in the film, were attached to the Denham Studios of Leslie Howard Productions for a few days so that indoor shots of dispersals could be taken. The young No. 118 Squadron 'film stars' stayed at the Savoy, and lived on champagne, oysters and caviare. Apparently the bill for their five days was in excess of £400, but was met by the film company.

## 1940-1941

Christopher "Bunny" Currant also recalls how he played the part of "Hunter Leader" the Squadron Commander, and that the scenes of him flying in an aircraft, taken in the cockpit of a Spitfire Vb, were actually filmed in the Denham studio. In another sequence he is filmed attacking a Heinkel with guns blazing. He said "only tracer bullets were used, but these completely ruined the guns, which did not please Fighter Command from whom he received an official mild reproof. However, the scenes were shot and on film.". "It was fun, so I didn't mind", said Bunny.

He also remembers that on Thursday, 9th October, whilst filming was being carried out on the airfield, they were scrambled. They dashed to their aircraft and were airborne with a dozen Spitfires. Flying at 18,000 feet, some ten miles South of Portland Bill, a Junkers 88 was intercepted. Bunny goes on to tell of how he was first in and blazed away, followed by all eleven aircraft. The Ju 88 crashed on rocks on the Cherbourg Peninsula, at Cap de la Hague, obviously the weight of lead from twelve Spitfires being too much to carry! Once again he received a mild reproof from Headquarters 10 Group who thought he was overdoing it, but he was determined that all pilots should have experience of an actual engagement, especially as some hadn't even fired their guns in anger.

Also in October, No. 118's Squadron Leader, Frank Howell, D.F.M., was posted overseas. He went to Singapore, aboard HMS *Prince of Wales*, where he was given command of No. 243 Squadron in December, just as the Japanese attack on Malaya commenced. He claimed one victory here but when escaping from the island in an Air Sea Rescue launch, with others, in February 1942, the craft was hit by a bomb and several were killed. Howell was among those picked up by other vessels, but was then captured and spent the rest of the war as a prisoner of the Japanese. He remained in the R.A.F. after the war, becoming a Wing Commander, but tragically on 9th May, 1948, was killed. He had been at Odiham filming a squadron of Vampires taking-off and landing, when he was struck on the head from behind, by the wing-tip of one coming in to land, and died instantly.

Squadron Leader Humphrey Russell, who had earlier been at Ibsley in command of No. 32 Squadron, which he had taken over from Squadron Leader Mike Crossley, replaced Frank Howell as Commanding Officer of No. 118.

## So Much Sadness, So Much Fun

No. 501 Royal Auxiliary Air Force, County of Gloucester Squadron, Ibsley 1941.
S/Ldr. Christopher Currant, D.F.C. (centre front), Sgt. Ray Dean, (extreme right front.)
Photo: Mrs D. Witt

"Betty" of St Leonards Hotel flanked by P/O Dickie Lynch and P/O Phillip Stanbury, 1941
Photo: W/Cdr. C. Currant

*1940-1941*

On 4th November Pilot Officer Eric Shore of No. 501 Squadron was shot up by a Bf 109 and was forced to put down on a French beach, and four days later, Pilot Officer Greenaway, also No. 501, did the same thing after clashing with 109's between Cap de la Hague and Alderney. Both became Prisoners of War.

A local lad, 19 year old Sergeant Pilot Raymond Frederick Charles Dean was not so lucky however, for whilst attacking German installations on the French Coast, on Monday 17th November, he was shot down by anti-aircraft fire and killed.

Raymond was born on 6th June, 1922, and lived at Lower Kingston Post Office, three miles South of Ringwood. He was educated at Bisterne School, Ringwood School and Brockenhurst Grammar School. After leaving school Raymond worked for a short while at Baker's Cycle Shop in Christchurch Road. He was a keen cricketer and played for the Ringwood town team. As soon as he was old enough on 13th June, 1940, Raymond joined the Royal Air Force Volunteer Reserve. After his flying training he was posted, during 1941, to No. 501 (County of Gloucester) Auxiliary Squadron at Ibsley, just a few miles from his home, as a Sergeant Pilot. Raymond is buried in the little village churchyard Brevands, France, near to where he fell.

When filming of "The First of the Few" was completed, at Ibsley, a party was held by Leslie Howard and David Niven at the Kings Arms in Christchurch, for those who had taken part in it. The menu included, in those wartime days, such unheard of luxuries as lobster, pheasant, mushrooms and so forth, with drinks ad lib. Some noisy but happy people returned to Ibsley afterwards, in the early hours.

Peter Howard-Williams remembered this party well and said their had been a reason for it being held at the Kings Arms. He had been on late readiness one evening when the airmen's food arrived. It was almost inedible which made him cross, so he sent for the Catering Officer and there was a bit of a bust up over it.

As a result of that, Wing Commander Norman Benge the Station Commander, asked what could be done to improve things. Peter H-W., happened to know Sidney and Mary Barber, who rang the Kings Arms, and he suggested that Sidney should be approached. Three weeks later he became Pilot Officer Sidney Barber and Ibsley's Catering Officer.

## So Much Sadness, So Much Fun

During the Summer term of 1942 children attending Rockford School were given their own special preview of "The First of the Few". Peter Smith remembered the day well. He said "a large Ministry of Information van arrived at the school. It was fitted out with seats, had a screen and a projector to show the film". The only problem for Peter was that he was seated at the rear of the vehicle, and being a small eight year old all he could see, now and again, over the heads of older pupils and staff was a Spitfire flying near the top of the screen!!!

The World Premier of this epic film, in aid of the Royal Air Force Benevolent Fund, took place at London's Leicester Square Theatre on Thursday 20th August, 1942. Peter Howard-Williams said that "anyone who had anything to do with the making of the film was there, and, of course, another great party was held afterwards".

Another favourite haunt of the pilots from Ibsley was the St. Leonards Hotel, on the main A31 road, about three miles West of Ringwood. Peter Howard Williams recalled how pilots on twenty minute standby would literally "scramble" from the bar. This fact was also mentioned in a Bournemouth Daily Echo article, more than twenty years ago, by reporter Roger Guttridge. It was at this hostelry, also, that a large number of pilots, of many nationalities, who served at Ibsley signed their names on panels fixed to the bar pillars. Their signatures are still there, although with the passage of time have become somewhat faded. A few years ago, however, the local district council placed a preservation order on them, so hopefully they should remain for many years to come.

In his Echo article on the St. Leonards, Roger Guttridge told of how it was also used as a base for wartime intelligence and counter espionage operations. Details of the intelligence work that went on there were obscured by the Official Secrets Act, and it was not until a number of years after the war that local people discovered some unusual things had gone on at the pub. The landlord at the time, Ted Harvey, was given no details until he had signed the Official Secrets Act. He then got together a team of about thirty trustworthy people, all of whom had to be vetted by the police, to work under him. It involved manning radio stations twenty four hours a day to listen for signs of enemy invasion. So, each night, after his customers had gone, Ted Harvey tiptoed to a clump of trees and entered the secret underground room, which hardly anyone knew existed. The entrance was under a tree stump, so well camouflaged that even a visiting general failed to find it. It was operated by means of a bolt and counter-weight in a nearby tree and a branch on the trunk which moved it aside. There were two underground rooms, connected by a tunnel. One contained a stock of food and the other radio equipment. During the day Ted Harvey continued to run the pub, but every night from midnight to six in the morning he would tune in his radio for ten minutes, every half-hour. Betty, a blonde barmaid at the St. Leonards, also worked regularly in the underground hideout. Unknown to the customers she had been trained to work as a cipher and coding clerk.

"Bunny" Currant remembers being shown around the hidden underground rooms by Ted Harvey, and recalls that Betty was a super young lady, who was both very intelligent and attractive.

Ibsley's Station Commander, Wing Commander Norman Benge was an ex-Royal Flying Corps man, and had rejoined the Royal Air Force on the outbreak of war. He knew many Air Marshalls well, and Peter Howard-Williams recalled how, to boost men's morale Wing Commander Benge managed to get the whole of the dance band from London's Coconut Grove Orchestra posted to Ibsley together with the top ranking comedians, the Lowe Brothers and Johnnie Lockwood. Most of them worked in the station headquarters and all performed at the big farewell party at the Kings Arms, which was where Leslie Howard, David Niven and many of the film crew stayed.

Also, during the Summer of 1941, it was discovered that there was a most talented artist in No. 118 Squadron, an L.A.C., Jon Doorne, who was employed driving a tractor and bowser. Almost certainly the camouflage expert Tom Smart referred to earlier. Squadron Leader Frank Howell took Doorne off driving and put him to work painting the portraits of the Officers and Sergeant Pilots of the Squadron. It is believed that about twenty portraits were painted by Jon Doorne, and this prompted a visit to Ibsley by Sir William Rothenstein, Art Adviser to the Air Ministry. Another visitor to the Squadron was Mr. Augustus John, who also showed considerable interest in the work of the 'Squadron Artist' and invited him to pay a visit to his (Augustus John's) studio in Fordingbridge. After the war Doorne became an Art Master. It has also been said that on occasions Squadron Leader Frank Howell would take Augustus John for a flight in the squadron's Tiger Moth.

## So Much Sadness, So Much Fun

*Oil painting by L.A.C. Jon Doorne of Squadron Leader Frank Howell, D.F.C., both of No.118 Squadron, Ibsley, 1941*
Mrs. J.J. Dexter

In November, 1941, Ibsley was honoured by a visit from H.R.H. The Duke of Kent, who also visited the Officers' Mess of No. 118 Squadron at Cuckoo Hill, where he was shown round by Peter Howard Williams.

November also saw the arrival of No. 234 (Madras Presidency) Squadron from Warmwell, Dorset, flying Spitfire Vb's, coded AZ. No. 234 were originally formed at Tresco (Scilly Isles) in August

## 1940-1941

1918, as a flying boat unit covering the Western approaches, and remained there until being disbanded in May 1919. It reformed as a fighter squadron at Leconfield on 30th October, 1939. The Squadron badge depicts a dragon rampant with flames issuing from the mouth, while it motto is "Ignem Mortemque Despuimus", "We spit fire and death". The dragon indicates the fighting role and the flames associated with the name Spitfire.

Now, together with No. 118 and No. 501, the commencement of operations as a Wing under the dynamic leadership of Wing Commander Ian "Widge" Gleed, D.F.C., began. Already in Fighter Commands's 10 Group, Gleed was initially given command of the Middle Wallop Wing, but plans were already in progress for him to take over at Ibsley. Setting up the Ibsley Wing kept Ian Gleed on the ground to some degree, something which tried a flyer of his aggressive calibre. He continued to live at Wallop, and every morning would fly the ten minute hop to Ibsley, to plan, administer, or fly on operations, then in the evening fly back to Wallop. However, as soon as he had all the paperwork flowing freely in the right directions, and the winter weather eased, he was able to get back into the cockpit more regularly. Gleed had earned great respect as a leader from all who served under him. Only five feet two inches tall, he was first commissioned in 1936 and had fought in France and the Battle of Britain. When appointed Wing Leader at Ibsley, and with the privilege of rank, he had his usual Spitfire Vb, AA742, coded "SD-A", re-painted with his own initials "IR-G". A Wing Commander's pennant was painted by the windscreen on both the port and starboard sides.

Of Ian Gleed "Bunny" Currant said, unhesitatingly, "he was one of the most courageous men I ever had the privilege to know. He may have been tiny in stature but by God he had a big heart and seemed not to have any fear. He was unflappable and unmoveable, and had a modest, unassuming manner. He always thought for his pilots, the ground crews and staff. A caring man, I remember him warmly with gratitude. A pocket size man with care for others and courage beyond compare"

Leading Aircraftsman, George Bowdidge was a ground crew member of No. 234 Squadron at Ibsley, who had recorded some of his personal memories.

In these George recalled that from what he saw of the interior of the Station Headquarters at Moyles Court the R.A.F. had made a bit

## So Much Sadness, So Much Fun

of a mess of the fine oak panelling by nailing up partitions to subdivide the large rooms. Also, that the Battle of Britain in 1940 had taught the need for dispersal and consequently their sleeping quarters were a mile away from the airfield, with the airmen's mess and ablutions situated about mid-way. Building contractors were still erecting huts here and there and the area, like Warmwell, from where No. 234 had come, was a sea of mud. Gum boots were worn all the time you were on duty and whenever possible men would try and keep to the few concrete paths. Sleeping quarters were in a Nissen hut, situated in the corner of a field down a muddy farm track, under primitive conditions. The only items of furniture were beds placed over hard, rolled down earth, and "we lived out of our kit bags placed on the damp ground". George reflected on the comforts of civvie billets back in Blackpool, but at Ibsley, at least, they didn't have to polish the floor! Heating was by means of a coke stove in the middle of the hut with a tin chimney going straight up through the corrugated iron roof. There was no water on the site. The nearest was at the ablutions half a mile away. After polishing the brass buttons on their walking-out best blue they had to seek a puddle, of which there were many, in order to wash their grubby hands.

"As Ibsley and the Spitfires of No. 234 Squadron was the raison d'etre of all the technical training I had received in the previous six months", said George Bowdidge. "I must admit to being a little concerned at what was expected of me. This was the real thing and I approached my first DI (daily inspection) of the aircraft for which I was responsible feeling like a newly qualified doctor about to see his first patient. As I signed the Form 700 (the book of responsibility) saying that in my opinion the Spitfire was OK to fly, I hoped that I had missed nothing. It flew all right, and the ice was broken."

"By the end of my first week at Ibsley I had settled into the routine. The aircraft were uncovered at dawn and the engines run-up in preparation for anything that might occur. If enemy aircraft were reported intruding into our area a red Verey signal shot skyward from the control tower brought the pilots rapidly out from their crew room. Their parachutes were already positioned in their cockpit and we strapped them in. A wheeled heavy-duty 24 volt battery was already plugged into the engine and as the pilot pressed his starter button we made contact by pressing ours on the trolley, then, as soon as the engine fired, we removed the plug and button-clipped the cover, buffeted all the while by the slipstream from the spinning propeller a few inches from our right ear. We had no chocks, the Spit's own Dunlop compressed air brakes holding the aircraft stationary, and then they would be away, lifting off in threes, and receiving instruction by radio as they became airborne."

"On their return, often quite soon, they were re-fuelled (100 octane petrol) and gun ports re-patched to keep out dust until the next time. Linen patches, doped over these gun ports, blew away easily as soon as the guns fired. At the day's end, at dusk, we carried out our DI's and signed the Form 700, the cockpit covers were put on and flying controls toggled to prevent damage should the wind get up during the night. And so to the airmen's mess for supper, and to the ablutions for our daily shave and clean up."

"A rota system gave us a day off in every three starting at 1 p.m. and ending at noon the following day. A lot of time was spent waiting for the aircraft to take off, and then waiting for them to return. On one occasion, perhaps we were a little bored, we saw a covey of young partridges in the next field, bobbing and nibbling between the ploughed furrows. So, just for fun, we started shooting at them with our .303 Lee Enfield rifles. We must all have been very bad shots for not one was hit, and the birds continued to feed in spite of the little spurts of dust being thrown up all around them. On reflection, what was even more reprehensible was the fact that we had been firing across the main A338 road that ran by the airfield. Luckily, being wartime traffic was sparse and none had wanted to pass in the few short minutes we were firing!"

"The R.A.F. Regiment had not yet been formed and the responsibility for Ibsley's defence at this time fell upon units of the Royal Artillery and their 40mm Bofors, a gun capable of firing 120 2-lb shells a minute."

Sid Watson recalled that while a member of No. 234 Squadron at Ibsley, their dispersal was close to the main A338 Bournemouth – Salisbury road, and that whenever a bus was passing, and a "scramble" taking place from the airfield, the bus would stop and all the passengers had ring-side seats.

"Because Ibsley was such a well dispersed station", said George Bowdidge "with some sites a mile away from the airfield, and some well hidden in wooded areas, it was soon obvious that a bicycle would be a valuable possession. There were a few obtainable on issue but not nearly enough to go round so I did what many others had already done and brought my own bike from home. Such was the demand for personal transport, when one pilot, Sergeant Gray, who owned a very nice, almost new bicycle, failed to return from a sortie and it became obvious that he was not going to make it back, there was an immediate unholy dash by his fellow pilots for the possession of the now spare bicycle."

"One day in December 1941, the Ibsley Wing was given the job of escorting three Lockheed Hudsons to Brest and back. The bombers came from a base up-country and needed to re-fuel at Ibsley, where they were also to join up with our Spitfires. Although three landed, unfortunately only two took off again. This was because earlier, on taking off from their home base one Hudson pilot had adopted an unorthodox retraction of the undercarriage. Normally the still spinning wheels struck the underside of the wheel bays with an uncomfortable thump felt through the aircraft. This the pilot avoided by braking the spinning wheels immediately on becoming airborne but he then forget to release the brakes. Landing with the brakes on was not recommended, especially as the Hudson's brakes were powerful hydraulic seven-plate discs. As the pilot touched down, at Ibsley, the tail lifted just sufficiently for the tips of the three-bladed propellers to strike the ground, and very neatly they were bent backwards. Although the pilot had reacted swiftly and prevented a greater mishap, he didn't take off again that day."

Christmas 1941 was an easy time for the ground crews, the whole Wing had flown off on Christmas Eve, and did not return to Ibsley for several days. They had departed on another Ramrod operation attacking Brest once more and were expected back later in the day. They had land at St. Eval, Cornwall, for refuelling, as usual, but on their return and before they could take off the weather worsened suddenly and they were grounded, so while Ibsley ground crews had it easy their opposite numbers at St. Eval had plenty to do.

George also said "My working party was off duty in the afternoon of Christmas Eve and the three of us decided to spend it in Salisbury. We tried to hitch a lift but only got as far as Fordingbridge, from where we completed the journey by taking a 1s. 9d. return on the bus. In order to decide which cinema to visit we marched into the library to consult the local newspaper and I'm afraid somewhat disturbed the respectful silence assumed in such a place. We decided on the Picture House which was showing a couple of American films. Later we called in at the Salvation Army services canteen where we had a meal of bacon, mash and fried bread, accompanied by a cup of cocoa and two small bars of chocolate. Looking back, we must have possessed iron stomachs, but there's more to come! By this time it was 8 p.m. so we visited the Woolpack pub for a couple of pints and while waiting for the bus to take us back to Ibsley we rounded off with a cup of coffee and a bun at the snack bar in the bus station. Instead of the expected bus they put on a special coach for us Ibsleyites, so in effect we had a free ride onwards from Fordingbridge."

"On Christmas morning there was egg, bacon and sausages for breakfast, but I overslept and was mad at myself for missing it! We got up around 10.30 and after a leisurely wash and shave went to dinner at noon. The dining hall was decorated with flags and bunting and the tables had cloths for a change. We were served by the Officers and NCO's and also pilots who had not gone on the trip to Brest."

"We had soup followed by fish, then came the main course of turkey and pork, stuffing, apple sauce and gravy, baked potatoes and brussels sprouts. The traditional Christmas pudding and brandy sauce followed, and the meal was capped with an apple, beer, minerals, nuts, and cigarettes. It should be remembered that food rationing was in force, so all things considered it was a grand affair."

"During the meal the station orchestra, normally reserved for the Officers' Mess, played dance tunes and swing numbers, then, when we arrived at the crew room to go on duty, even though we had no aircraft, we each had a mince pie and two bottles of ale. I put one bottle on the window-sill behind me and a few minutes later when I looked round in order to finish that one off some smart Alec had swiped it."

When our dinner had settled we went on to the edge of the airfield and punted a football around. It wasn't very exciting, nobody had much energy. But then it was livened up by a pilot of No. 118 squadron who took up their pet Tiger Moth and chased the ball, flying at about eight feet off the ground. We left the ball to him. Once, when he banked, his wing tip creased the short winter grass, the pilot grinning from ear. Rain stopped play just before tea when we went to eat again."

## So Much Sadness, So Much Fun

"In the evening professional performers now in the R.A.F. put on a polished and enjoyable performance and I crawled into bed at 11.30 p.m., the end of a Christmas Day to remember.

"No. 234 Squadron also had a Tiger Moth for its use and usually it was flown by an off-duty pilot, official of course, both for relaxation, as a change from a Spitfire, and for conveying, when necessary someone or other between airfields in the Group."

"One of the sergeant-pilots of the squadron who had a W.A.A.F. girlfriend decided that he would take her up for a flight, but wrongly chose not to seek official permission. So, very early one morning, at the crack of dawn, she climbed into the front cockpit while he cranked the propeller. Unfortunately he had set the throttle a little too wide and as soon as the engine fired the bi-plane, which had no chocks or brakes, started to move forward. It was a long way to the controls in the rear cockpit around the wing tips and he had to run after it as it moved away from him. He couldn't run fast enough, and there was the Tiger Moth taxiing out on to the field with a desperate W.A.A.F. in the cockpit. Eventually an extra large tuft of grass caused the tail to lift and the aircraft was over on to its nose in no time. It had stopped alright. When we arrived, shortly afterwards, the girl had gone, none the worse for her adventure, but the Tiger Moth's wooden propeller was lying splintered on the ground and its tail pointed sadly skywards. We never knew if the pilot was disciplined, probably not."

There were pilots of many nationalities serving with the Royal Air Force, and in December 1941, Commander Andre Jubelin of the Free French Navy was posted from training unit at Heston to No. 118 Squadron at Ibsley.

In his book "The Flying Sailor", (Hurst and Blackett, 1953) he recalls his arrival at Ibsley, early on the morning of Christmas Eve, 1941. Jubelin tells of how, as he started on the way to his first operational airfield, his old Standard motorcar skidded in all directions on the icy roads. It had been snowing for three days. After leaving Winchester he entered the forest. It was a strange experience driving along an unknown road between huge trees covered, apparently, with stalactites. He recalled coming out on to a dismal, empty plain, the road then descended in a gentle gradient towards the valley. Jubelin said he found the little village of Ibsley and a few minutes later drove on to the runways which had been swept clear of show, that had been heaped in low banks on either side. They were grey strips in the white expanse. At the North-East corner of the airfield some fine elm trees motionless under their shell of frost sparkled in the sunshine. The chimneys of a long line of huts were all smoking at full blast. Facing them, in a well-dressed row, a dozen sheeted Spitfires awaited their next flight, and at the end of the runway stood two others, their engines still, but with the pilots seated in the cockpit ready to take off at the first warning. Men were obviously at war here.

Jubelin goes on to describe his first impression of the dispersal hut "a smoke-filled room, smelling of dust and cold tobacco ash, bandy legged armchairs, a split divan that trailed its springs like intestines. The cast iron stove in the middle of the room which emitted snaky and sulphurous coils of smoke from its crevices with a dented copper kettle about to splutter. Models of German aircraft hung from the ceiling and along one of the walls, on shelves, were Mae Wests and parachutes.". On his arrival Andre Jubelin recalls some ten R.A.F. pilots getting up to salute him, then returning to their various occupations, reading, cards, or a game of darts.

Jubelin spoke little English, but found there were two Dutch naval officers in the Squadron, and the three of them were soon gossiping together in excellent French.

There was still a lack of accommodation for personnel and, of necessity, many of No. 234 Squadron's pilots were billeted with local villagers.

At daybreak of December 30th, a glorious frosty morning lit by stars scintillating from a cloudless sky, the Ibsley Wing went down to Predannack, from where at 1315 hours led by Wing Commander Ian Gleed, with Squadron Leader John Carver, then a tactics man from Group, as his No. 2, they took off on a Circus operation against Brest, called "Veracity". The job of the Wing, which was stepped up at intervals of one thousand feet, was to see that the Halifax bombers reached the flak area without attack from enemy aircraft. Some Me 109's were seen and a straggling aircraft paid the price. Gleed led the bombers into the flak area, and one Spitfire was hit by a bomb which crashed right through one wing, (but luckily did not explode). The pilot managed to bring the plane home safely. The operation cost three bombers and three fighters. It was on this mission that Sergeant Pilot A. E. "Teddy" Joyce of No. 234 Squadron was lost and posted missing. He had parachuted from his plane, was wounded and taken prisoner of war. It was later learned he was in Stalag Luft

## So Much Sadness, So Much Fun

III, the notorious Prisoner of War camp from which the great escape was made in 1944.

The first news, heard by Teddy Joyce's parents, that their son was safe but a prisoner of war, came during a broadcast by "Lord Haw Haw", the official confirmation came later. Could it have been because Sgt. A.E. "Teddy" Joyce had the same surname as "Lord Haw Haw (William Joyce) that the information was broadcast?

*Sgt. Pilot A.E. "Teddy" Joyce, 234 Squadron, R.A.F. Ibsley,1941*
Photo: Mrs. S. Dooley, Mrs. P. Marrable, Mrs. J Simmonds

# 1942

## Backs to the wall

Andre Jubelin took part in a Rhubarb on 14th January, 1942 and recalls that when they reached the harbour mouth at Port-en-Bessin a crowd of fisherman waved their caps to salute them, and some also climbed their mastheads to get nearer to them. Jubelin goes on to say that he was often asked, "Can you really identify a house or a vehicle from such a height?". His reply: "People don't seem to know much about it. Not only can we recognise a house but we could describe anyone standing at the door and know whether a girl has a red or blue blouse on as we fly over her at 250 miles an hour."

Jubelin goes on to tell of how during a flight his seat came unscrewed, being held by only the back legs, so that it rocked every time he shifted position. He had to land without the use of rudder pedals, and with his toes tucked under the seat. A subsequent enquiry found the fitter guilty of neglecting to lock one of the spring loaded plungers into position. The fitter was later court-martialled.

Early in January, only a matter of weeks after taking command on No. 118, Squadron Leader Humphrey Russell was posted to No. 82 Group, Northern Ireland. Johnny Carver, D.F.C., a Squadron Leader Tactics at 10 Group was then posted in to lead No. 118.

During an air-to-sea firing exercise in January 1942, a very cold month, Sergeant Pilot Eric Campbell was lost when his Spitfire (BL568) broke-up in mid air and crashed at Rockbourne near Fordingbridge, on Saturday 10th and he was killed. This was an untimely death because during this exercise a message was received at Ibsley that Eric Campbell's commission had finally been approved and so, as the inscription on his War Grave in Bristol (Canford) Cemetery reads, he died a Pilot Officer.

On 15th January the airfield at Ibsley was under snow, but by daybreak the runways had been swept clear using bundles of heather, probably collected from Ibsley Common.

*So Much Sadness, So Much Fun*

Three weeks after being taken Prisoner of War Sergeant Pilot Teddy Joyce, in a letter sent from Stalag Luft III wrote home, and the following are some extracts from his handwritten letter.

*"You will have to excuse the writing as I have to prop the pad up on top of my legs. This is quite a good place we are in now, the "doc" seems to know his stuff.*

*I was not planning to get shot down on the wrong side of the New Year but things went wrong that day. I thought it might be a good idea to have a ME 109 on my birthday (although the actual date was 30.12.41) and after having a crack I hit some heavy flak from Brest, I think. Things really started humming then. One of my ailerons was blown off and a shell burst right under the wing of the kite and bits of hot shrapnel were whistling around the cockpit, great fun. The aileron loss resulted in my being unable to stop her spinning. Then it became difficult to stay awake so I had to bail out over France. I did fall asleep on the way down and woke up again on the ground. The army then took me into hospital in Brest where they got busy with the jolly old knife and cat gut. Actually I finished up with 23 splinters in the left leg and 15 in the right all below the knee. Then in another hospital somewhere else. The pins will be a little while yet before they will walk properly."*

On Thursday, 29th January, 1942, No. 118 Squadron's Commanding Officer Johnny Carver, Sergeant Frank Brown, Pilot Officer Ted Ames and Sergeant Hardy Kerr took part in a successful sweep on the distillery at Corseilleur Sur Mur. On the return journey Sergeant Kerr was seen to be lagging, then his aircraft suddenly shot into the air, turned on its back and crashed into the sea. Kerr was seen to bail out at 400' with his parachute opening before he hit the water. Subsequent searching by Coastal Command and his fellow pilots proved useless and Kerr was lost.

In February the fitter who had forgotten to lock Andre Jubelin's seat properly came before a court-martial. He was charged on two counts, the first of endangering a pilot's life by gross negligence – a very serious offence – and secondly of negligence in endangering His Majesty's Spitfire while on active service by leaving two starboard pins undone. He pleaded not guilty to both, but was cleared of the first only. The sentence was twenty-one days detention.

*1942*

W.A.A.F. Ambulance Driver, Hazel Sims (maiden name Sheppard), known as "Johnnie", on ambulance outside the Station Hospital, the 'As You Like It', at North Gorley, 1941
Photo: H.Sims

Dr. Gordon, No. 234 Squadron Medical Officer, standing alongside ambulance.
Photo:H. Sims

*So Much Sadness, So Much Fun*

On Monday, 2nd February, No. 118 Squadron lost Pilot Officer Ted Ames during a dog fight whilst on a "Rhubarb" with Flight Lieutenant Peter Howard-Williams to whom he was flying as No. 2.

That same evening there was another tragedy when Nurse Orderly, Aircraftman Second Class, Frederick Jones of the M.I. room was knocked down and killed by a car, while walking on the nearside of the A338 road, back from the cinema at Fordingbridge. The story was that only half an hour before the accident he was discussing the loss of Ted Ames with a pal, and Jones had said, "thank goodness I am in a safe job on the ground".

When Ron Rutter was posted to 2763 R.A.F. Regiment at Ibsley in February 1942, the weather was, in his own words, really b....y terrible. He was on a Bofors Gun on Three Tree Hill at Rockford and remembers how he enjoyed doing the cooking for about six people up there, and that they often had roast lamb.

There was yet more tragedy for No. 118 Squadron on Wednesday, 11th February, when Sergeant Pilots Thomas Mathers and Keith Buettel (Australian) collided whilst flying at 5,000 feet in the vicinity of West Grinstead near Salisbury. They were both buried at Ringwood Cemetery, with full Military Honours on 17th February. The officiating Minister was the Rev. Major, Wesleyan, who was assisted by Ibsley's own Station Padre, Rev. Catley. The band of the Oxford and Berkshire Light Infantry were in attendance.

Fred Fox was an armourer at Ibsley with No. 3042 Servicing Echelon, attached to Nos. 234 and 66 Squadrons, and married his wife Dorothy on 28th February. He remembers how Fred "Chiefy" Hando said all available people were to gather at the Royal Oak at North Gorley to give him a wedding present, and a few beers. His own N.C.O. at that time was Sergeant Lewis, a somewhat morbid man, who lived out, and said he wouldn't be able to make it. He was somewhat henpecked. Chiefy Hando went atomic and ordered him to turn up. Sergeant Lewis had a few beers – Strong of Romsey – terrible stuff at the time – at any time! Used to think it was really Reckitts & Colmans. However, at the end of the evening Lewis staggered out, got on his bike – well nearly, careered over the bit of grass, straight into the slimy green pond opposite the pub. Sergeant Lewis forever afterward treated me with a certain amount of disdain and until he was posted overseas I always got the mucky end of the stick when jobs were dished out. It seemed that somehow I was to

*1942*

*Pilot Officer Roderick McKenzie and "P/O" Sally-Anne Mullington.
McKenzie killed in action 9th March, 1942
Photo: Mrs. S-A. Salm*

blame for the state of the pond that caused him to cut such a ridiculous figure.

Three German battleships, Scharnhorst, Gneisenau and Prinz Eugen, had been trapped in Brest Harbour for several months, and had already been the subject of attacks by bombers, escorted by fighters, including those of the Ibsley Wing. On 12th February, however, in inclement weather the German Navy seized an opportunity to break out of Brest and steam up the English Channel at speed in an attempt to reach the port of Wilhelmshaven, Germany, for a safer refuge. Heavy morning fog over the airfields of Southern England had precluded any R.A.F. reconnaissance flights, enabling the convoy of three capital battleships, heavily escorted by destroyers, 'E' boats and flak ships to slip out of Brest Harbour undetected.

## So Much Sadness, So Much Fun

A request for a "Rhubarb" over the area, and a shipping recce at dawn had been rejected. This was a most unfortunate decision as the weather began to clear a little and the warships would probably have been seen. As it turned out, however, it was not until several hours later that the convoy was spotted, entering the Straits of Dover, by two pilots from R.A.F. Kenley.

Wing Commander Ian Gleed and his Ibsley Wing were quickly alerted, as were many other operational units in the South of England. The Ibsley pilots were sent off to West Malling, Kent, for re-fuelling and a briefing on what was now Operation "Fuller". The plan was to fly from West Malling in an attempt to secure air superiority over the retreating German ships and allow the vulnerable torpedo bombers time to execute their attacks without being interfered with by enemy fighters.

By this time, however, the main sacrifices had been made in attacks against the ships. Lieutenant Commander Eugene Esmonde, D.S.O., of the Fleet Air Arm and his six gallant Swordfish crews had made their suicidal attack. All six Swordfish were shot down by flak or fighters, and Esmonde (who was subsequently awarded a posthumous Victoria Cross, for valour and resolution in action against the enemy, died along with eleven of his men.

Other bombers and torpedo aircraft made repeated attacks, but all failed. The weather by then was extremely bad and the Germans had put up a mighty air screen over the convoy. Added to this, smoke screens from the ships made the task even more difficult.

The only successes for the Ibsley Wing were two Messerschmitts destroyed by No. 234 Squadron. No. 118 Squadron lost Pilot Officer Ivan Stone of the Royal New Zealand Air Force, and No. 234 Squadron Pilot Officer Dennis Pike and Sergeant Pilot Don McLeod. The latter ran short of fuel and made a forced landing in Northern France, only to be taken prisoner and subsequently end up in Stalag Luft III.

A disappointing day for Gleed's Ibsley Wing and the other R.A.F. units involved in the operation, for the German capital ships had escaped without too much damage.

On 9th March the Ibsley Wing, 118, 234 and 501 Squadrons went over to Redhill, Surrey, for an 11 Group "Circus", bombers escorted by fighters with the intention of bringing enemy fighters into

## 1942

combat. No. 118 were engaged in a dog fight with Focke Wolf 190s and Messerschmitt 109E's. Pilot Officer Roderick 'Mac' McKenzie got five cannon shells in the fuselage of his Spitfire and was also wounded. He made a gallant effort to get his aircraft back, but after crossing the English coast crash landed on the Dover to Canterbury road and was killed.

It was at this time too, that No. 501's Squadron Leader, Christopher "Bunny" Currant, while on a mission to attack a fuel depot in Northern France, received a bullet wound to the head, when attacked by FW 190's. Although in severe pain he managed to get back across the Channel and landed at Lympne airfield in Kent. He was unaware that the tyres on his aircraft, Spitfire W3846, SD-Z, (W3846) had been punctured by bullets from the Focke Wulf 190's, which caused the aircraft to somersault on landing. Ground crews were quickly on the scene and he was dragged from the wreckage and taken to hospital in Folkestone, where he had an operation to remove shrapnel from his skull, but he was flying again within a month. However, seven pieces of shrapnel still remain, even now, as a permanent reminder of that day.

A few days later there was yet more gloom and doom for No. 118 when their Commanding Officer, Squadron Leader Johnny Carver was shot down into the sea five miles West of the Casquettes. Whilst it was hoped he might be picked up there seemed little hope as he had been shot down so near the French coast.

The Wing was soon escorting bomb carrying Hurricanes, 2 Group light bombers and the heavies of Bomber Command. Many of the "Circus" operations were very successful, but a long range sweep of 300 miles, made on 15th March, 1942 nearly ended in disaster. In bad weather, and short of fuel, 28 Spitfires landed at Exeter, four scraped into Bolt Head and four crash-landed in various parts of Cornwall with the loss of one pilot, Sergeant James Hogg, of 234 Squadron.

The following day, 16th, brought some great and unexpected good news, 118's C.O. Johnny Carver had been picked up, full of cheer, floating steadily in his dinghy a few miles off Portland. He had made about 70 miles as the crow flies and had been at sea for nearly 57 hours before being picked up by H.M.S. Tynedale. His Intelligence Report on what happened reads as follows:

## So Much Sadness, So Much Fun

Wing Commander Ian 'Widge' Gleed, D.S.O., D.F.C., Wing Leader, R.A.F. Ibsley, 1941/42.
Photo: R. Gleed

*1942*

## Intelligence Report, S/Ldr. J. C. Carver, 118 Squadron
## Roadstead Operation, Middle Wallop Wing, 13/3/42

"At 1725 hours, Red 1, (S/Ldr. Carver) when at sea-level, saw a twin engine aircraft passing behind from port to starboard at about 1500 feet at 3 o'clock. He turned to port, climbing steeply, and closing up identified it as a Ju 88 from the fine rear starboard quarter. He then gave a one second burst of cannon and machine gun from the rear starboard fine quarter, travelling at 240 A.S.I. and closing from 200 to 150 yards. Accurate return fire was received from both the upper and lower rear gunners and Red 1's aircraft was hit in the radiator, probably by machine-gun bullets. Continuing the attack from dead astern, Red 1 used up all his ammunition (there was a stoppage in one cannon) from 150 yards closing to 120 yards, still at 240 A.S.I. He observed de Wilde strikes on the a/c. He claims that this aircraft was damaged by him. Owing to glycol fumes in the cockpit and glycol temperature of 120, Red 1, setting course for home attempted to jettison the hood. The rear portion became detached but hood was still held by the catch in the front which, despite every effort of the pilot failed to become detached. Glycol temperature stabilized at 110 but oil temperature rose steadily to 100 and became very rough. Red 1 meanwhile had been giving distress calls on the R.T. and had attempted to gain height but condition of engine would not allow him to go higher than 2,000 feet. No reply was heard from ground control but contact was maintained with Blue 1, which went up to 8,000 feet to give a fix. Suddenly the rest of the hood became detached and struck Red 1 a stunning blow in the face, which knocked him out for a short period. On recovering himself, aircraft was sat 1,300 feet and unable to maintain height, so Red 1 turned the aircraft on its back and bailed out at a point 3 to 4 miles west of the Casquettes. Red 1's watch stopped at 1728 hours when he hit the water.

On leaving the aircraft, head-first, the first pull at the ripcord failed to open the parachute but a second more determined pull opened the parachute at about 400 feet. Just as he was entering the water, Red 1 attempted to release his parachute by striking the quick release box. He apparently did not strike hard enough and struck the water attached to the parachute. He held his nose as he went into the water, the entry being quite smooth. He came up immediately and did not bother to blow up his Mae West. He then got rid of the parachute harness, got the dinghy out of its pack and proceeded to inflate it. Everything worked perfectly and the dinghy

## So Much Sadness, So Much Fun

was well blown up. He had considerable difficulty in climbing into the dinghy and discovered he was entangled in the shrouds of his parachute. He managed to disentangle the parachute and then had no difficulty in climbing into the dinghy. On entering the dinghy, he proceeded to bale out all the water and found that there were no leaks. He decided not to open his aid-to-escape box until he was really hungry as he expected that since the box was not water tight, the contents might be useless. He had covered himself over with the aprons and hood cover by about 1800 hours and, although his clothes were wet, he was not unduly cold. Thinking it possible that boats might be sent to his rescue, he kept awake all night blowing his whistle at short intervals. There was a South wind blowing at the time. On the morning of the 14th, Red 1 discovered that the wind was still blowing from the South. By timing roughly the pieces of seaweed passing the dinghy he decided that the wind was contributing a speed of three quarters of a mile per hour (or a foot a second), also that there was a following sea. The distance to be covered was thought to be 70 miles and he estimated that with the same weather conditions continuing he would make English coast in three days. As he continued to feel quite fit, he decided to allow seven days for the journey, and opening his emergency tin rationed the contents to one-seventh per day. The edible contents were slightly soggy but quite palatable, but the compass was useless through water. The compass in his button was also damaged by water and u/s. He forgot about the compass in his foreign purse. A further compass in his belt could not be used as it was of the hanging type and impossible to keep stead under the circumstances. Checking his course, by the sun during the day and the North Start at night, he was able to fix his progress. On the 14th two unidentified enemy aircraft were seen to the South at about 2,000 feet. Nothing else was seen that day.

On the morning of the 15th three unescorted Hudson aircraft passed one mile to the North and what might have been a Lysander was seen to the West. In the afternoon a convoy of ships carrying balloons was seen to the North. These signs satisfied Red 1 that he was making progress according to schedule. During the day of the 14th the weather was fine, the sun shone, but it was not possible for Red 1 to become completely dry as however much baling was done there was always a certain amount of sea being shipped between the two aprons. As the dinghy drifted at right angles to the wind it was found that by unfastening the apron on the windward side and

## 1942

holding as a sail a slight increase in speed was obtained, but more sea was shipped in consequence. It was worth while to hold up the apron during the day although this meant baling out every half hour. At night it was found advisable to close everything up and sleep. Red 1 managed to get four to five hours sleep at night. He used the special paddles whilst awake at night as these could be used with both aprons done up. During the night of 15th to 16th Red 1 was awakened by the noise of approaching ship's engines and found himself in the middle of a convoy. He signalled S.O.S. on his whistle and heard an acknowledgement shouted from the nearest ship which was passing 150 yards away.

The escort vessel H.M.S. Tynedale (Hunt Class destroyer) turned round and re-appeared ten minutes later, showing riding lights. As soon as these were seen Red 1 blew continuously on his whistle and, when the ship was 100 yards away, a searchlight was shone on him. Ladders were lowered at various points on the ship's starboard side. The destroyer came alongside the dinghy, and Red 1 thinking that all that was now necessary was to climb up the nearest ladder, proceeded to try and do so. He found, however, that he was very weak and could do no more than get his arm through the rung of the ladder and hold on. The dinghy meanwhile had drifted away. One of the ships crew jumped into the water and fastened a lifebuoy round Red 1, who was then hauled aboard, at 0310 hours on 16th March, 1942, about seven miles South of Portland.

At no time did Red 1 feel thirsty during the 57 hours that he had been in the dinghy, but when it rained on the 15th he sucked the rain water off his rubber apron. He said it would have been possible to collect rainwater in the apron and transfer it to the rubber bottle in the emergency tin if necessary. Less water was shipped if the dinghy was kept fully inflated at regular intervals with the hand bellows. The aprons of the dinghy were found to be absolutely invaluable. On the evening of the 15th it was found that the effect of the salt water had caused a split at the point where the soft rubber of the hand bellows joins the harder rubber of the end pieces making inflation of the dinghy by this means a good deal hard, though it could still be managed by holding the thumb over the split portion of the bellows.

When baling out Red 1 lost his left boot but otherwise kept all his clothes on. The right boot was kept on and although always damp, kept his right foot warm whereas the left foot, minus boot, became numb. He kept on his wet gloves the whole time but his hands

## So Much Sadness, So Much Fun

remained quite warm and pliable. One benzedrine tablet was taken on the second day as the tablets were getting mushy having been blown overboard whilst they were spread out to dry.

On being picked up by H.M.S. Tynedale Commanding Officer Carver was taken to Haslar Hospital at Gosport, but insisted on coming back to Ibsley. Peter Howard-Williams went down to fetch him and he arrived back in triumph at lunch time. He was carried in and put to bed, but was remarkably fit considering his ordeal and very cheerful. His achievement is bound to have a terrific effect on the morale of fighter pilots.

The Daily Mail published the story of Johnny Carver's feat on 27th March, 1942. The report by Colin Bednall, Daily Mail Air Correspondent, was headed "R.A.F. Men Told: Study This Story. Cool Head Carver Beat the Sea". It went on to say *"Young fighter pilots have been recommended to study the story of 26 years-old Squadron Leader J. C. Carver, who was picked up near Portland after 56 hours, paddling across the Channel in a rubber dinghy. It has been described by a high air officer as a classic example of what a pilot in trouble can do to help himself."*. It then went on to give Carver's account of his ordeal.

Daisy Porter recalled how March, 1942 came in like a lion and it was a very windy month. There was a incident when a Spitfire coming in to land was blown by a heavy gust of wind and hit one of two stationary Spitfires that were waiting at readiness, and with a member of the squadron ground crew at each. The landing Spitfire bounced off, cutting one plane almost in two, but not injuring the pilot, then bounced in the air and almost on the other stationary plane killing one Aircraftman. It was said that it was a local lad, from Ringwood, Cecil Bowey of No. 234 Squadron, who was attending to the pilot at the time, while the other airman sustained a broken ankle. Station ambulances and fire engines were quickly on the scene.

Also on Friday, 27th March, Sgt. Childs of No. 501 Squadron, flying Spitfire AB965 was killed. During a practice interception he lost control of his aircraft and it spun into the ground near Burley, in the New Forest.

André Jubelin told of how at nearly midnight on 3rd April, 1942, there was a bitter wind blowing through every crack in the dispersal hut. It did however reduce the reek of the stove that made one's

## 1942

head go round. Black-out curtains were only half drawn, all lights were out and there were pallid gleams through the misted panes of the huge airfield, covered with a light layer of snow.

No. 118 Squadron pilots Commander Jubelin, and Sergeant Pilot Micky Green, who was dozing, were comfortable in their dispersal hut armchairs. Behind them in the gloom was the usual pile of disorder, life-jackets and parachutes, newspapers on the floor, cards still scattered over the table, and curled up at their feet, Duke, the squadron's bull mastiff, growling in his canine dreams. The three of them are the night section. Three? Well, when the warning sounded Duke would gallop beside Jubelin and Green and supervise their final adjustments with shrill yelps. He would watch them taking off and then return to drop into his place in the hut, which would have still been warm, and resume his canine dreams, with a sigh of resignation. Jubelin goes on to tell of how on this particular evening he himself was dreaming, then "Ting!" Operations were calling. The klaxon wailed, hurling them as though by a spring from their chairs. The night struck an icy blow, snow crackling under their boots. The covered lorry, sprinkled with white simply flew along. Two mechanics rose out of the night and helped feverishly. Parachute straps, leather helmet. Where are my gloves? A quick rub with a rag over the windscreen. The routine accelerated. Red lamp, green indicator, engine primer. "All clear? Contact!". The propeller began to turn fitfully. One could still hear familiar sounds – a barking dog, a thicket shuddering under a gust of wind, the rumble of the starter. Then suddenly everything was obliterated by the tremendous outburst of the power of a thousand horses. There were mauve plumes from the exhaust. The brakes were off and the machine came to life, dancing over the inequalities in the ground and rolling towards the start of the runway. Jubelin requested permission to take off. A green eye winked showing him the way. With slight jerks the Spitfire began to roll along in the snow, while the navigation flares slid over the white plain and the tops of the trees rose, in menace, against the pale sky. Full throttle. The machine shuddered, then bounded proudly forward. The barrier of the hostile woods dropped back into the jumble of the landscape. Jubelin extinguished the navigation lights, pushed in a lever, and two slight bumps told him that that the wheels were in place. He was flying.

## So Much Sadness, So Much Fun

Heather Cottage, Rockford, where there was always a warm welcome for the pilots of No. 118 Squadron. Wooden Rockford W.I. Hut, demolished when P-47 Thunderbolt crashed on it, in 9144, visible on the left.
Photo: Mrs. S-A. Salm

"Robbie the tea taster"
Flight LieutenantRobson, No. 118 Squadron, relaxes to music from a wind-up gramophone in the garden of Heather Cottage
Photo: Mrs. S-A. Salm

*1942*

"We'll keep the home fires burning"
Jean Mullington and Ena Elliott collect wood for the fires at Heather Cottage, 1941/42.
Photo: Mrs. S-A. Salm

Ground crew, No. 66 Squadron at N.A.A.F.I. van on Ibsley airfield, 1942
Photo: T. Hamer

## So Much Sadness, So Much Fun

Jubelin was alone at last, in a sense at any rate. The ritual had been performed. The cockpit was open, lamps were out. The graduations and phosphorescent indicators were illuminated on his instrument panel and he had picked out a star so as not to have to consult his compass. Away at sea a convoy was steaming with all its lights dimmed, and Jubelin and Green's mission was to defend it against the nocturnal Junkers which they successfully did.

With the Royal Air Force now on the offensive, sweeps over occupied Europe code-named "Rhubarbs" and "Ramrods" were the order of the day at Ibsley, although its position, not far from the coast ensured a regular share of convoy patrol work.

Wing Commander "Bunny" Currant remembers the day, early in April 1942, when No. 501 Squadron were spectators to the tragic 'Battle of Imber'. An army co-operation exercise was being held on Salisbury Plain, and the squadron flew several rehearsals in preparation for the main demonstration which was to be held on 13th April.

He went on to say that "During this event No. 501 was detailed to attack dummy troops on the ground with cannon after the twelve gun Hurricanes had done their stuff. A week was spent, in good weather, on rehearsals over the target area."

"On the fateful day we were circling above at 1,500 feet and I had a grandstand view of the crisis as it happened. An American pilot Flight Sergeant William McLachlan, Royal Canadian Air Force, serving with No. 175 Squadron from Warmwell, fired upon what he thought were dummy troops on the Imber Range. What he had actually fired upon was a large gathering of Army, Navy and R.A.F. top brass. Forty-two were killed. The only man to remain on his feet, firing a Verey pistol at the attacking Hurricane was Jimmy Ronald (the Wing Commander Armament Officer at No. 10 Group)."

"We were immediately ordered to return to Ibsley. To watch that lone Hurricane dive on those officers and open fire was sickening. I felt so sorry for the pilot whom I subsequently discovered had never had the opportunity to fly over the target area beforehand. He was a last-minute substitute: such situations portend tragedy."

Flight Sergeant McLachlan, the pilot of the Hurricane, who was found guilty of an error of judgement by a subsequent Board of Enquiry was himself killed in action on Monday, 29th June when attacking enemy shipping in the Channel.

## 1942

Also, in early April Wing Commander Ian 'Widge' Gleed led six Spitfires from No. 501 Squadron, plus six from No. 118, on a shipping reconnaissance over Cherbourg, reporting on his return that there were two armed trawlers sitting in the harbour with larger ocean going vessels nearby. Shortly afterwards a strike was organised against them.

On 7th April, Flight Lieutenant John "Robbie" Robson and Commander André Jubelin of No. 118 Squadron, at cockpit readiness, were scrambled when an unidentified aircraft was reported over the Channel at 20,000 feet ten miles South of Portland. After climbing they spotted a plane high above, heading South. The two pilots chased after it, but the 'bogey' had the advantage of height and speed over them. However, with throttles wide open they gradually began to close the gap, finally getting within range. It looked like a 109, but Jubelin was unsure, so climbed a little and then recognised it as a Spitfire. In his book, The Flying Sailor, André Jubelin records that it turned out to be a Wing Commander out for a morning spin and he hoped that the man would get a dressing down appropriate to his rank, for presumably not having proper authority for his flight nor letting 'ops' know that he was out on his own. However, perhaps Jubelin was a little put out at having to rush after this machine and be put in the invidious position of nearly shooting down a friendly Spitfire and its pilot. It later transpired that the offending Wing Commander was none other than their own Ian Gleed!

Another occasion, recalled by George Bowdidge, of No. 234 Squadron, was when three brand new Spitfires were delivered, marked out with a small flag of Denmark painted below the cockpit. The arrival of these three Spitfires at Ibsley was reported on the front page of "FREE DENMARK", The Free Danish Monthly, published in London. Under the heading Danish Spitfires, Churchill's Message to Free Danes, "Denmark will be Free", it stated: *On 9th April, 1942, Mr. Winston Churchill honoured the Free Danes throughout the world by personally accepting, at 10 Downing Street, a cheque for £38,300, the final sum raised by the Danish Fighter Fund.*

On 10th April the first flight of fighters paid for by the Danish Fighter Fund were presented to the Royal Air Force, at a fighter aerodrome in South West England, (which we now know to have been Ibsley) where they flew with No. 234 Squadron.

One Spitfire was named after Neils Ebbesen, the Danish hero who, in 1340, killed Count Gert the Commander of the German

*So Much Sadness, So Much Fun*

Armies which had occupied Denmark. Another was called Valdemar Atterdag after the Danish King who completed Neils Ebbesen's work by expelling the Germans and re-uniting the Danish provinces. The name of the third machine was "Skagen ind" which means "Homeward bound through the Skaw".

Following the presentation the Danish Spitfires then took off on their first flight and disappeared in close formation into the blue sky. When they returned they broke formation, one of the pilots bringing his Spitfire down in a steep dive and pulling out of it into a steep climb, just over the heads of those watching from the airfield. At a considerable height the pilot did a few turns, flew upside down over the airfield, and righting his machine joined the other two planes to make a perfect landing.

After this first trip the Danish pilots expressed their gratitude to their fellow countrymen who had made it possible for them to fly their own machines. Now that they had these new Spitfires all they wanted was a chance to fight the "Jerries".

No. 118 Squadron learnt, on 9th April, that Royal Australian Air Force Sergeant Pilot Hardy Kerr's body had been washed up at Friston, in a very decomposed state (he was lost on the 29th January) after so long in the sea. It is believed that two pilots from the squadron were sent to identify the body, which they did mainly by a model Spitfire, about an inch long, which Kerr always carried on him. Two days later Sergeant Hardy Kerr, from Queensland, was laid to rest in Ringwood Cemetery. The Pipe Band of the Irish Fusiliers was in attendance and the service was conducted by the Station Chaplain, Rev'd Catley.

On 15th April Ian 'Widge' Gleed led the Ibsley Wing on their first No. 10 Group Circus. No. 118 Squadron flew as close escort to nine Douglas Bostons bombing Cherbourg. No. 234 and No. 501 flying above, and above them were two Polish Spitfire squadrons. Heavy flak was encountered over the target area and No. 234, who were attacked by enemy fighters, lost two aircraft, and their pilots. They were Spitfire Vb, AB987 flown by Flight Lieutenant Denys Mileham, aged 22, and Spitfire VB, W3967, flown by an American serving with the R.A.F., Pilot Officer Michael Simon, aged 26, from Pennsylvania. Both are commemorated on the Runnymede Memorial. They were claimed by Me109's of JG26.

## 1942

After the battle Gleed dropped down to search for a pilot in the sea and in his log book later recorded: 'Nearly got shot down when searching for a pilot in the sea, but how or why we do not know.

The following day Gleed led No. 118 Squadron and Wing as escort to six Hurribombers attacking the aerodrome at Maupertus. There was a brief exchange with some enemy fighters but no claims were made. One Hurribomber went into the sea with glycol streaming and a Spitfire went down in flames. Although the Hurricane pilot managed to get into his dinghy, and several Spitfires stayed over him for as long as possible, including Wing Commander Ian Gleed, but Flight Sergeant Bricker Forman, Royal Canadian Air Force, of No. 175 Squadron was not rescued. No. 175 Squadron had only been formed as a fighter-bomber squadron at Warmwell, Dorset on 3rd March, 1942, becoming operational a month later, and flew on its first bombing raid, to Maupertus airfield, on 16th April, when tragically Forman was lost.

On the same day Sergeant Maurice Costello, Royal New Zealand Air Force, of No. 118 Squadron was wounded while on an ASR sorties off St. Albans Head when attacked by enemy aircraft, his Spitfire Vb, AB846 was damaged, but later repaired. No. 234 Squadron lost two pilots, Pilot Officer George Bland, aged 20, while on a Ramrod near Rauville, and Pilot Officer Ralph Woolass, who was attacked by an Me109 while on an early evening ASR sortie off Cherbourg.

Wing Commander Ian Gleed later put himself on the readiness rota. This was a job that could have been left to junior officers but Gleed believed that he should share every job with his men – even down to the boring job of cockpit readiness.

During his time with 3042 Servicing Echelon at Ibsley Derek Haselwood also recalled there was a sad incident when a Spitfire of No. 501 Squadron coming into the airfield bounced on another, which was on readiness near the Ellingham end of the runway, killing the flight mechanic who was attending to the pilot. He also said that "Wing Commander Ian Gleed was well known to us. His aircraft, which bore the letters IR-G, would come in requiring several hours work on it, for which he allowed about ten minutes".

Milton Jowsey, a Royal Canadian Air Force pilot, was with No 234 Squadron at Ibsley from November 1941 to April 1942. He remembers how he arrived at Ibsley as a nineteen year old, one year out of secondary school, in a new country with a very different living environment and all kinds of new things to do (Ringwood pubs and Salisbury pub crawls) plus several short passes to London. Visits to pubs in Poole netted baskets of fish for breakfast as the locals were going to educate this poor young Canadian. "I couldn't take fish to start the day off but the rest of the mess certainly did them justice" said Milton. I was a very busy boy.

"A bad weather experience found Lady Luck looking after me. One Sunday afternoon in early April, 1942, several squadrons, in excellent weather, left on a Sweep over the Channel Islands where we found no targets. Coming back the weather deteriorated while we operated under the control of a more western group. The C.O. couldn't raise anyone on the R.T., so we let down through the cloud in tight formation in three lines of fours, line astern. I was last in the centre four, so I was concentrating straight ahead. Suddenly the plane ahead of me was just clearing a hedge and there was a blue flash on either side. I broke off and my low flying training came to the fore with me dodging trees and telephone poles, then flying down some small river and on through a whole mass of ships. Fortunately, for my nerves, I couldn't see the cables and balloons in the cloud which would have increased my unease, as I was in Plymouth harbour. I then found myself following the coast line below the cliff elevation as the cloud just curled over the edge. The water looked cold, rough and uninviting and I could raise no one on my R.T.

I needed a few nervous pee's and used the funnel and hose for the first time and this apparently just ended up in the bottom of the fuselage.

Things looked pretty grim when suddenly a green verey flare came off the cliff edge (turned out to be Bolthead, Devon). Lined things up and did a circuit below runway elevation, nipped up over the edge and plonked down on the runway.

A Polish Squadron was stationed here. While I recuperated the ground crew refuelled and checked out the plane, they all seemed to tower over my six foot one inch height. There was a commotion around my plane and I was invited over to help solve the problem. There were half a dozen gigantic ground crew dipping their finger in this liquid sloshing around in the fuselage and tasting for oil or glycol leak, but found this very strange liquid – could I help them? I was sorry I couldn't help at all. It had to remain a mystery !!"

## 1942

Milton also recalled a memorable session with the R.A.F. Ibsley Station dentist, which would have been at the Station Hospital and Dentistry at the 'As You Like It', North Gorley. "At the time, the Royal Canadian Air Force officers medical and dental needs were looked after, but the Royal Air Force only looked after the dental needs for other ranks. While Royal Canadian Air Force aircrew were assigned to Royal Air Force squadrons the R.A.F. had to supply all required needs. I had a dental appointment just before noon (I think a Saturday) and found myself in the dentist's chair confronted by an angry dentist. He went into a tirade about North Americans being spoiled and demanding too much dental work. He stated that he intended catching the train from Salisbury in an hour. To make his point he wore his great coat while fixing a cavity. I can't remember whether he kept his cap on – I think he did. That, of course, was my last visit there which I am sure suited him."

Incidentally, we always took the bus to Salisbury to board the train as the Exeter to London route never seemed to be touched by bombs while trains out of Ringwood or Bournemouth went through Southampton and always had delays, diversions, etc. very unreliable."

Friday 17th April was a busy day for the Ibsley Wing. A daring daylight attack on a factory at Augsburg, deep in enemy territory, was made by a force of Avro Lancasters. Raids by light bombers of No. 2 Group acted as diversions, while "Widge" Gleed's Wing flew a sweep over Cherbourg, taking off from Ibsley at 0900 hours and returning at 1025 hours.

The morning was hazy, 5/10th cloud to 10,000 feet. Three Messerschmitts were spotted by Gleed flying towards the Spitfire formation from below. Gleed immediately turned to starboard and commenced a diving attack. The Me109's began a steep climb and also turned, frustrating Gleed's attack as he failed to get within range of them. He therefore ordered Bunny Currant and No. 501, being the medium cover squadron, to have a go at them. Seeing the 109's, No. 501 then started to turn towards them which enabled Gleed to climb hard and close with the three Germans.

Seeing the danger from both sides, two of the Messerschmitt pilots dived away and No. 234 Squadron, who were high cover, peeled away after them. The remaining Me 109 was surrounded by Spitfires. Bunny Currant opened fire at it and so did Pilot Officer R.

## So Much Sadness, So Much Fun

"Dickie" Newbery, Pilot Officer A. E. Drossaert (Belgian) and Sergeant Pilot Miroslav Rocovski (Czech). Gleed also entered the fray and fired, observing hits on the Messerschmitts belly and centre fuselage. After the attack the Me 109 stalled and was then seen to fall away vertically. Although Gleed was of the opinion that the Me 109 pilot had been hit, and possibly killed, but as the plane was not seen to crash they could only claim it as a probable. No. 234 Squadron managed to engage the other two Me 109's, with one being claimed as damaged by Flying Officer B. Wydrowski.

The Wing then reformed with Ian Gleed leading his Spitfires back across the Channel but they were followed by other enemy fighters. Fuel was running low so they could not afford to engage, but when the English coast came into sight Gleed turned towards them, putting his Spitfire into 12 boost and 3,000 revs. The Germans however turned back and he was unable to get closer than six hundred yards, but it put the wind up the Me 109's.

The following day Wing Commander Ian 'Widge' Gleed led No. 234 Squadron as high cover to No. 118 and No. 501 in a sweep, again over Cherbourg, but nothing was seen. The operation was not a success, for on returning home Pilot Officer Cameron and Sergeant Edward Fairman, of No. 234 Squadron, collided in mid air, near Ringwood. Cameron managed to bale out of his crippled Spitfire (BL693), but Fairman (AA938) was not so lucky and was killed. Both pilots were at 1,000 feet and this incident happened directly in front of Bunny Currant whose squadron, No. 501, were following No. 234 back to Ibsley.

R.A.F. Ibsley was still being developed in the early months of 1942 and offices, station armoury, firing butts and miscellaneous buildings were springing up in the midst of an operational station at the same time as it was in operational use. Also, hard work by a Works Flight had provided double fighter pens around the airfield perimeter.

It was at this time too that the large house belonging to farmer Mr. Fred Lambert, which had been used as a Squadron Office, had to be pulled down. This was because it was directly in line with the Mockbeggar – Ellingham runway and was a landing hazard. However, the Ministry built the large bungalow at the Cross Lanes Green end of Mockbeggar Lane to replace it.

Also in line with the North East/South West runway was the bungalow home of Frederick and Dorothy Smith at Mockbeggar, and

*1942*

Pilots of No.234 Squadron, Ibsley, 1942.
Back, L-R ?, P/O Milton Jowsey (Can). Sgt. Hesselyn (N.Z.)
Front, L-R, Sgt. Webster (N.Z.), ?, Sgt. Tim Goldsmith (Aus), Sgt. Foster Fisher (Can).
Photo: F. Fisher

F/Lt Don Mckay, 234 Squadron, R.A.F. Ibsley,1942. By this time he had destroyed 16 enemy aircraft, including two Messerschmitts on February 12th whilst flying from Ibsley.
Photo: F. Fisher

their son Peter vividly remembers the day when an aircraft, towing a drogue (air firing target) got it entangled round their tall outside wireless aerial pole and pulled it down. It was soon replaced by the Ministry. Luckily, the Smith's bungalow didn't need to be demolished!!

Sergeant Pilot Foster Fisher, Royal Canadian Air Force, of No. 234 Squadron was billeted with the Smith family, at their Mockbeggar home, and it was while on a Wing Sweep on 24th Arpil, 1942, that he was shot down and taken Prisoner of War.

On the afternoon of 24th Wing Commander Ian Gleed led Nos. 118, 234 and 501 Squadron on a sweep along the French coast to Berck-sur-Mer where the Luftwaffe had a fighter base. Seven of the pilots became separated from the main formation doing a turn and were bounced by Focke Wulf 190's which dived down from above and behind. Before they knew what had hit them four Spitfires from No. 234 Squadron, who had been split up, went down. Flight Lieutenant Vivian Watkins, an American, from California, and Pilot Officer Axel Svendsen, a Danish pilot, were killed. Flight Sergeant Foster Fisher and Sergeant Machin, both Royal Canadian Air Force, were lost, but taken Prisoners of War.

Fifty years on, in 1992, and for the first time, Foster Fisher, still living in Canada, wrote details of what happened to him that fateful day. He recalls: "The Ibsley Wing crossed the French coast somewhere near Abbeville with No. 234 flying top cover for Nos. 501 and 118. Our Squadron were at 26,000 feet. I was acting as weaver, flying about 200 feet above and keeping an eye out for enemy aircraft. Near Aire the first group of Focke Wulf 190's were detected coming from the south-east and making contrails at an altitude that I guessed would be about 5,000 feet above us. Our Wing Commander called ground control station in England to ask if they were plotting any enemy aircraft in our area. Ground control soon confirmed that they were plotting eighty plus in our immediate vicinity.

By this time the Focke Wulf 190's had circled around and started their attack from above and behind. I turned to see them and while I was in the turn I heard a loud bang and there was a bright flash in the cockpit which must have been a cannon shell. The cockpit immediately filled with smoke and liquid which must have been glycol. I opened the hood. When the cockpit cleared enough I could tell that the aircraft was spinning. I initiated normal recovery procedure but there was no response to the stick so I assumed the

## 1942

control lines had been shot away by canon fire. Smoke was still thick in the cockpit and I was afraid flames would start at any moment, so decided I had better get out fast. This was not a very easy task. The only safe way to get out of a Spitfire is to turn it upside down, push the stick forward and fall out. This would not work in my situation and I am still not sure how I got out. I was being held in the seat by the force of the spin and couldn't get my body up. All I remember is that I got my elbows up on the sides of the cockpit, and using their leverage while pushing with my legs managed to ease my body up until my shoulders were out of the cockpit. The next thing that I knew was that I was free of the aircraft.

The trip down, after I had deployed my parachute, wasn't too bad. I was still fairly high and guess that I got out of the aircraft between fifteen and twenty thousand feet. It was a clear day and I could see the channel to the North and some towns down below.

Two Focke Wulf 190's were flying around but all other aircraft had disappeared. All was quiet except for the sound of these two aircraft and some gun firing in the distance. I was afraid these two German aircraft were going to start shooting at me so I started to swing in my parachute, hoping it would present a more difficult target for them to hit, but I need not have worried for in a few minutes they flew off and left me. About this time I noticed that the heel and side of the flying boot on my right foot had been shot away and blood was running out. Blood was also running down the side of my face and neck.

There was a strong wind blowing from the South which was carrying me towards the coast and I thought that I might drift all the way to the coast and come down in the Channel where I could be picked up and taken safely back to England. However, I soon found I was going down faster than I was going horizontal. As I got closer to the ground I could see some people running across a green field. I decided these were French civilians who would rescue me and hide me from the Germans. This was not to be either. In another few minutes I could see that I was going to land in a military compound. In fact, I landed directly in the parade square of a German Army Camp. On landing I activated the release button on my parachute harness but two of the straps caught around my leg. The wind was strong at ground level and was keeping the parachute full so that it was dragging me across the gravel parade square on my rear end while three or four German soldiers were running after me. I was

## So Much Sadness, So Much Fun

very glad when they finally caught up with me and released the parachute to end a rather painful experience.

I was then taken, by car, to a small village where I was given medical treatment at a Red Cross facility, which I believe was manned by French civilians. From there I was taken to a country estate, a large house with well maintained lawns and gardens, probably the Luftwaffe H.Q. There a Luftwaffe corporal told me, in good Canadian dialect, that "For you the war is over". He had lived most of his life in Winnipeg and had gone back to Germany in 1938 to get on Hitler's bandwagon.

Later I was taken to a hospital in St. Omer where they operated on my foot and removed shrapnel from my head. I spent three weeks with about a dozen other pilots in a room with locks on the windows and two soldiers guarding the doors twenty four hours a day. From St. Omer I went to another hospital at Frankfurt where I was kept in solitary confinement for two weeks for interrogation. About a month after arriving at Frankfurt, I was moved to a permanent Prisoner of War Camp, Stalag Luft III.

Peter Smith remembered how upset his mother was when someone came to collect Foster Fisher's belongings from their home, after he had been shot down, even taking the small piece of soap which he had been using.

In 1999 Sid Watson paid a nostalgic return visit to Ibsley, from where he really started his operational service with No. 234 Squadron. He recalled the events of 24th April saying "we were directed to Tangmere from Ibsley that day for re-fuelling before making a Sweep over the Abbeville area of France. I thought Abbeville was just an area chosen, I did not know at the time that it was the home base of some very experienced German fighter pilots!"

"On take off 'A' section, which included Flight Sergeant Foster Fisher, Flight Lieutenant Vivian Watkins, Pilot Officer Axel Svendsen and myself proceeded to cross the Channel towards France. Some way out my Merlin engine started to play up, the revs started to rise without any change in the throttle setting being made. I realised something was wrong and aborted the mission to fly back, landing at Ford, the nearest airfield."

"Little did I realise that when the remaining pilots arrived in the Abbeville area what a disaster it would be for No. 234. The Germans were operating FW190's and just one, so it is believed, shot down

*1942*

F/Lt. Peter Howard-Williams (right) and P/O Donald Claxton (left) (Canadian), with No.118 Squadron scoreboard. On 25th April, 1942, only three days after this photo was taken, Claxton was killed in action, shot down by an Me109 after escorting Bostons to Cherbourg.
Photo: P. Howard-Williams

four of the squadron including Fisher, Watkins, Svendsen and Sergeant Machan, who was from 'B' Flight. Only Fisher and Machan survived that day to become Prisoners of War, which left No. 234 Squadron so depleted they were sent to Portreath for rest. (In fact they lost eleven pilots inside one month when at Ibsley)."

Sid Watson soon returned to Ibsley, being posted to No. 118 Squadron who with Nos. 501 and 66 Squadrons now formed the Ibsley Wing. He is sure that if his Spitfire's Merlin engine had not played up that day he could well have been lost also, since his experience was so limited at the time, especially against the FW190.

When Sid arrived at Ibsley he found that Peter-Howard Williams, 'A' Flight Commander, had just departed No. 118 Squadron. He went to Group to become Squadron Leader Tactics. One day he was arriving over the airfield at Ibsley flying a small tri-cycle type aircraft (maybe a Tri-pacer) said Sid, intent on visiting his old squadron. I arrived at the same time in a Spitfire at about 3,000 feet, and commenced to dive to enter the circuit at 1,000 feet. I did not see Peter's aircraft and upon levelling out I missed hitting him by the slightest of margins. I was really shaken how close we had come and when I arrived in the crew room he wanted to know who had "shot him up". I admitted it was myself but did not have the temerity to admit that I have never seen him.

Another pilot of No. 234 Squadron who was billeted with Fred and Dorothy Smith was 25 year old Pilot Officer John Webster of the Royal New Zealand Air Force who had a very strange habit. He refused to use either the front or back door of their bungalow, but would always enter and leave through his bedroom window. Sadly, on 23rd July, 1942, he was shot down whilst on a mass Rhubarb to Lannion, from Portreath. Although he managed to bale out of his Vb Spitfire, AR285, off the French coast he was not found, and is commemorated on the Runnymede Memorial.

Squadron Leader Johnny Carver, who had been recuperating at the R.A.F. hospital at Torquay after his ordeal in the Channel was discharged from hospital on 22nd April. Before returning to Ibsley he visited the company who had made the dinghy in which he had sat for fifty six and a half hours, Messrs. P. B. Cow and Co., to thank them for their good work and to tell them how much the pilots of the R.A.F. valued the reliability of their product. The visit was much appreciated by both workers and management. Carver then

*1942*

returned to Ibsley to resume 'his command', where everyone was pleased to have him back.

Six more Ibsley pilots were lost on Saturday, 25th April. In the morning the Wing, Nos. 118. 501 and 402 (deputizing for No. 234 after their losses of the previous day) escorted Bostons to Cherbourg. No. 118 lost Pilot Officer Donald Claxton and Sergeant Landon Mooney during a morning Circus, following combat with enemy aircraft, of JG2, South of Bournemouth.

During the afternoon No. 501 Squadron also had a bad time. Whilst returning from a sweep over the Cherbourg Peninsular they were attacked by six Me 109's who were making the most of cloud cover. Pilot Officers Robert Wheldon and Antony Palmer-Tompkinson were shot down and killed instantly. Sergeant Miroslav Rocovski (Czech) baled out from his severely damaged aircraft but his parachute failed to open and he was lost. Sergeant Karel Vrtis (Czech) was still at the controls of his Spitfire, AB251, when it hit the sea.

Sergeant Pilot Ian Blair's aircraft, Spitfire Vb, AB179, had been hit by flak over Cherbourg but he managed to get back to the Dorset coast before his engine finally failed. Ian Blair recalled how he was too low to bail out so attempted a wheels up crash landing, in a field near Worth Matravers, but unfortunately the Spitfire went on to its back. Luckily some local men and boys were on hand to lift the tail, which enabled him to open the cockpit door. However, in doing so he inadvertently touched the firing button and there was a burst of machine-gun and cannon fire which frightened those lifting the plane so much they immediately dropped the tail back down again. Once they had recovered from their shock, however, they managed to extricate Sergeant Pilot Blair who was then taken to Bovington hospital.

The following day the Adjutant visited Ian Blair in hospital, and after the usual sympathies asked what had happened to the other four pilots. This was the first time Ian was aware of the squadron's losses. He went on to tell the Adjutant that his own loss of engine power, shortly after leaving the French coast, resulted in him becoming a "straggler", not a nice position to be in alone, and over the Channel. Ian Blair was "non-effective" for eleven months before returning to operations.

Research by a colleague of Ian Blair's into the German archives has shown that two German pilots were responsible for destroying the four Spitfires on 25th April, 1942, and that each pilot was flying a Bf.109 F2 which belonged to III Gruppe/Jagdeswader 2 "Richtofen" unit. The pilots were Hauptmann Hans "Assi" Han, Gruppen Kommandeur III/JG2-2, and Oberleutenant Egon Mayer, Staffel Kaptitaen, 7/JG2-4.

Hans Hahn, who was taken Prisoner of War in Russia on 21st February, 1943, survived the War and died in 1982. Oberleutenant Egon Mayer was shot down by a P.47 Thunderbolt and killed on 2nd March, 1943.

In 1994 Ian Blair visited the area of Worth Matravers where his Spitfire crashed. Through enquiries at the local pub, he was able to trace, and subsequently meet, members of the family, some of whom were small boys in 1942, who assisted in his rescue, and to whom he will always be grateful.

Whilst in the Prisoner of War Camp, Stalag Luft III, Foster Fisher sent a postcard to Mr. and Mrs. Smith at Mockbeggar expressing thanks for all they had done for him while he was billeted with them. The family still have this postcard. Throughout the years Foster Fisher has kept in touch and has paid nostalgic visits to Ibsley when in this country on holiday or for Prisoner of War reunions.

It was while in Stalag Luft III that Foster Fisher met up again with two pilots from No. 234 Squadron who had already been shot down and taken Prisoner of War whilst flying from Ibsley. They were Sergeant Pilot A. E. 'Teddy' Joyce, who was lost on an Escort mission on 31st December, 1941 following combat with German fighters off Brest, and Pilot Officer Don MacCleod, who was one of twenty pilots from ten squadrons of Royal Air Force Fighter Command lost during 'Operation Fuller', an action that became known as 'the Channel Dash', on 12th February, 1942.

Foster Fisher and Teddy Joyce had done their flying training together in Canada, and both were posted to No. 234 Squadron at Ibsley, in November, 1941.

In an effort to find out more about how her brother Teddy Joyce met his death in the prison camp, Sheila Dooley, one of his three surviving sisters, and on behalf of the other two, Pat Marrable and Jane Simmonds, made contact with Foster Fisher who wrote giving her the following information:

"Our fighter squadron was a very small group in that at any one time it consisted of not more than fifteen to eighteen pilots and we

## 1942

spent a lot of time together. During the day when we were on readiness, we were together from dawn till dark, and in the evenings we frequently went to the local pubs together. It was during this period that I got to know Teddy very well, and was sad when he was shot down.

This happened on an operation where we escorted bombers to Brest to bomb a large Naval facility being operated by Germans. The area around Brest was heavily defended by anti-aircraft batteries so, in the target area, the sky was black with bursts of flak. With the heavy flak and many aircraft flying around it was difficult to keep track of everyone. Consequently, no one saw Teddy go down and it was not until we got back to base that we were certain that he was missing.

I was shot down on 24th April, 1942, during an operation over Northern France and when I arrived at Stalag Luft III was pleased to find that Teddy was in fact alive and in good health and spirits. We were housed in different buildings within the camp but saw each other frequently. He did not mention any definite plans. For this reason, I believe that his attempt to escape was a spur of the moment decision to take advantage of an opportunity that appeared to be feasible, but a decision had to be made quickly because the opportunity was not going to last very long.

It all started with the Germans digging a hole, the reason for which I cannot recall, about mid-way between the warning wire and the perimeter wire surrounding the compound at the South end of Centre Camp. The hole appeared to be about six to eight feet in diameter and perhaps four to five feet deep. This hole was located about twenty feet from the perimeter fence, which consisted of two rows of barbed wire, about six feet apart, and ten feet high. The area between the two fences was filled with coils of barbed wire. The soil in the area was coarse sand and Teddy and his partner probably reasoned that if they could get to the hole without being seen it should be possible to dig a trench under the perimeter wire in a short time and make their escape. It was a hazardous plan because just getting to the hole without being detected presented a lot of risks. The nearest building to the hole, Barrack block 66, was at least two hundred feet away across an open area that was scanned frequently by searchlights mounted on sentry towers on the perimeter of the compound. In addition, sentries accompanied by dogs, patrolled the outside of the perimeter wire. Any proposed escape bid had to be approved by the Camp Escape Committee and it is assumed that they must have considered this proposal and given it their blessing.

The evening of the attempted escape I was in sick quarters, which were located in the Vorlager, outside the main Centre Compound. As I recall, it was staffed by a British Army Major, a medical doctor who was also a Prisoner of War, and a German doctor. Most of the support staff were allied Prisoners of War who had some medical training. I was in a room with about half a dozen other Prisoners of War.

Early in the evening, between nine and ten p.m., we heard shooting from the Centre Compound and speculated that it was probably someone trying to escape. The shots were spaced as though fired from a rifle rather than from machine guns, such as were mounted in the guard towers. About one half hour later, there was a commotion at the front entrance of the building, which sounded as though someone was being admitted on an emergency basis. A short time later, one of the medical orderlies came to our room, and when questioned about the shooting confirmed that there had been an attempted escape and that one person involved had been injured. When we asked the name of the person who had been admitted he said that it was Ted Joyce.

As soon as I heard that it was Teddy, I went down the corridor to find out how badly he was injured and if there was anything that I could do to help. He was in a single bed against the wall, in a room by himself, and I assumed that the medical staff had already attended to his injuries. He was moaning and moving his arms and body around as though in great discomfort.

I pulled up a chair beside his bed and said "Teddy, it's Foster, what can I do to help?". His eyes opened and recognized me, and he replied: "Oh Foster, my throat hurts something terrible". I asked him if he would like some water and he said that he would, so I gave him a little water but he continued to be in pain. I looked at his throat and examined his chest and head, but there was no external sign of injury. There was some blood such as might occur by biting the lip or tongue, but nothing to indicate any major injury. He continued to complain about his throat and I thought it might have been twisted in some way or received a blow but there were no bruises to suggest this was the cause of the problem. I sat with him for two to three hours, giving him a sip of water from time to time.

## 1942

After a while, it appeared that he was dropping off to sleep and since there was nothing more that I could do I returned to my room. It was a great shock to me the next morning when the orderly told me that Teddy had died during the night.

Later I was told that an autopsy had been done and the cause of death was a bullet wound. It was determined that the bullet must have entered his mouth, gone down his throat and lodged against his backbone. The ultimate cause of death was likely internal bleeding and shock.

One point I would like to make clear is that I cannot fault the medical staff who attended Ted in any way. The medical facility was more of a first aid station than a hospital and lacked any of the diagnostic equipment such as we have today. I feel that they probably did as well as they could with the tools they had to work with."

Foster Fisher also said that he had thought long and hard before deciding to mention all the facts to Sheila Dooley, but finally decided that she would like to know everything possible. He ended his letter by saying, "I know that you will continue to think about him just as I do. He was a special friend who I continue to remember from time to time, just as I do many other pilots who served with us and died so young."

In 1943 the Prisoners of War Department of the British Red Cross Society and Order of St. John of Jerusalem, somehow obtained photographs of the funeral of Sergeant A. E. "Teddy" Joyce, held at Stalag Luft III, which were then sent to his parents. Teddy Joyce now lies in the Military Cemetery at Poznan, Poland.

Just two days after Foster Fisher was shot down No. 234 Squadron left Ibsley on April 26th/27th bound for Portreath.

No. 118 Squadron met with disaster on 9th May. They went to Tangmere for an 11 Group Circus. The sweep was to St. Omer and the role of the Middle Wallop Wing was that of target support. The main attack was to be by Bostons, on the marshalling yards at Hazebrouck. However, when some ten miles North of St. Omer No. 118 was jumped by twenty-five plus F.W. 190's of JG26. Sergeant Michael Green went down in flames. Supernumerary Squadron Leader John Walker was shot down and killed, as was Sergeant Franklin Hough, Royal Canadian Air Force, who is buried in the Military Cemetery at Dunkirk. Sergeant Geoffrey Shepherd who

## So Much Sadness, So Much Fun

*Funeral Procession, Stalag Luft III, June 1942 for Sgt. Pilot A.E. "Teddy" Joyce, from No.234 Squadron Ibsley*
Photo: Mrs. S. Dooley, Mrs. P. Marrable, Mrs. J. Simmonds

*Burial of Sgt. Pilot "Teddy" Joyce, Stalag Luft III, June 1942*
Photo: Mrs. S. Dooley, Mrs. P. Marrable, Mrs. J. Simmonds

was also shot down was taken Prisoner of War. Although wounded in the leg Pilot Officer Thomas Thomas managed to return and crash landed at Manston in Kent, his Spitfire being badly damaged by 20 mm cannon, while Pilot Officer Gerrit Aalpael, Dutch, also managed to get back but crash landed at Tangmere when his aircraft ran out of fuel.

On Friday 16th May the Station played cricket at Bournemouth. It was a remarkable match for L.A.C. May of the Parachute and Cable (installation), who took five wickets with successive balls. Bournemouth were 18 for 1, then 18 for 9, and they added only two further runs. Needless to say the Station won comfortably.

In May 1942, No 66 Squadron, with Spitfire Vb's and Vc's coded LZ replaced No. 234 Squadron. Among their pilots were Lieutenant Victor Nissen and Lieutenant Andrew 'Killer' Morum, both South African Air Force, Andrew Deytrikh, and Leroy Gover (U.S.A.).

Of his time with No. 66 Squadron at Ibsley, on two separate occasions, Andrew Deytrikh says:

"Squadrons stationed at Ibsley considered themselves extremely fortunate to have moved nearer the 11 Group area as this was where most of the operational flying was taking place, rather than the somewhat boring, endless "Readiness" and Convoy patrols which had to be undertaken in 10 Group (i.e. Cornwall to Hampshire)."

"To begin with" said Andrew, "we were re-equipped with Spitfire Vb's which suffered from constant cannon stoppages and had to be fitted with 30 gallon belly tanks. To remedy this took some little time, and after endless short cannon test trips, consisting of firing ones guns into the sea off Bournemouth and ensuring that the newly fitted 30 gallon tank worked correctly, we whiled away our time with numerous Convoy patrols and practice Wing formations. Finally, the armourers won the battle of the linkage extractor mechanism and the Engineers were satisfied that all extra tanks fitted did deliver the 30 gallons of fuel they were supposed to."

Peter Smith recalled the day in 1942 when he was cycling South from Mockbeggar along the Gorley road to Rockford School. He was overtaking a long column of airmen marching down towards Moyles Court. Unfortunately, coming from the other direction was a W.A.A.F., also on a bicycle. Well, the W.A.A.F. thought Peter would stop, and Peter thought she would stop, but neither did until they hit one another. Peter said he had never heard a scream like hers, and always remembered it. He vividly remembered how he lay in the road with his own bicycle, the W.A.A.F. and her bicycle, on top of him, and how the laughter from the marching airmen did nothing to help their embarrassing situation.

Children attending Rockford School from the Gorley area (no school transport in those days) were issued with passes. These had to be shown at the guard-room at Cross Lanes and again at the Sentry Box at the brick bridge, over Dockens Water at Moyles Court, the road through the ford having been blocked off with barbed wire entanglements.

Another incident, recalled by Daisy Porter was when a Jeep with three high ranking officers came through the water splash at Linbrook, not far from her home in Ringwood, as she was cycling towards the narrow footbridge there after duty at Ibsley N.A.A.F.I. One of the men called out to her to stop. Daisy carried on, making out she hadn't heard them, until a very loud voice shouted out; "will the lady in uniform please come here". She went back to them and the officer said: "We want to know the way to Ibsley Aerodrome, are we heading in the right direction?". She said "I'm not really sure". His reply:. "Oh, come now, lady, you must know you are wearing N.A.A.F.I uniform. We believe you've just come from there.". Daisy said "no, I'm a local girl, I've just come home on leave and am having a ride round". They looked at one another, then had a good laugh and said "alright". In my mind they were testing me to break the strict wartime rule of 'not to tell strangers'. "I didn't dare tell them, and so they went on their way, and no doubt found Ibsley airfield".

No. 66 Squadron was now fully operational at Ibsley, commanded by the New Zealand tennis champion, Cam Malfroy, followed by Bob Yule, and finally Harold Bird-Wilson.

"Andrew Deytrikh also recalls that there were many occasions when the Ibsley Wing had to take off at dawn, no doubt waking the local residents, and make their way to an 11 Group station to join up with other Wings in order to escort Boston aircraft bombing targets in Belgium or Holland. Sometimes they would meet up with Flying Fortresses over Belgium and escort these safely back to the U.K. Once operations were completed the Wing would return to Ibsley to resume normal readiness status and study operational orders for the following day."

## 1942

"He also remembers that when the Germans mounted night bombing raids over most of England their aircraft seemed to have been routed over Salisbury, and despite the fact that the squadrons based at Ibsley were day fighters, those in authority decided to use them as temporary night fighter interceptors. This was not a very popular move amongst the pilots who were used to day operations only, devoting the evenings to relaxation, visiting the St. Leonard's Hotel or pubs in Ringwood, and making dates with the local girls and W.A.A.F.'s."

"However, orders were orders and the routine, at least for a short time had to be altered. The general idea, as far as Andrew can recall, was to have a number of aircraft circling over Salisbury, separated by about 2,000 feet in height, up to 15,000 feet, in the hope of catching the Hun on his way to Bristol, Birmingham and Coventry."

"The Spitfire was not really adapted for night fighting, so for this purpose it was necessary to fit exhaust screen deflectors, as the exhaust stubs of the Merlin engine produced a very bright light at night which was inclined to make night vision extremely difficult. The experiment lasted for about a month and with no results to show for all the fuel expended on this night standing patrol, then the exercise was abandoned much to the relief of everyone," said Andrew.

He goes on to tell of how "they were now entering a more serious phase of aggressive sorties and that the tempo of their life was changed with the odd aircraft failing to make it back to base, or one that ditched in the sea, after which a hurried air sea search would always be laid on".

"Close escort to "Hurribombers" was always an exciting exercise and they always thanked their lucky stars they were in Spitfires, as the anti-shipping operations always seemed to claim the odd Hurricane, fitted out with a five hundred pound bomb. Little did they know then that two years later they were going to carry out similar shipping strikes".

American, Brigadier Philip D. Caine, in his book 'Spitfires, Thunderbolts and Warm Beer', put together the stories and diary entries of LeRoy Gover's wartime efforts, a number of which concern time spent at Ibsley, and so, are reproduced here.

"Gover was determined to be a fighter pilot but lacked the qualifications that would guarantee him U.S. Army Air Corps

## So Much Sadness, So Much Fun

Wings, so the young Californian signed on with the Royal Air Force. LeRoy Gover arrived in England on 7th December, 1941, and after disembarking at Liverpool made his way to Bournemouth to get processed into the Royal Air Force. He was then posted to the Operational Training Unit at Llandow, South Wales. In March 1942 LeRoy Gover found himself joining No. 66 Fighter Squadron who at that time were stationed at Portreath.

On 27th April, 1942, LeRoy's diary entry read. "Up at 7.00 a.m. Got everything organized and caught the train. Arrived at Ibsley at 8.00 p.m. and on up to the billets.

LeRoy Gover's first impression of Ibsley was that it was rather isolated and there was no transport available for the pilots. When No. 66 Squadron arrived at Ibsley, most of the eighteen pilots were sergeants and had quarters very near the base. Since there were only eight officers, they had a four bedroom farmhouse about half a mile away. The Royal Air Force had a large number of non-commissioned officers who were pilots. Because they were not officers, the sergeant pilots had separate living and dining facilities, although they flew the same aircraft in the same formations as the officers. The formation was always led by an officer, however. This system was often criticized, because isolating the sergeant pilots kept them from sharing in all the combat experiences of the unit. Discussion about a certain mission or new tactic usually took place at the Officers' Mess, since the flight leader was always an officer.

Going to the base at Ibsley meant a walk unless the lorry was not being used by the squadron commander, in which case it could be despatched to bring the pilots to the flight line. Ibsley also had hard surfaced runways, but with a very unusual feature. At the end of the runway was a huge net, about sixty feet wide and seventy-five feet high. The net, which was normally in the collapsed position at the end of the runway, could be shot into the air in case of a strafing attack in the hope of snagging some of the German aircraft and causing them to crash.

On 29th April LeRoy Gover wrote home describing his move to Ibsley and what he was doing. When his letter arrived in San Carlos so much of it had been cut out by the sensor's scissors that it was just a blue paper border framing the air, signed "Love Lee".

About 6.00 in the evening the phone rang and it was Fighter Command releasing the squadron until dawn. They all hurried back

*1942*

*LeRoy Gover, an American Pilot with No. 66 Squadron, R.A.F. Ibsley, 1942, relaxes while waiting to scramble.*
Photo: A. Deytrikh

to the house and Vic Nissen said, "Let's try to get the C.O.'s lorry and go to Bournemouth. I haven't been there since I left for Operational Training Unit, and I know this great little bar". We got into our uniforms and six of us (all pilots who lived in the little house) jumped into the lorry and took off for Bournemouth. It was raining and there was mud everywhere. We parked the lorry behind Vic's little pub and had just started walking round the building when we heard an aircraft coming. Thought nothing of it until a bomb hit about sixty yards in front of us. We all hit the ground, and when we got up we were covered with mud. We looked at each other, turned around, got back in the lorry and came home. So went our big night out in Bournemouth.

One of the requirements levied on No. 66 Squadron at Ibsley was to provide a pilot to ferry aircraft throughout England for various purposes, and probably because he was one of the least experienced combat pilots in the squadron, on May 1st, LeRoy was detailed for three weeks of that duty. During that time he flew the Miles Master

## So Much Sadness, So Much Fun

(a trainer), Miles Magister (another trainer), Spitfire, Tiger Moth, Defiant, and Hurricane. He crossed all of England, including going to Northern Ireland and Scotland, and had two forced landings because of engine failure. On May 19$^{th}$ Gover returned to his squadron at Ibsley, and the following day, while on a reconnaissance mission near Cherbourg, Gover shot down his first German aircraft, an Me 109.

On May 31$^{st}$ LeRoy embarked on the most ill-fated mission of his career in the R.A.F. He said "I was Red Two and we were strapped in our Spitfires, on cockpit alert, on the edge of the runway". He goes on to say: "Shortly after the alert period began a red flare sailed through the sky and off we flew. Immediately after take off Red One called and said he had to abort as he had a bad power surge. Control vectored me toward the Huns at Angels two zero (twenty thousand feet). I saw two Me 109's, approximately half a mile ahead, flying line abreast about two hundred feet apart. I closed at a pretty good rate and just as I got in range the one on my left started a steep turn to the left and the one on my right a steep turn to the right. I caught on too late to what they were doing. I could only go after one of them. As soon as I had latched on to the one on my left the one on the right swung in right behind me. We went round and round, then one of them hit my engine. I had no choice but to bail out, so I jettisoned the canopy, unbuckled my shoulder harness, took off my helmet, climbed out on to the wing and away I went. Had I stayed with the plane and crash- landed with no power, I am certain I would have been killed. I came down OK and was soon taken back to base, given a medical check-up, and was flying missions again next day. The entry in LeRoy Gover's Log Book read: "Shot down by two Me 109's. Bailed out near the coast at Bournemouth.

Knowing how much his mother worried about him, LeRoy says "I would have liked to tell my folks about all our survival equipment. Each of us had a personal bail-out or escape kit in our breast pocket. It had silk maps of France and the Low Countries, a file, several kinds of currency to use if you were able to evade capture, a compass, a box of waterproof matches and a three-inch knife you carried in your boot. The knife was interesting because it had one blade and a long needle in it. The needle was to puncture your dinghy in case it accidentally inflated on crash-landing or in combat and kept you from being able to move in the cockpit or get out of the

## 1942

plane. We actually had three compasses. One a plain navigation compass in the kit, another was a collar button on your shirt. You could take it off, scrape off the paint on the back of the button and there was a compass. The other was a small one that could be inserted into any body orifice to hide it for future use.

Eric Moore was with No. 501 Squadron at Ibsley during the Summer of 1942, and recalls some memories of Spitfire Mk Vb EP120 which was at Ibsley at that time.

Eric went on to recall that EP120 was flown mostly by Philip Stanbury, who had a test flying background. Squadron diaries show he would do lone night sorties over the Channel on shipping reconnaissance. At the end of his operational tour he was posted to Boscombe Down where new aircraft for the R.A.F. were evaluated. He was injured there in a high speed dive in a jet, when the hood blew off. In his latter days with 501 squadron he had a powered glider, although personally I never saw it fly. I am sure that his flights on EP120 would have been to check trim etc. 'SD' were the squadron letters. The R.A.F. moved these squadron letters around just before the war to confuse the enemy but at least two squadrons ended up with the same letters, the only people confused were the R.A.F.

Dicky Lynch also flew her on a regular basis. Only recently commissioned, Dicky's experience placed him as deputy flight commander. After repairs, following a runway collision at Ibsley EP120 changed from SD-L to SD-Y.

Eric also recalled how he regularly did the first turn on convoys. He said, "a Canadian pilot, MacDonald, and I would sleep at dispersal, in the far corner of the airfield, which could be accessed through a hole in the fence, on the way back from the pub in Ringwood. Doing the first stint gave us the rest of the day to ourselves. Take off at first light, or I believe then referred to as "sparrow fart", flare path on and passage to convoy at low level, those cottages en route would have an early call and the wispy smoke from their chimneys pushed back again. Low level around the convoy was maintained to avoid radar attention from across the Channel."

The Ibsley Wing escorted twelve hurribombers to Maupertus on 6th June, where bombs were dropped on the aerodrome. On the return journey, while flying at sea level, Squadron Leader Johnny Carver, D.F.C., Sergeant Lloyd Jones (Royal Canadian Air Force)

*So Much Sadness, So Much Fun*

and Flight Lieutenant John "Robbie" Robson, all No. 118 Squadron, were jumped by 9 FW 190's. In the resultant combat only Robbie managed to get back to tell the tale.

That such a fine Commanding Officer as Johnny Carver, D.F.C., should be lost in this way was a tragedy, especially after his earlier escapade. Three days later Squadron Leader Ernest 'Bertie' Wootten, D.F.C., took over as No. 118's new Commanding Officer. He had been at Ibsley earlier, with No. 234 Squadron.

On Saturday, 13th June, there were 14 flights by 40 aircraft of No. 118 Squadron. These consisted of formation flights, aerobatics, section attacks, camera gun, cannon tests and practice interception. It was the latter that led to tragedy. Pilot Officer Dirk Klink (Dutch) who had only joined No. 118 on 23rd May, was following his Section Leader, Flying Officer Ian Stewart, up through cloud, when at 3,300 feet he was seen to be lagging. Pilot Officer Dirk Klink who was flying in 'Perfect', the presentation Spitfire proclaiming the products of H. J. Heinz Ltd., crashed in Alderholt Park, near Fordingbridge, the aircraft bursting into flames and the pilot burnt to death. Pilot Officer Klink died on his thirtieth birthday, and the tragedy was all the more poignant because his wife had arrived at Ibsley only the day before to spend his birthday with him. Dirk Klink was the second husband she had lost during World War II, the first having been killed by a bomb. Even to-day some marks are still visible on trees which Dirk Klink's Spitfire struck, in privately owned Alderholt Park.

Pilot Officer Klink was laid to rest in the Churchyard at Ellingham the following Wednesday. Rev'd Catley officiated at the funeral service which was attended by Klink's widow and other relatives, representatives of the Dutch Government, No. 118 Squadron Officers, escort and firing parties. Sometime later, Dirk Klink's body was exhumed from Ellingham Churchyard. He now lies in the Dutch War Graves section of a cemetery in Middlesex. Some years ago two wooden Commonwealth War Grave crosses were found in Ellingham Church, where they still remain. One bore the name of Dirk Klink, the other of an unknown German soldier who died in May, 1943.

There was yet another major disaster for No. 118 Squadron, resulting in the loss of four more pilots on Saturday 20th June. When ten miles North West of St. Omer, whilst returning from a

*1942*

*"A" Flight, No. 501 Squadron, R.A.F. Ibsley, June 1942*
Photo: E. Moore

diversionary sweep to Le Havre, the Squadron was jumped by FW 190's and Me 109F's of JG26 and JG2. Pilot Officers Johannes Veen, and Paul Stenger, together with Sergeant Cornelius Van Houten were shot down and killed, while Robert Noel, Free French, was taken Prisoner of War. Veen, Stenger and Noel had been with the Squadron for some time, but it was van Houten's first sweep with No. 118, although he was said to have made about forty with No. 11 Group. Having survived as a Prisoner of War, Robert Noel was killed in action in Vietnam in 1953.

The 30th June, 1942 saw a change in Station Commander at Ibsley. Squadron Leader Christopher "Bunny" Currant was promoted to Wing Commander, replacing Wing Commander Norman Benge who went to Group as Group Captain. A huge farewell party for W/C Benge was held at Chatley Wood.

Following a week's leave, spent in London, Leroy Gover was admitted to the R.A.F. Hospital at Wroughton, Wiltshire, where he underwent a tonsillectomy. When he arrived back at Ibsley on Monday 20th July he found many changes. Five members of the squadron had been posted to the East, while the Commanding Officer, Squadron Leader Cam Malfroy, D.F.C., and the Flight Commander had been posted to other squadrons.

Andrew Deytrikh also remembers how No. 66 Squadron was gradually introduced to participating in "Rhubarbs". This type of operation was, or should always have been carried out with good visibility and a ten tenths cloud coverage in which to escape should one be unfortunate enough to be bounced. Just such an operation had been laid on for Friday 24$^{th}$ July, and four planes took off for a fast sweep of Northern France, to attack anything of substance. Andrew remembers this sortie well, not because they inflicted great losses on the enemy but because it turned out to be a complete shambles due to the leader being over zealous, much to the detriment of the other three. Andrew cannot remember who the leader was, the others with him were a supernumerary squadron leader, J. Cridland, attached to the squadron from Training Command, and South African Lieutenant Albert 'Killer' Morum, aptly named because of his size and strength.

All set out with great hopes of blasting anything of note and using their 20mm cannons which had remained silent for some time. Halfway across the Channel they found to their dismay that all the cloud cover had disappeared. Cherbourg peninsular came into sight and the German radar station there was already picking them up, as the familiar sound of their radar came through on their earphones quite plainly. Radio silence continued and so did progress towards the French coast, much to our concern, recalls Andrew. It wouldn't be long before the Focke Wulfs in Cherbourg would be scrambled and our retreat cut off smartly in beautiful ten tenths clear sky.

"There was still no word from the leader so on we went, over the coast with adrenalin flowing," said Andrew, who was flying with supernumerary Squadron Leader Cridland who had little experience of flying, having just left Flying Training Command for a short taste of operational flying. Morum was flying with the leader. The two sections separated and were free to pick out their own target.

Flying down a railway line they finally came across a train, stationary at some local station, and both gave it a good dose of 20mm cannon fire and left it steaming out of places where no steam should be seen, and with a very bewildered porter or station master, gaping up at them as they flashed past never to return again. Their only hope was that the shells left him intact to sort out the mess,

*1942*

Chatley Wood, No. 118 Squadron Officers Quarters, 1941/1942
Photo: A.S.C. Lumsden

No. 118 Squadron, Pilots and Officers, pictured outside Chatley Wood, Rockford, 1942.
Back: L. to R. F/O LeMesurier, F/O Wilson, F/O Veen, F/O Gibson
Front L. to R. P/O I.Jones, F/L. Corfe, S/L. Wootten, D.F.C., F/L. Robson,
W/C Gleed, D.S.O., D.F.C, P/O Stenger
Photo: P. Howard-Williams

*So Much Sadness, So Much Fun*

with the train now parked fairly permanently at his station. Well, from there they went on until they reached the approximate location of Deauville where they turned North to cross out of France.

It was still gin clear with R/T silence now breaking and the other section in trouble and no cloud into which to escape. The Cherbourg Focke Wulfs were not far from us but had obviously found the others. "By this time," recalled Andrew, "I had lost my No. 1, Cridland, so by constantly weaving and keeping as close to the sea as I could, made my way back northwards. I heard Morum in trouble, but I did not know his position and was unable to assist, but as we were flying in pairs, his leader should have been somewhere near him.

A quarter of the way back I came across some low cloud and immersed myself into it as quickly as my aircraft would take me, and there I remained until I made a quick dive out of it to see the Isle of Wight on the horizon. Back at Ibsley the story unfolded. For the price of that one train put out of action, my colleague Morum never returned and my No. 1, Cridland, severely damaged his aircraft while force landing due to technical failure caused by enemy flak. It would appear that we had attacked a flak train. Young though I was at that time, I cannot but pose the question of whether it was really worth it. Two aircraft lost, one valuable pilot killed, all because the leader failed to turn back when it was obvious that there would be no cover for our return trip. The press on type, we had many of them, but not to be practised when others are involved and when no important target can be envisaged."

Charlie West, who served with No. 66 Squadron also has vivid memories of the day that Morum was killed, and says, "early on the morning of Friday 24th July, 1942 the W.O. Engineer Officer of 'A' Flight informed all trades that four Spitfires were to be airworthy and ready for "take-off" – D.I.'s signed – for a special "sortie" was to leave Ibsley later that morning.". As an Air-Frame mechanic Charlie had been allocated to do the necessary duties, i.e. petrol tank (full), oxygen bottle (full), cowlings (secure), all controls (working), tyre (correct pressure), trolley accumulator (plugged-in), chocks (in place at wheels) – on Spitfire Vc AB455, LZ-F.

For this special "sortie" all was ready for "take-off" at the appointed time. As a "lot to learn" 19 year old, Charlie felt proud that Lieutenant 'Killer' Morum – the six foot four inch South African

– would be flying LZ-F on this mission. Charlie helped him fix the seat and his parachute harness and "turned-on" the oxygen bottle before stepping down from the port wing, ready to press the button on the trolley accumulator. The engines of all the planes started, Charlie walked carefully along the front wing of LZ-F to remove the plug, also "double checking" that the camera patch was removed, pulled the chocks away and gave the 'thumbs up' sign to the pilot who slowly revved-up the engine, started to pull away with the other planes, then stopped. The propeller slowed and the perspex hood slid back on its runners. Lieutenant Morum called Charlie back on to the port wing. "I've left my silk and leather gauntlet gloves" were his words – "please fetch them from my locker". Charlie rushed to retrieve these from the Pilots Room and running out of the building saw the planes moving across the airfield for "take-off" – one pilot minus gloves.

Just over two hours later LZ-F failed to return to base, and it was with a sad heart that Charlie returned Lieutenant Albert Morum's gloves to the locker. "Although over fifty years have passed since then, vivid memories still remain", says Charlie.

Andrew also recalls that they had members of the Free French Air Force flying with them and that one particular pilot, by the name of Maurice Claisse, was an ex-test pilot. He was slightly older than the rest of them, at least thirty years old, and considered to be the "Daddy" of the squadron. Andrew says he flew as his Number 2 on numerous occasions and that he taught him many things, amongst the most important was "how to stay alive".

On one particular high level interception the aircraft were fitted with 30 gallon belly tanks and Andrew was flying Number 2 to his Flight Commander at the time, whose name was none other than Wilbur Wright, newly posted in from Training Command.

As they were nearing 30,000 feet, the vectors to fly were coming in fast and furious which meant that they were fairly close to their quarry, and in the excitement of this interception Andrew's leader forgot to put him into either line astern or echelon starboard, and being on the inside of the turn and at this great height, the aircraft went into a spin, and Andrew remembers very vividly that the Isle of Wight was going round and round at quite an alarming rate. He was in a right hand spin with a belly tank still attached, and it took him about 12,000 feet to recover normal flight. Whilst his personal

## So Much Sadness, So Much Fun

*No. 66 Squadron, Ibsley, 1942.*
*Back: Tommy Tomblin, Jenkins, Bob Mann, Banning-Lover, Wilbur Wright, Bob Yule (C.O.), Dickie Durant, Danny Magruder, Kevin Barclay, Vic Nissen, 'Killer' Moran*
*Front: Andrew Deytrikh, Passmore, BooBoo Borossi, McSpedden, Zulu (Sqdn. Dog), Loyns, Saunders, ?, LeRoy Gover*
*Photo: Andrew Deytrikh*

*1942*

*Briefing the pilots of No's. 66, 118 and 501 Squadrons, Control Tower, R.A.F. Ibsley*
Photo: I. Jones

battle with gravity was going on, an Me 109 fled southwards and too fast for Wright to catch him up. According to our listening out posts the Hun was exceedingly worried and transmitted to his base for assistance, which never came.

"I was told later" said Andrew, "that it was the first time that a Spitfire had been spun with a 30 gallon tank attached and that the authorities were very pleased to learn that it was possible to recover from a spin with the tank still attached."

In August, the Station Commander, Wing Commander Christopher "Bunny" Currant was married at All Saints Church, Ellingham, close to the airfield. Cynthia Brown, his bride, an evacuee from Southampton, was, at the time, living at Poulner, near Ringwood.

Another wedding also took place in August, that of Sergeant Pilot Ivor Jones of No. 118 Squadron, who married a Ringwood girl Anne Ward, at the local Parish Church of St. Peter and St. Paul. Best man was John "Robbie" Robson. On this happy occasion a flight formation from 'B' flight, 118 Squadron, flew over the Church during the ceremony.

There was no let up in the action during the month and on the 15th August, No. 66 Squadron was told to pack and be ready to leave for Tangmere the following dawn.

For a five day period, also during August, No. 421 (Red Indian Canadian) Squadron under Squadron Leader Frank C. Willis, R.A.F., were at Ibsley with Spitfire Vb's, code letters AU. They came from, and returned to, Fairwood Common. Three months later, on 8th November, Frank Willis was killed in action, shot down by a FW 190.

Tim Hamer, a pilot with No. 66 Squadron recalls the night in August 1942 when he was returning from leave on the Paddington to Salisbury train, due to arrive at Salisbury on Saturday evening at 9.30 p.m. but, owing to enemy action, didn't arrive until 1.40 a.m. on Sunday morning.

He was hoping to catch the last Salisbury – Ringwood – Bournemouth bus on the Saturday night. However, when he arrived at Salisbury there were no buses or taxis which meant that he had to walk the 13 miles or so to Ibsley.

During his walk he didn't see any cars and only met one person en route; he was an American soldier on guard at the gate of a U.S.

## 1942

camp, who had only just arrived in the UK and didn't even know where he was. Tim had only travelled from Salisbury to Ibsley once before, and as there were no signposts, these had been removed in case the Germans invaded, he wanted to check that he was on the right road. Then it started to rain!

Tim eventually arrived at Ibsley at 7 a.m. and at 8 a.m. No. 66 Squadron were off to Tangmere for four days. Tim also recalled that when he was talking to a 118 Squadron pilot about the unexpected hike he found that he too had had to walk from Salisbury to Ibsley. He said that he had put his feet in a brook at Fordingbridge to cool them down. Tim went on to say he was sorry to learn that the pilot to whom he had spoken was killed in 1943 when two No. 118 Squadron Spitfires collided in mid-air over Coltishall. The pilots killed in this accident were Pilot Officer Eric Buglass and Flight Sergeant Joe Hollingworth, both had been at Ibsley with No. 118 Squadron.

Gover recorded that there were six Squadrons at Tangmere, on Monday 16th. Late in the day on Tuesday, however, his diary entry reflects both relief and concern at knowing what was to come. They were not allowed off camp that evening, in any circumstances. So when the word came that it would be in support of a landing at Dieppe, in France, the mission took on a new seriousness. The danger of the day was certainly not lost on any of the young pilots as they realized that the Luftwaffe would put up everything it had to show the British that any invasion of the Continent would simply have been too costly.

LeRoy talked with his squadron mates, Vic Nissen and Tommy Tomblin about what the next day might bring. He said Tommy Tomblin thought it might be just a small fake invasion to keep the Germans on their toes and probably wouldn't last more than one day.

The losses to those poor chaps on the ground could be horrible, and Lee didn't think they had much chance of protecting them.

As it happened the three of them, Vic Nissen, Tommy Tomblin and LeRoy Gover were fairly accurate because the one-day operation was planned by the British to test the German's defences and keep them off guard, and casualties ran to nearly fifty per cent among the commandoes who made the raid.

Reminiscing, Gover records that the action of 19th August 1942 was his most memorable experience while in the R.A.F. It is also one of the longest entries in his diary:

## So Much Sadness, So Much Fun

"This has been a very exciting and also sad day. Our Ibsley Wing, 66, 501 and 118 Squadrons, had to escort twelve Hurribombers over to Dieppe this morning at first light. We all flew at sea level the entire mission. We took them in through flak that cannot be described. There were hundreds of planes screaming through the sky. Dozens of dogfights going on. Planes plummeting to earth on fire. Pilots who had been shot down were floating in their dinghies. I saw nine or ten Spitfires just shooting hell out of a Jerry Dornier. We fought off attacks on the Hurribombers, but four were shot down by the shore batteries. We were attacked twice more, by Messerschmitt 109's as we crossed back over the coast of France. I got strikes on a Messerschmitt 109, but I was flying about fifty feet off the water and couldn't manoeuvre to finish him off. Three of our Spitfires were so badly shot up they were out of the fight but did manage to fly back to England.

There were five planes left in our squadron for the second mission at 11.00 a.m. and we went back across the Channel to shoot up any gun emplacements we came across. By this time Dieppe was a real mess. The Germans were sending Dornier 217's to bomb the landing craft that were trying to take men off the beach. Seven Focke Wulf 190s attacked us as we hit the French coast. The only advantage we had was to outrun them. I got strikes on two, but did no real damage. We lost two more of our Spitfires. I was now out of ammo., so broke away and headed home.

In the afternoon our squadron, which now consisted of three aircraft, was detailed to fly close escort on four Bostons, who were to lay a smoke screen along the shore to cover the withdrawal of the commandos. We went in at sea level, and two of the Bostons were shot down right in front of me. I was about two hundred and fifty yards from shore and the German machine guns were spraying hell out of things. Large cannon shells were bursting all around, and cannon shells were hitting the water and shooting up tall columns of water. As the Bostons finished laying their smoke, one more was shot down. As I was now being shot up, I lost track of the other Boston and do not know his fate. The beach was covered with fallen commandos. About two miles out, on the way home, we were jumped by a gaggle of Focke Wulf 190s. One was right on me and getting hits, so I pushed full left rudder and his bullets struck the water beside me. He turned and shot my number two, Vic Nissen from South Africa straight into the sea. The third man in our

## 1942

threesome, Ronald Loyns, Royal Canadian Air Force, was shot down, and I was now all alone. I weaved to beat hell and came home balls out. Saw three more pilots in the water in their little yellow dinghies. They looked lonely bobbing about in that mess."

Records show that on The Dieppe Raid Royal Air Force Fighter Command lost one hundred and eleven aircraft, comprising seventy Spitfires, twenty seven Hurricanes, nine Mustangs, four Typhoons and one Boston. Forty five pilots paid the supreme sacrifice while many others were wounded and a number taken Prisoners of War.

Those from the Ibsley Wing who lost their lives were two No. 66 Squadron pilots, Flight Sergeant Ronald Loyns, aged 20, of the Royal Canadian Air Force, from Saskatchewan, and Lieutenant Victor Nissen of the South African Air Force, while No. 501 lost Sergeant Pilot Allan Lee, aged 21, who, in low cloud and poor visibility was unable to locate base and crashed into the side of a hill at Billingshurst, twelve miles North of Tangmere.

Pilot Officer W. Lightbourne, 501 Squadron, had the luckiest escape of the day. Deciding to abandon his badly shot-up Spitfire (AB402) he was thrown violently against the aircraft's tail-plane by the slipstream. With a broken leg and entangled against the aircraft as it dived towards the sea, he struggled to free himself. After frantic efforts he managed to part company with the Spitfire and parachuted into the sea close to a convoy, which despatched a small vessel to pick him up. He was later transferred to another ship for medical treatment.

The only mishap to No. 118 Squadron was when Flight Sergeant Sid Watson, Royal Canadian Air Force, taking off at 0747 hours, in Spitfire EN964, on the first sortie of the day, burst a tyre. The aircraft went up on its nose, and although damaged Category B, Sid Watson was uninjured.

Charlie West remembers how one day a Spitfire of No. 66 Squadron was late returning from a mission. Because Charlie had a bicycle he was told to wait for the said Spitfire and then go to the cookhouse for dinner on his cycle. On landing the Spitfire pulled up too close to the runway, the pilot got out and ran off, obviously in a state of shock, probably from being bounced by enemy aircraft. Unable to do anything about it Charlie left the Spitfire and went for his meal. Unfortunately, Wing Commander Currant saw where the Spitfire had come to rest and been left, and ordered Warrant Officer

## So Much Sadness, So Much Fun

Robinson of No. 66 Squadron to put Charlie, as the person who allowed it to be there, on a "fizzer", for being in charge of aircraft LZ-F parked too near the perimeter track, being in a dangerous position, liable to be knocked by passing vehicles, such as lorries and bowsers.

Charlie was brought before Wing Commander Currant at the Station Headquarters at Moyles Court, and remembers well what happened there. He recalls the conversation that took place like this:

W/Cdr.: "Do you realise airman that Spitfires cost five thousand pounds each."
Charlie: "Sir".
W/Cdr.: "Have you anything to say before I pass sentence upon you?"
Charlie: "Well it's like this Sir".
W/Cdr.: "That's enough. 14 days confined to camp, 14 days privileges. Corporal, take him out."

So from the second floor of Moyles Court House Charlie was marched out and given his hat again. But what Wing Commander Currant did not know was that Charlie's home was in Fordingbridge and that he had a living out pass, and also took his meals in the cookhouse in the wood. When Charlie returned to his Squadron, then stationed near Ibsley Church, Warrant Officer Robinson asked him how he got on and the conversation went like this:

Robinson: "How did you get on West?"
Charlie: "Not very well Sir".
Robinson: "What is it then?"
Charlie: "Well 14 days confined to Camp, 14 days privileges".
Robinson: "Oh that's a bit unfortunate. Did you tell the Commander you lived out, and that your home was in Fordingbridge?
Charlie: "Indeed not, he didn't seem to know".
Robinson: "Well we'll see what we can do for you West, it's a bit harsh. In the evenings at 7 o'clock when you're supposed to report to the guardroom, come into my office".

For many days Charlie would go into Warrant Office Robinson's office and say "it's now 7 o'clock Sir". W/O Robinson would pick up the telephone – "is that the Guardroom?" "West won't be able to come

*1942*

tonight, he's working on the flight". Phone down, to Charlie W/O Robinson then said, "Bugger off home West".

The day after Dieppe, LeRoy Gover was told that he "was posted to Eagle Squadron (Number 133)". He packed his belongings and went out on a beer binge to celebrate, because he had never really thought he would belong to one of the famed units. All U.S.A. airmen serving with the Royal Air Force were being posted to the Eagle Squadron, and on Friday, August 21st, LeRoy caught the train from Ringwood station on his way to Biggin Hill, Kent.

Only a few days later the Ibsley Wing dispersed. No's. 66 and 118 Squadron went to Zeals (Wiltshire), and No. 501 to Group Headquarters at Middle Wallop (Hampshire). Tragically, while on convoy patrol off the Isle of Wight September 17th, Dicky Lynch, who was at Ibsley with No. 501 Squadron, died in action. He had just returned from leave after visiting his wife and new born child.

W.A.A.F. Accountant Officer Rowena Foster (maiden name Hulland) remembers arriving at Ibsley, getting off the bus at the Church and walking to the station headquarters. Very shortly after arriving, days rather than weeks, the R.A.F. personnel were posted, but the Accounts section remained to pay the R.A.F. Regiment personnel and the owners of the billets where personnel were sent to live. Rowena was first billeted in Ellingham Vicarage where she stayed for a few weeks, and then in Ringwood itself. At that time the Accounts section was in a large house near what was known as the Mockbeggar barrier.

L.A.C.W. Maura Gorman (nee Kiely) from 1942 to 1943, was a Teleprinter Operator in the Signals Section. Maura recalls the memories she has, of Ibsley being a very pleasant and happy station. One unfortunate incident, however, caused her some inconvenience. On her way to attend Pay Parade Maura met a herd of cows coming towards her. Being terrified of cows, she turned and retraced her steps – at the double! So, Maura missed Pay Parade, which left her 'Broke' for a week!

With the departure of the three squadrons of the Ibsley Wing in August, came the arrival of the U.S.A.A.F. 8th Air Force, 1st Fighter Group under Station Commander Col. John Stone. The American advance party arrived at Ibsley on 27th August, two squadrons No. 71, commanded by Major Raymond Ruddell, and No. 94 under Captain James Harman, flying their P-38F Lightnings in from

Goxhill. The third squadron in the Group, 27$^{th}$, were to be based at Colerne.

The move to Ibsley from Goxhill is recalled by Sgt. Ken Fritz, a recruit radioman with 71$^{st}$ Squadron. He says the move came in mid-August and while loading the 40 and 8 vehicles a problem arose, the NCOs said no bicycles could be taken. Now if this were to happen in today's society things would get a bit testy but back then, after a lot of quiet bitching, the bikes did not go. Oh! mine did go all right. I stashed it in the homing truck and retrieved it in Africa several months later with two flat tires and no pump.

Our new station was Ibsley, down near Bournemouth on the South coast. Our bivouac was in a dense grove of trees up on the hill; the mess hall was half way between on the way to the airfield. It was a good walk several times a day till we could afford another round of bicycles. Our cooks were relatively proficient at serving American food but had absolutely no knowledge of how to handle mutton and boiled cabbage. The British cooks were called in to help with the same results. Gradually a bit of GI staples of canned Spam and Corned Willie was obtained in large enough quantities to stave off a mutiny.

Whilst the P-38 Lightnings were at Ibsley, Peter Smith recalled how one pilot had a one pound bet with another that he could fly a P-38 Lightning between two of the large elm trees in Gorley road, just South of Cross Lanes Chapel. This he accomplished, but not without losing four feet of the plane's wing tip!! Ken Fritz also remembers this incident and wonders if anyone knows who the pilot was. He says they were playing cat and mouse with a couple of Spitfires that were still at Ibsley.

"Work at Ibsley doubled", said Ken, "as everyone prepared to get everything tip top to engage the enemy, the missions so far being really only practice.

The real thing, in the radio section, the shortage of test instruments caused problems that had been replaced by American ingenuity, bugs in equipment causing shorts were getting weeded out, this put a strain on everyone plus the inescapable duty of KP and guard duty was not leaving extra time for that new Physical Training that was expected of everyone, to run around the perimeter of the airfield. It was amazing there was very little bitching, almost an exciting mood of actually getting into action".

## 1942

"Out of the blue I received a three-day pass, and went bike riding no place in particular, just pedalling, and I might add not paying attention to where I was going. As night was approaching I looked for lodgings, ending up in a grassy ditch sleeping with my bike. Morning arrived and I admitted that I was lost. With two days of pass left I did not panic. I spotted a Beaufighter landing nearby and pedalled in that direction. The guard said, "come with me", they would not tell me where I was but put me in their plane with my bike and flew me home. A very embarrassed soldier had to explain where he had been. All road signs had been taken down for fear of an invasion attempt.

The road up the hill to our bivouacs was rather steep, in an 'S' curve, and near the middle and along one side was a very soft spring which meant a very muddy slide as our American finest came down that hill too fast on unaccustomed bicycles and missed the road, it happened quite often.

I went to Ringwood on a special mission. That little lady waiting at home, wanted some incentive to remain attached. What could be better than a diamond? It depleted my meagre savings but anything to keep harmony for a few more months. It was not good enough. A bit later she met up with a sailor stationed in the States. She was kind enough to spend three cents postage for a "Dear John" letter to write and tell me".

The Group's first operation took place on 29th August when the 94th scrambled two aircraft to intercept a Luftwaffe bomber, but no contact was made.

On Tuesday 1st September the 71st and 94th made, what was believed to be, the first mission to be flown by all American Forces from British soil. This was a fighter sweep over occupied France, but not an enemy aircraft was seen.

2nd Lieutenant Roy Russell was a pilot with 71st Squadron and says that his log shows three combat missions flying escort for B-17's, on September 1, 2 and 26. An entry in Roy's diary shows that they lost their first 71st pilot in combat, William "Sleeper" Young, my classmate and dear friend. He just failed to return from the mission – no one knew what happened to him.

Roy also says that when returning from one of their missions they found the field at Ibsley to be fogged in and were unable to land. Several landed at another R.A.F. Spitfire airfield, no record of the name, where we they were cordially received. They spent the night there and were entertained royally at dinner, served with wine and brandy. They were put up in private rooms with batman service. Roy goes on to say they found the English people, both military and civilian, to be courteous and friendly wherever they went.

During their stay at the base at Ibsley they had quite a lot of free time to explore the beautiful countryside, which Roy did on his English bicycle and his crew chief's motorcycle. He says he made several trips to London, taking the train from nearby Ringwood.

Roy also recalls, while doing duty as Officer of the Day in the control tower at Ibsley, the visit of a Brigadier General, small of stature. I didn't know until sometime later that he was the famous Jimmie Doolittle, who went on to become the Commanding General of the 12$^{th}$ Air Force in Africa and later of the 8$^{th}$ Air Force in England.

Despite more flights into enemy territory the next casualty was the result of a tragic accident at Ibsley. Training exercises involved making low level strafing passes on one of the Bofors anti-aircraft gun positions close to the airfield. Unfortunately, whilst on one such exercise, Lieutenant William Pennington, of No. 94 Squadron, due to some miscalculation, pulled up too late and crashed on the gun pit causing the deaths of two gunners of 439 Light Anti Aircraft Battery. Sadly Lieutenant Pennington was also killed.

This incident was also recalled by Dewey Prince of No. 71 Squadron, who says "One day I was walking across the field on one of the taxi strips which ran alongside the fence near the road on which the church stood, on the corner of the airfield. I heard a loud noise. I looked up and saw a P-38 Lightning which looked like it was heading straight for me. I immediately fell to the ground. The plane passed right overhead. There was a windsock on a pole attached to the fence. The plane was so close to the windsock it caused it to spin on the pole. I then watched the plane pull up and then dive towards an ack-ack gun which was on the edge of the field. When the plane pulled up it was too close to the gun to clear it. The P-38 was a large plane which weighed nine tons. Instead of pulling up quickly the plane "squashed" (that is the best word I can think of) and continued downward. The horizontal stabilizer (the flat surface of the tail that connected the fins on the end of the booms) hit the barrel of the gun which was pointed upward. The

*1942*

plane crashed in the field opposite. One of the engines fell close by. The part of the plane containing the cockpit was quite a bit farther on, and the other engine was even farther down the field. We all ran to the crash site. Although the cockpit section did not appear to be badly damaged the pilot was dead, and as I remember there were two of the soldiers on the ack-ack gun who were killed too.

Ron Rutter, of the R.A.F. Regiment remembered seeing several accidents when the Americans were at Ibsley with their Lightnings, and later Thunderbolts.

"The Americans were also a great help to the R.A.F. Regiment lads at Ibsley as they were able to use their PX like our NAAFI and there were plenty of American cig's. cartons and cartons of them, when you could afford them. Not that they were expensive, but your cash ran out," recalled Ron. "There was also loads of Yanky chocolate and other goodies."

Late in October the two American squadrons of the 8th Air Force, 1st Fighter Group, 71st and 94th, learned they were to go to Gibraltar, then to Egypt via Algeria, North Africa.

The first ground contingent left Ibsley on October 25th, and travelled by train to Glasgow where, the following day they boarded an English troopship. Other contingents also left Ibsley and went by train from Ringwood to Liverpool and boarded ships there.

In early November all the air echelons moved to Portreath, Cornwall, in readiness for departure to Algeria. After delays caused by bad weather the Lightnings took off from Cornwall on 13th November, on what would be an eight hour trip to North Africa. Sadly, somewhere along the route two aircraft from No. 27 Squadron were lost, Lieutenant John Wolford went down in Spain, and was safe, only to be killed in action in May 1943, but Lieutenant Robert Chenoweth apparently crashed in the sea and, tragically, was killed.

Jackie Gilbert was a small boy in the war days, and remembers his parents telling him of a few incidents which occurred at Ibsley.

One incident he recalls was of the time when his father and a colleague were hay making and they found the cockpit of an aeroplane. They wanted to keep it but were apprehended by Americans and had to hand over their "prize", after an argument and threatening of pitchforks.

Another incident Jackie recalls being told of, was when his Mother held at pitchfork five R.A.F. men who had been taking apples from the orchard at Moyles Court where she worked. Eventually the Military Police arrived and the situation was defused.

In those days Moyles Court gardens had greenhouses and orchards, now school playing fields, and Jackie's mother Mrs. Minnie Gilbert, worked there for a Mr. Miles. One particular day there had been a lot of heavy rain and water had got into the brakes of his 1937 Vauxhall. He left the nurseries at Moyles Court and proceeded round to the hump bridge where there were Sentries on guard. On reaching this point he was supposed to stop and show a pass, but because of the steep bridge and wet brakes, could not. This led to a shot being fired into the boot of the car, which came to rest at the bottom of the bridge, but all was well when its occupant explained about the wet brakes.

As the Americans left in November, Sandy Fraser, who worked on the Direction Finding station arrived at Ibsley, from Fairwood Common, South Wales.

He recalled how a mobile V.H.F. Station was set up in Somerely Park, the Earl of Normanton's estate, off the main Ibsley to Ringwood road, but that the site proved to be useless, and too far from the airfield for communications to be satisfactory. It was then transferred to Ibsley Common, above the airfield, which proved to be an excellent site, the only major difficulty being the D/F tender which was inadequate, to say the least.

Sandy went on to say that due to the tender being unreliable, they eventually took over the D/F tower, which was then under the control of Middle Wallop, as by this time squadron activity from Ibsley was steadily on the increase.

Having inherited the D/F tower, they also inherited the Ginger Tom Cat, from a Corporal Barham, who was in charge and about to depart. The cat was very lazy, always asleep, his usual resting place being on top of the signal generating set, which was always warm, giving out a nice gentle heat. The only time the animal would descend from his place of comfort was for food amply supplied by the mess hall.

While the cat rested in his lofty position it was noticed that he was disturbed only by transmission from aircraft, never ground station transmission, the aircraft signal would cause much ear twitching and head shaking, and general movement, so by hanging a spare set of headphones near the cat they had a very alert operator.

## 1942

When activity increased across the Channel the cat came into his own. "We would take our cue from the cat and were alert to the activity. Even if transmission was inaudible we despatched a bearing transmission irrespective, as the cat was a very accurate piece of equipment, and generally an aircraft was in need of assistance,"

One particular summer evening, in 1943, recalled Sandy; "I was alone on duty, activity was nil, despite the fact that it was a beautiful summer evening. All of a sudden the cat started to perform, and was restless, so searching for a transmission, I eventually heard a faint break in the background noise. A homing bearing was despatched and obviously received, because the faint break was once again heard, but the cat was still agitated. Eventually the process came to a realization, this was an aircraft in distress, transmitting a "Mayday". For a considerable time his only contact had been with Ibsley, despite the fact that his nearest base was Exeter, where it was eventually able to land."

"The aircraft was a P-38 Lightning with an American pilot. His plane was losing height, one engine on fire and the other running rough. Obviously it was bounced on the other side of the Channel and it was remarkable that he had made Exeter and a satisfactory end, thanks to a Ginger Tom Cat."

Many pilots of various squadrons would be very surprised to learn that the cat at Ibsley was the alert operator who set in motion the answer to their request for a homing bearing on numerous occasions.

"When I was posted from Ibsley I went to Predannack in Cornwall and met up again with Corporal Barham. I remember the first thing he asked me was about Ginger the cat. I assured him that the W.A.A.F.s at Ibsley found him a very good home. He was very fond of the animal as he had got it as a kitten from Mr. and Mrs. Bennett at Mockbeggar Farm."

Fred Turner also worked on the Direction Finding Station on Ibsley Common, and he remembers how it comprised of a thirty foot tall tower, of wood and felt construction, situated inside a seven foot high hexagonal blast wall. The tower itself was bolted down on to the concrete floor inside the protecting wall. Surrounding the Direction Finding Station, in a circle, approximately thirty yards from the blast wall were sixteen concrete blocks representing the points of the compass. Twelve of these compass points still remain, as does the hexagonal blast wall. Near the site of the D/F Station there is still brick rubble and concrete from the derelict living quarters structure and also remnants of the underground air raid shelter.

In December 1942 Ibsley was transferred back to 10 Group, Royal Air Force, and the first squadrons to return were No's. 66 and 118 on 23$^{rd}$ December, flying in with Spitfire Mk Vb's.

It is understood that on their return to Ibsley things were found to have been left in a pretty messy state by the "Yanks", and the beautiful mossy woods around Moyles Court had been churned up by their transport. Messing Officer Sid Barber had been posted, there were hardly any staff, they had to feed in a dismal Nissen Hut, and fetch their own food. According to a member of No. 118 Squadron, they were billeted at Chatley Wood, Rockford, but had to feed at the W.A.A.F. site at Gorley, more than two miles away.

Three days later, on 26$^{th}$ December, No. 504 (City of Nottingham) Squadron arrived from Middle Wallop, under Squadron Leader R. Lewis. They too were flying Spitfire Mk Vb's, code letters TM.

Vic Sellings recalled how he had just completed an armourers course at the dreaded Credenhill Camp, Hereford, and was posted to No. 504 Squadron at Ibsley.

He remembered arriving at Ibsley with a fellow refugee from the course, late into the evening, and what did they find – bods still working! "Little did he know. Come the morn and they climbed aboard the transport (bikes came a little later) and still in shiny blues with a brand new Judgeware mug, a pressy from Mum, surveyed the other inmates, and being a naïve eighteen year old he thought, God, what a shower of tramps, and wasn't really impressed when later one of them chucked a large flint into his mug so that it looked a bit more like theirs. A few more weeks and he was also an oil stained octane smelling tramp.

At the Squadron Office they were told to report to 'B' Flight, and after a hike round the perimeter of the airfield, were welcomed with open arms, as being a shortage of their breed, the present incumbents had four Spitfires each to worry about.

So, they then got a tool box each, containing a screwdriver which had seen better days, and a bit of twisted wire with a loop at one end and a lump of wood at the other, known as a cocking toggle; plus a

## 1942

cocoa tin with a wire handle and a brush with a couple of hairs left in it, for brushing anti-freeze on breech blocks. Then they got two kites each to look after. Well, being keen lads, they thought they ought to go and look at their charges, joined forces and found one of their Spits just outside the Flight office.

They climbed up on to the main plane and proceeded to undo panels, practised removing 20mm magazines. "My mate was underneath with .303 magazines out and yards of ammo trailing", said Vic. Oh, great fun! Then suddenly a klaxon blares, somebody shouts 'scramble', and a pilot comes haring round the bay, hotly pursued by fitter and rigger. "Oh! Effin Ell!!!! Over to 'D' quick.". We said "what was all that about?". Well, no one told us about instant readiness. We were of course told politely later, and wondered who actually had the rollickin' for it. Mind you, we were pointed out in the cookhouse for a few days. "That's them!!"

The winter inflicted many problems on the airfield staff. Due to lack of good drainage on the south side of the airfield, flooding was a frequent occurrence. Also, exposure to severe gales damaged aircraft hangars. A fire in the clothing store (a requisitioned building near to the Station Headquarters at Moyles Court) caused much damage and loss.

*So Much Sadness, So Much Fun*

*Artist's Impression of the Direction Finding Station on Ibsley Common*
D. Williams

# 1943
## A busy year, many comings and goings.

The year opened on a busy note for No. 118 Squadron, as they were preparing to leave Ibsley for the last time, and on Saturday, 2nd January, they moved to Wittering.

The 31st Works Flight were now based at Ibsley, and G. Allott, an L.A.C. in the Royal Air Force was attached to this. He recalled that they were at Ibsley for only a short time, probably during the winter months of 1942/43.

According to former L.A.C. Allott, they were engaged in the construction of landing strips along the coast which were for the use of gliders, etc., in the invasion of France on "D" Day, and were commanded by Warrant Officer Butcher.

R.A.F. Ibsley was used as an accommodation base and 31st Works Flight travelled each day to the site where they were working at the time, which could be several miles away. They took over farms, filled in ditches, removed trees and anything else which was in the way, and when the area was level laid what was called Sommerfield Tracking. This was a kind of wire mesh reinforcement laid on the ground with metal bars which were tensioned. This was laid for whatever width and length was required for an airstrip.

The 31st Works Flight did not get a good reception from the Commanding Officer at Ibsley, mainly because of their appearance, and also because they were not actually contributing to operations at the airfield. Although they were R.A.F. personnel, due to the nature of their task they dressed in khaki Army uniform during working hours. This got very muddy after working all day in the fields and their vehicles made an awfully dirty mess when they returned to Ibsley at the end of the day.

In 1943 B. W. D. Cooke was posted to Ibsley from Technical Signals at R.A.F. Valley (N. Wales). He didn't know where it was

## So Much Sadness, So Much Fun

but his railway warrant said Salisbury. He was six hours late because of the bombings in London. He asked the only Great Western Railway man at Salisbury station where Ibsley was and set out with knapsack. The G.W.R. fellow ran after him and said "By the way, the signpost says Mockbeggar!". Cooke arrived after 10.00 p.m., but was anxious that his new C.O. should know he had at least arrived on the right day.

It was for this reason that he went, with misgiving, to the mess – stood inside the door discreetly and waited for the C.O. to pause in conversation at the bar, with three Wing Commanders. Before Cooke could take one step the C.O. turned and beckoned him forward. As he reached him and saluted he was given such a surprise!! The C.O.'s gloved hand shot out and hit him harder that he had ever been hit before. Cooke fell backwards for a few yards till he hit a mess table and fell on his back on that, and not on the floor. He sat alone for a few minutes, then the C.O. disappeared for bed. One of the Wing Commanders then came, tapped him on the back and said "Don't look so worried old man, you haven't defied protocol or anything like that, but at this time of the night the C.O. likes to relate – we've heard it many times before – how he was shot down as a fighter pilot, by a Messerschmitt; had to have an arm amputated to release him from the wreckage, and he *always* concludes by saying", "but gentlemen, there is nothing I can't do with my false arm that I couldn't do with my real one.". "At that time", said the Wing Commander, "you showed up, so you were the obvious Aunt Sally".

A different Wing plan was now used at Ibsley in the shape of the high altitude Spitfire MkVI, brought in from West Hamptnett on January 3rd, 1943, by No. 616 (South Yorkshire) Royal Auxiliary Squadron, led by Squadron Leader Colin F. Gray, D.F.C.

No. 616 was formed at Doncaster on 1st November, 1938, as a bomber squadron with Hawker Hinds. It was the last of the Auxiliary squadrons to be initiated, and in June, 1939, was transferred to Fighter Command. At the end of the War No. 616 became the R.A.F.'s first jet fighter squadron, with Meteor F.1's. Its badge carries a Yorkshire rose, commemorating its association with Yorkshire, and the squadron motto is; "Nulla rosa sine spina" ("No rose without a thorn").

Unfortunately on their arrival at Ibsley the Spit VI's were still giving the odd problem and the squadron was grounded for four

## 1943

days whilst a carburettor problem was sorted out. The engine had developed an unpleasant tendency to cut out during tight turns – something that was not ideal for a fighter! However, the experts from Rolls Royce soon came up with a cure and the aircraft were back in business again.

The latter part of January brought a change in Commanding Officer for 616, Squadron Leader G. S. K. Haywood replacing Squadron Leader Colin Gray. Six new pilots also arrived in January, including four Belgians and one Australian.

Flight Lieutenant Jack Cleland of the Royal New Zealand Air Force was with No. 616 Squadron at Ibsley and later flew with with the U.S.A.A.F. Eighth Air Force's 357th Squadron. His time with the U.S.A.A.F. was to make his wartime experiences unique, as he was the only Kiwi to fly with the Eighth Air Force. In 1999 Tim Neilsen published a book, in Australia, 'Jack's Adventures' which tells the full story of Flight Lieutenant Jack Cleland, and with Tim's permission we have been able to incorporate excerpts relating to Jack's time with No. 616 at Ibsley.

Jack's first operation in the New Year was a convoy patrol on the 4th. Squadron Leader Barthold (Yellow 1) and Jack (Yellow 2) took off at 0955 hours. They completed the uneventful flight one and a half hours later. Over the next week Jack didn't take part in any combat operations, but instead practised attacks on bomber formations, and then he flew to Tangmere for three days, returning to Ibsley during the morning of 11th January.

Then, at 1445 hours, Squadron Leader Haywood (White 1) and Jack (White 2) started a standing patrol which would cover the area between Portland Bill to The Needles. Sometime during the operation they flew to Cherbourg where they attacked a German military barracks. After making repeated strafing runs over the complex the two pilots noticed that many of the soldiers were seen to fall. One hour five minutes after take off they landed safely back at Ibsley. The two men weren't given long to rest, for just over and hour later they were both airborne again as White flight. After fifty minutes patrolling over a convoy they returned with nothing to report and brought their Spitfires in for a night landing. In between Jack's two flights Pilot Officer Cooper (Red 1) and Sergeant Dolton (Red 2) were scrambled. They were sent to 20,000 feet to intercept an unidentified aircraft. The German turned back before he could be sighted by the pursuing Spitfires.

*So Much Sadness, So Much Fun*

Shortly after this Flight Lieutenant Maclachlan (Yellow 1) and Sergeant Pearce (Yellow 2) who were on standing patrol over The Needles were vectored by Control to try to catch the bandit. After searching their assigned area they couldn't locate the aircraft either.

Only one flight was made on 12th January and that was a convoy patrol by two aircraft. The following day saw No. 616 Squadron fly a series of convoy patrols. Jack Cleland (White 1) and Sergeant Dean (White 2) filled their part of the day's proceedings by spending one hour five minutes patrolling above the ships. All the pilots returned from the day's operations with nothing of interest to report. The rest of the month, as far as Jack was concerned, was taken up with three more uneventful convoy patrols, formation flying and some aircraft testing which occasionally involved firing the Spitfire's weapons.

Escorts continued to be flown from Ibsley and on one such mission Flight Lieutenant Peter Wright threw his dinghy to the ditched crew of a Ventura. Wriggling round in the cockpit of his Spitfire to free the dinghy and then throw it out was no easy task. This was not the first time that a Spitfire pilot had thrown his dinghy to someone in the sea, and over the following months 616 squadron pilots did so on a several occasions.

On 26th January 'A' Flight of No. 257 Squadron arrived at Ibsley, on detachment from Warmwell, with Hawker Typhoons Mk 1B, but their stay was short and they left on Monday, 8th February.

The first operation in February for No. 616 Squadron was on the 2nd. After an early morning briefing twelve Spitfires flew to Tangmere. On their arrival they were refuelled so that they would have the maximum range possible. Jack Cleland moved YQ-A into position, he was Yellow 3. The other members of his flight were Flight Lieutenant Maclachlan (Yellow 1), Sergeant Rodgers (Yellow 2) and Sergeant Fowler (Yellow 4). At 1040 hours Red, Yellow and Blue sections received the green light, the operation was under way. Jack brought his aircraft to full power, released the brakes and on reaching take off speed lifted his Spitfire's nose into the air.

The task was to escort twelve Venturas on a bombing operation off Abbeville. The Squadron crossed Beachy Head at zero feet and on reaching the French coast they were passing through 10,000 feet. The bombers made their run over the target at 12,000 feet and were engaged by very limited flak. On completion of their assignment the

## 1943

escorting fighters returned to Tangmere. Once they had been refuelled they made their final flight back to Ibsley. The next day Jack enjoyed himself, practising air to air firing with live ammunition.

On Thursday, 4th February, No. 616 Squadron had twelve aircraft over the Cherbourg Peninsula at 20,000 feet. Jack was flying YQ-K as part of Yellow section, he was Yellow 3. The Germans fired a substantial amount of flak at the formation but fortunately for the pilots it all exploded harmlessly behind.

Jack Cleland (White 1) and Sergeant Dolton (White 2) were the only No. 616 Squadron flight airborne the following day. They flew a routine and uneventful mid-afternoon convoy patrol.

On Sunday 7th, No. 616 squadron was given the honour of providing an escort for the Prime Minister's Liberator 'Commando' on his return from the Casablanca Conference, and later for His Majesty King George VI coming home from North Africa.

On 9th February Jack Cleland was back in business with two convoy patrols. He was in the cockpit again on the 11th with a shipping reconnaissance at zero feet around the Cap de Barfleur area, but no enemy ships were observed. The next day saw him back at zero feet but this time around the Channel Islands. He was on an escort operation to protect an ASR Walrus as it searched for a downed airman. February 13th started with another convoy patrol but finished with No. 616 Squadron flying rear cover to twelve Bostons on a bombing operation to St. Malo. It made a nice change for all involved not to be engaged by flak batteries. Another day of no flying for Jack followed the escort flight.

No. 66 Squadron left Ibsley for Skeabrae on Tuesday 9th February, then, on Saturday 13th Nos. 616 and 504 Squadrons were joined by the Spitfire Vb's of No. 129 (Mysore) Squadron, under Squadron Leader Henri Gonay. Their code letters were DV.

For Jack Cleland and No. 616 Squadron February 15th saw a routine and uneventful convoy patrol, but 16th was to be different. Exeter airfield was where the operation was to start from, and the Squadron was to provide close support for seventy Flying Fortresses and twelve Liberators on their journey to Guincamp. The formation was attacked by flak but luckily for the bombers and their escorting fighters it wasn't accurate. Jack and the other pilots landed back at Exeter before making their way back to Ibsley.

Tragedy struck on Jack's next flight. The Squadron was practising line abreast formations on 18th February when Flying Officer Peter Blanchard left the group to shoot down a drifting barrage balloon. When he made his attack somehow his aircraft became tangled in the balloon's trailing steel cables and he was killed.

Over the next week Jack took part in more formation exercises but didn't participate in any combat operations. At dawn on 25th February Jack took off in heavy fog to fly a convoy patrol. On his return forty five minutes later he had to divert to Warmwell due to the extremely poor visibility at Ibsley. He made it back later in the day once the fog had lifted.

The operation on 28th February was to hold a surprise for Jack. It was the third visit by No. 616 Squadron to Cherbourg-Maupertus airfield as escort to Whirlwind bombers. He had missed the first two trips but to-day was to be different. He was to lead a flight for the first time. The twelve Spitfires which made up Red, Yellow and Blue sections took off at 1500 hours. Jack took his assigned position in the formation at the head of Yellow section, the other pilots were Sergeant Davies (Yellow 2), Sergeant Rodgers (Yellow 3) and Sergeant Fowler (Yellow 4). No. 616 Squadron flew with No. 602 Squadron as high cover while No. 504 Squadron flew a free lance operation. Close escort duties for the six Whirlwinds was handled by No. 130 Squadron. They were the only people to spot the enemy, and one of their pilots was lucky enough to destroy a Focke Wulf 190. The three flights were back on the ground eighty five minutes later. Jack noted in his log book that his wingman, Sergeant Davies 'went mad and caused a shambles in Yellow section'. What transpired is not known or recorded in any documents. It must have been fairly serious to be noted. Later in the day Jack spent forty five minutes on a convoy patrol and landed at dusk.

This was the last day of operations for No. 616 Squadron before they took part in Exercise 'Spartan'. No. 129 Squadron who were at Ibsley with No. 616 left for Tangmere for the duration of the exercise. It was noted in the Squadron's record book 'pilots are busy getting gen on servicing their aircraft, the intention being that on this exercise Squadrons will not have the benefit of established station maintenance and servicing facilities.

It is frequently forgotten that even during wartime, time and effort has to be put into training, either at squadron level or in respect of major exercises. A particular army exercise, named 'Spartan' called for intensive air participation and No. 616's Spitfire, together with those of 504 and 129, were heavily involved with intercepting the 'bad guys' in addition to providing escort to Hurricanes on ground strafe. During this exercise the squadron notched up a healthy tally of 'kills', mainly on Mustangs and Typhoons, although in the process was, on paper, reduced to less than half strength.

Jack Cleland took part in Exercise 'Spartan' which was an Army and Air Force combined operation. It was a war game that was designed to see how the two branches of the service would cooperate. The exercise was staged from the 1$^{st}$ to 12$^{th}$ of March. Day one dawned with very little cloud and plenty of sunshine. The Squadron pilots spent the day practising formation flying and dog-fighting. On their return the pilots refuelled their own aircraft. This was certainly a new experience for them and it must have been strange for the ground crews to sit back and watch the pilots do their job. The next day Air Marshal Leigh-Mallory visited the Squadron. At the dispersal he stressed to the assembled pilots the importance of working with the Army. This was one of the main aims of operation 'Spartan'.

Unfortunately, the only operation undertaken for the day was beating up the airfields gun posts. Heavy cloud cover was the reason for the limited amount of activity. March 3$^{rd}$ started with the Squadron being at 'readiness', but because of the weather this rating was soon down graded to sixty minutes. 'B' Flight were given detailed instruction on the recognition of armoured fighting vehicles. The day before it had been Jack and the other pilots from 'A' Flight.

Jack's part in operation 'Spartan' started on 4$^{th}$ March. Nothing happened until 1030 hours when four aircraft were scrambled, but they were recalled before becoming airborne. At 1150 hours sixteen Typhoon fighter bombers raided Ibsley. They were credited, on paper, with destroying one aircraft, damaging two and wounding six pilots. Thirty minutes later four Spitfires were scrambled to intercept two Mustangs and a Typhoon that were observed South of the airfield. As a result of the camera gun footage that was shot during the dog-fight that ensued, No. 616 Squadron claimed all three aircraft destroyed for no loss. Jack was airborne once during the day in a Spitfire Mk VI (YQ-K). He flew this aircraft on all of his flights throughout the operation.

No. 616 took off at 1455 hours to rendezvous with twelve Hurri-bombers, which they escorted on their operation to attack fifty to sixty vehicles housed at a military transport park. On the way to the target 'Red section' spotted, attacked and then destroyed a hostile Mustang. Once the Hurri-bombers had left the target area No. 616 Squadron strafed Kidlington airfield. Approximately thirty Spitfires, fifteen Mustangs and some Tiger Moths were parked close together on the ground, which made them easy targets. The pilots claimed twelve of these aircraft destroyed or damaged, while the umpires ruled that three 616 Spitfires and their pilots were lost. After the Hurri-bombers had landed at their base and the escort operation was drawing to a close, twelve Typhoon bombers with hostile markings were spotted. The enemy aircraft took no evasive action of any kind and their losses were assessed by the umpires as seven destroyed for no loss to No. 616 Squadron aircraft or personnel.

On Friday, 5th March it was an early start for the Squadron. They were at 'readiness' thirty minutes before dawn. Jack Cleland flew only one operation and was airborne for one hour thirty minutes. The following morning everyone was up again before dawn, but owing to ground haze no flying took place until 1715 hours. When the haze lifted twelve Spitfires took to the air as high cover to twelve Bostons and their dozen close escorting fighters. After the Bostons had carried out their bombing run, and the formation was making its return flight, twelve army vehicles were spotted travelling East on the Buckingham to Bletchley road. Each pilot executed a strafing run, but none of the army personnel made any attempt to seek shelter and no return fire was experienced. All the transport attacked was claimed to have been damaged. An enemy Mustang was spotted by Squadron Leader Haywood, who engaged and destroyed it, and 616 Squadron came through the day's activities with no losses to aircraft or pilots.

A point that was noted in the Operations Record Book was the difficulty during the day of obtaining full details from the exercise Controller as to (1) targets, (2) rendezvous time, (3) operation altitudes and (4) operational frequencies. The final notation read 'Although ample preliminary warning is given, final details are not usually received until aircraft are required to be in the air, leaving not enough time to rendezvous with the bombers.'

## 1943

Jack was at 'readiness' from dawn on March 7th. Three sections of four aircraft took off at 0740 hours to carry out a low-level attack on Heston airfield, and with the other pilots finally located the target in fog. Their arrival wasn't noticed and when they lined up their Spitfires to strafe the base they weren't met by any defensive fire. They had achieved complete surprise which resulted in three Spitfires and three Bostons destroyed plus two Spitfires and three Bostons damaged while a number of the airfields personnel were machine gunned as they moved around the aircraft under attack. The umpires ruled that No. 616 Squadron suffered no losses.

The Squadron including Jack were airborne again at 1437 to shoot up tanks and motor transport in the vicinity of Byfield (South West of Daventry). The twelve Spitfires located a column of tanks moving North and in the distance another column of military vehicles was seen heading South. Each aircraft made one pass at the tanks and then headed after the trucks. These attacks reaped the pilots six vehicles put out of action and one Churchill tank (which was astride a canal bridge) shot up. The two operations had Jack at the controls of his Spitfire for a total of two hours thirty minutes.

On March 8th No. 616 Squadron flew just one operation with Jack leading one of the flights. The aim was to provide high cover for thirty minutes while eighteen Mustangs made a reconnaissance of military vehicles. The areas that needed observing were Dunstable-Bedford road, Thame-Aylesbury-Linslade road and an ammunition dump in a wood East of Bletchley. After the pilots had completed their escort task they made a sweep over Cranfield airfield, Bedfordshire. Many aircraft were observed dispersed around the base. Leaving a section to act as top cover, the remainder dived down and scored five Beaufighters, three Typhoons and one Lysander destroyed or damaged on the ground for no loss.

Jack took part in two operations on Tuesday March 9th, the first being at 0715 hours when twelve Spitfires made a low-level attack on Duxford and Debden airfields. He led one of the flights. When No. 616 Squadron arrived at Duxford eight aircraft broke from the formation and in the ensuing battle destroyed five aircraft on the ground. The remaining four Spitfires continued to Debden where they accounted for a further three destroyed on the ground. Airborne again, at 1200 hours, Jack and seven other pilots had to provide top cover while two Mustangs performed a reconnaissance for military transport in the Princes Risborough area. The Spitfires rendezvoused with the Mustangs over Dunsfold. No combats took place even though a substantial number of vehicles were see moving along the roads. During one of the flights on 9th March the Umpires (Air Commodore C. E. V. Porter and Air Commodore H. K. Thorold) judged that Jack had been 'killed in action'. He was told to go back to his normal duties with the Squadron while the other pilots kept flying. At the time he was oblivious to what was about to unfold, but it was to cause him a few headaches. The authorities forgot to mention that it was an exercise, so Jack's death became official and a cable was sent to his parents informing them of his death, but they never received it, thankfully.

Jack did not realise anything was amiss until he went to London on leave. He first called on the New Zealand Base Post Office to collect his mail. When he walked in he saw his friend Tassie Whitehead. Tassie looked up in horror. "Good God Jack, we've been notified of your death and have distributed your food parcels!"

After Jack had sorted this out he called on MGM's head office, (he had been with them in New Zealand). He walked into the General Manager's office. When Joe Goldman saw him he went as white as a sheet,. "My God Jack, we've just published your obituary!"

The obituary appeared in the MGM magazine "The Lions Roar". It read:

*A saddening shock this Wednesday was the news that Pilot Officer Jack Cleland had been killed the day before when his aircraft was shot down. It was his first flight after recovering from bronchitis in hospital, which he left on Monday. Leo's British organisation offers deep sympathy to his family and friends in New Zealand where he was a booker for MGM.*

After clearing everything up with Joe Goldman Jack went to the bank to cash a cheque. Suddenly he was being interviewed by police from Scotland Yard, who had been called in by the bank to investigate why he was cashing a dead man's cheque. Once Jack had produced the relevant identification and a telephone call had been made to No. 616 Squadron, at Ibsley, the problem was resolved. He now realised what had taken place, and knew the chain of events this mistake would cause, so he hurriedly cabled his parents 'Am fit and well'. He received in return 'Didn't know you'd been sick'. When Jack finished his leave and returned to the Squadron, the pilots greeted him with, "Hello 'Jack', we'd heard you had gone for a burton!". Jack replied,

## 1943

with a smile, "I'm OK, but it's not often you get to read your own obituary".

With the end of the exercise on March 13th it was back to operational duties with an escort for Whirlwinds the following day. A similar mission was planned for the 15th and the squadron were deployed to Harrowbeer, Devon, in readiness, but four days later they were still there waiting and so returned to Ibsley.

Jack didn't fly his next combat mission until 19th March, when at 1755 hours twelve Spitfires took off to escort the same number of Whirlwind fighter-bombers on a shipping strike West of Alderney. On the way they were joined by No. 504 Squadron who were also assigned to help in protecting the fighter-bombers. Jack led the second flight of four aircraft, he was Yellow 1, Pilot Officer Mullenders (Yellow 2), Sergeant Fowler (Yellow 3) and Sergeant Dean (Yellow 4). Because of thick haze no ships were located and everyone returned to Ibsley without incident.

The following day Jack Cleland spent forty five minutes patrolling the Portland Bill area at 25,000 feet when No. 616 Squadron received an order to 'scramble'. They were recalled when the enemy aircraft turned back. Jack flew again on March 28th when he undertook a shipping reconnaissance around the Channel Islands at 18,000 feet, but nothing of interest was observed. Later in the day he patrolled above Ibsley airfield at 27,000 feet but one again the enemy wasn't sighted. Jack's last flight with No. 616 Squadron before his posting to to North Africa was on April 4th when he flew from Ibsley to North Weald.

No. 616's pilot strength continued to build at Ibsley with the arrival of another six pilots, mainly Canadian and Australian. Eleven major operations were flown in April, four of them on consecutive days at the end of the month. There was yet another change of C.O. with the arrival on 4th of Squadron Leader Peter LeFevre, D.F.C.

An escort for Venturas to Brest, on the 5th, brought the first air combat for some time. One Ventura ditched and the area was promptly investigated by four Fw 190's. Without delay the Spitfires went down after them and battle was joined. More 190s arrived and Flight Lieutenant Peter Wright was shot down. In return Flying Officer Mike Cooper claimed a damaged as the engagement came to an end.

## So Much Sadness, So Much Fun

Mike Cooper recalled how, in the early part of 1943, while stationed at Ibsley he was courting a young lady who lived in Oxford and who later became his wife. Mike said "she had a brother, a Company Sergeant Major in the Royal Marine Military Police, who was stationed near Bournemouth, I think, at the time. I promised him that I would give him a flight in the Squadron Tiger Moth if he came to the aerodrome. One day he did just that, but gave no warning that he was coming. He turned up at the aerodrome guard house on his motor bike and in full military uniform. At the guard house he stated that he wished to see Flying Officer Cooper of No. 616 Squadron. The guard Sergeant said that he would phone our dispersal to find out if I was available. However, the message we got at the dispersal was, "Tell Flying Officer Cooper to get the hell out of sight because the Military Police are after him". The Sergeant then told my girl friend's brother that Flying Officer Cooper was flying and not expected to be back for at least an hour, perhaps longer. The Marine Policeman then left. He told me his side of the story when I next saw him. We laughed when I told him my side. So, once more I promised him a flight if he could come again, but he must give me warning of his visit. This he did a few weeks later. In fact, he turned up on 29$^{th}$ May 1943 (I know the date because it is in my Pilots Log Book).

This time I was ready for him and had warned our Guard House. I duly got a flight in the Tiger Moth authorised, and borrowing a flying helmet for my friend I got him installed in the front cockpit. Unfortunately it was not possible to connect our operational helmets to the inter-cockpit communication system in the Tiger Moth, so we could not speak to each other. Nevertheless we set off and I flew him over the New Forest on our way to have an aerial view of Bournemouth town. We were flying happily around there when I suddenly saw four FW190's flash in from the sea; presumably to bomb Bournemouth. I did not stop but dived down to house top level and high tailed it for base. I kept low down, weaving between trees, skimming over roof tops and scraping the grass on hill tops. We soon arrived safely back at Ibsley where I landed and taxied to the dispersal. On getting out of the plane I helped a very white faced Military Policeman to get out. Clinging on to the plane for support, he turned to face me and, obviously very angry, said, "My God do you always do that to your first time passengers? You frightened the b....y life out of me!". When I explained the reason for our mad hat return to base he cooled down, and we remained the best of friends".

A mission to Brest on 16th April saw both the C.O., Squadron Leader Peter LeFevre, D.F.C., and one of the Flight Commanders, Flight Lieutenant Gordon McLachlan being shot down by flak. LeFevre evaded capture and returned via Gibraltar on 13th July, but was killed in action on 6th February, 1944, when leading No. 266 Squadron. McLachlan was also killed, claimed by JG2. Two days later while on an ASR sortie off Swanage (yet another engine failure), Sergeant S. J. Fowler ended up in the water. Safely in his dinghy he waited, protected by the orbiting Spitfires, until collected by an ASR Walrus.

During his time at Ibsley with No. 504 Squadron (County of Nottingham), Sgt. Pilot Brian Eyre kept a diary about life in 1943, and the following are some extracts from this.

Thursday 1st April: "To-day is the 25th anniversary of the R.A.F. – twenty five years of progress from the 1st World War SE25's to our Spits – quite an advance and I feel it something of an honour to be flying these lovely aircraft in the company of such a gallant crew as 'A' Flight, No. 504 Squadron, so ably led by Flight Lieutenant Geoff Richards, an officer whose valiant efforts to keep the morality of his flight above rock bottom is match only by his unique and inventive command of the English language. In this endeavour he is well supported by his second-in-command, Flying Officer Jackie Pearson. Then there is 'Bis' otherwise Domenico Gregory Blassissi, who takes a lot of fun about his name in good part and has the reputation of being an expert in overturning Tiger Moths! The phrases 'He hasn't a clue' and 'Wizard prang' spill freely from the lips of Flying Officer Barry from whom, it is most reasonable to suppose, all R.A.F. slang originates. He is at his most prolific during mess parties – which occur at the drop of a hat – where one only has to cock an attentive ear to hear the words 'a veritable locking-piece' used to describe the outcome of a bit of mess wrestling won by our noble Flight Commander. Pilot Officer Milne, the bright Anzac and devotee of the Brighton course for undisciplined pilots is another character in our unruly mob of officers.

The N.C.O. side of the outfit is equally bright. Perhaps the outstanding personality is our mad I.R.A. merchant; Paddy Filson famed for claiming full responsibility for each and every event at

Ibsley since his arrival. His keenest effort, he alledges, was to return to the flight one night after dark to bore a hole in the petrol tank of a Spit. It wasn't until his engine cut out next morning that he found out whose plane it was. Half-a-crown in the 'line box' for each such story has so far failed to stem the flow. Other members include the tough New Zealander, Bill Warwick, the 'gunnery king'; Flight Sergeant Roberts; the 'brutal and licentious' Bailey (to quote the Flight Commanders), Gerry Locke and my sabre, foil and squash partner and co-member of the entertainment's committee, Gerry Gough. There are also three pilots from Ceylon, M. R. 'Rex' De Silva, L. S. Flamer-Caldera and the third, I think, named Jaywardena who has joined us recently together with F. Cowling. Altogether a highly motivated and splendid crew".

Friday 2nd April. "A beautiful morning, true herald of spring. Gerry tells me I woke about 5 a.m., dressed, went down to the flight and subsequently took off to find myself with him stooging along with a convoy a mile or two off the coast. All was peaceful until a couple of planes dived on us from up sun. My hours of Aircraft-Recognition study now paid off – just in time we identified them as Typhoons – and peace returned to that part of the Channel."

Saturday 3rd April. "Readiness all day:. A late abortive scramble to 13,000 feet as the sun was setting."

Sunday 4th April. "Went to sea in a tanker with Flight Sergeant Gordon on a navy liaison exercise from Poole to Southampton which was both interesting and helpful in seeing the receiving end of our frequent convoy patrols. The Captain of 'Shelbrit LL' gave us breakfast in his cabin before hoisting the balloon and setting sail down the harbour and thereafter hugging the coast for a couple of hours. Passed moored Sunderlands before we docked at 3 p.m. and drove back to Ibsley. Bags of activity on our return. Our Squadron, while searching for a pilot of No. 129 Squadron, in the sea off Cherbourg, came across several 190s. In the ensuing battle Squadron Leader Leslie Ivey was shot down, while Sergeant M. Harding of 'B' Flight was wounded, though he brought his plane back. We claim two probables and a possible but so far none have been confirmed. Bags of 'panic' all evening with two raid alerts and many scrambles but no firm combats were reported though two Huns were seen at a distance.

Another show rehearsal for 'The Mystery of Moyles Court' in the theatre at night. We had so much fun with it that we really never

*1943*

got through the sketch. It seems funny, and with a couple of amendments to the script it should go quite well. Gerry and I stayed up till after eleven to make the necessary alterations and I played the piano for a while before going back in the cold night air."

Monday, 5th April. "After yesterday's losses, we were ready for a repeat run in the afternoon but the 'powers that be' decided we should stay at home on aerodrome defence so everyone was cheered when the other two squadrons took off. We were left with stooge patrols in the rear of the operation at 17,000feet, but landed without seeing anything. However, in the early evening, we were shaken to see only eleven aircraft straggling back, presumably some pancaked elsewhere according to the Intelligence Officer who dashed past. He said that each Squadron had lost one man, while the Wing-Commander and Squadron Leader Henri Gonay each claimed one probable and one damaged FW 190."

Friday, 9th April. "Coming back from a 'do' my wheels wouldn't come down. I flew away, juggled with the selector but without effect, then tried to shake them down by violent 'wing waggling' and finally did a bit of 'upside-downing', but all to no effect. In the end I was forced to use the CO2 bottle which happily, worked, but of course it put the kite u.s.

The 'do' itself was a shipping reconnaissance which brought up a goodly amount of enemy flak from Alderney and Cap de la Hague, which was pretty accurate. It's a wonder there were no holes afterwards and Paddy Filson ahead of me disappeared in a cloud of black ack-ack smoke just before I went through it, but we both came out apparently none the worse. I wonder, on reflection, if this had anything to do with the failure of my wheels to come down on my return. We did remain on readiness until 9.30 p.m. and are on again at half-past-six tomorrow morning. Thank goodness I am going on leave at mid-day tomorrow!"

During the evening of April 9th, Sergeant Arthur Jeffreys (Equipment Section) arrived at Ringwood Railway Station on posting from R.A.F. Valley. An R.A.F. Jeep was there, waiting to take him to the camp. Arthur recalls how the Military Transport driver took him to one of the Camp's Sleeping Quarters where he was fixed up for the night. The next morning transport was provided to take him into Ringwood, which surprised Arthur, but the driver told him that the Equipment Senior N.C.O., and W.A.A.F.'s were using the requisitioned Avon Guest House (now demolished), close to the River Avon, and alongside the main A31 road, as their administration headquarters.

After being introduced to the Equipment Officer, Flight Lieutenant Broomhead, Arthur learnt that he would be replacing Flight Sergeant Hall, (who was being posted to Middle Wallop), as N.C.O. in charge.

In the grounds of the Avon Guest House was a large building which was used for storage of items (Class "C") which were of an expendable nature. In the house itself only one room was used for equipment, namely bed-linen for R.A.F. Officers.

Arthur remembers that Flight Sergeant Hall and the W.A.A.F.s were billeted with families in Ringwood, and when the days work was done just two W.A.A.F.s were left in charge as duty storekeepers for any emergencies that might occur. He says he was lucky enough to exchange billets with Flight Sergeant Hall at Manor Road in Ringwood, and was with a lovely lady, the late Mrs. Ada Tanner, who was in her nineties when she died, in 1996.

This arrangement with the Equipment Section, recalled Arthur, was unusual to say the least, as on the camp itself was the petrol storekeeper, and a corporal W.A.A.F. who was in charge with the other W.A.A.F.s. Their admin. office was the single cottage which laid back off Ellingham Drive (still there to-day). The clothing store at Moyles Court was ably looked after by Corporal Haynes (W.A.A.F.).

The Barrack Store was the large brick built barn in the grounds of Moyles Court House.

The set-up for the Equipment Section at R.A.F. Ibsley, was, in Arthur Jeffrey's words, as follows: "The Equipment Officer and N.C.O. in charge operated in Ringwood with the remaining sections three miles away at Moyles Court. To my knowledge, there were no serious problems on account of this. I always attended Clothing Parade, although this was not really necessary as Corporal Haymes was a tall, well built W.A.A.F. who could handle any R.A.F. airmen who tried to pull a fast one on her!!"

Arthur also had the responsibility to keep an eye on all requisitioned properties around the airfield.

He remembers an amusing experience which happened when he was on night duty at the Avon Guest House. He says: "On this

## 1943

particular night two of our equipment W.A.A.F.s, I think their names were Edith King and Lorna Higgins, decided to go to Fordingbridge for a dance but missed the last bus home, and so had to walk the seven miles back to Ringwood. They were unable to wake Mr. and Mrs. Jarvis of College Road, with whom they were billeted, so could not gain entry to the house, they were locked out. They decided they would explain their predicament to me, provided they could wake me. This they did, and I let them in. I believe the time was about 12.45 a.m. I said "you two W.A.A.F.s, sleeping quarters, for tonight only, in the bed-linen room.". Before I left them to continue my interrupted shut-eye, I gave them strict instructions to be out of the house by 7.30 a.m. They slept like babes, so they told me when reporting for duty next morning – and no wonder after their escapade!! As I think about this incident now it seems so funny, but it could have been tricky for *me* at the time, had the Equipment Officer arrived for work early!!

Another incident I remember could have been a disastrous one. The Avon Guest House was on the banks of the River Avon and it was common practice for the W.A.A.F.s to take a dip in the river. On this occasion one of them got into difficulties caused by the strong currents and it was fortunate that a number of W.A.A.F.s were swimming close to her, for together they were able to pull her to the bank and get her out. After that I decided that swimming in the River Avon would be out of bounds.

Because of the many friends made and the kindnesses shown to him by many Ringwood families, Arthur and his late wife, Rosa decided that the New Forest area was ideal for their retirement, and he now lives not many yards from the old airfield at Ibsley where he served during World War II.

Brian Eyre's diary on his return from leave continues:

Tuesday, 20th April. A fine clear day, obviously calling for something intrepid, so we were not too surprised in the early afternoon to see a squadron of Venturas roar over the field in neat vics of three, break away and pancake. Very soon afterwards, the mess phone rang calling us to readiness for a briefing at 4 o'clock p.m. We climbed into the truck outside the mess and were soon heading swiftly around the perimeter track, now lined by the bombers; their crews lounging around them on the grass beside the briefing room while starting to empty their pockets of personal possessions and fastening the cords of their Mae-Wests. An air of tension seemed general, yet it was an accustomed tenseness born of experience. Mingled with the bombers were the visiting fighters, two Squadrons of Spitfires with their pilots, many of whom were swarming all over the Venturas and asking all manner of professional questions about them. The bomber crews seemed rather less interested in the Spits, as if they took their presence for granted. Ground crews hurried about, some cleaning the guns, others with necklaces of cannon shells and bullets, swarming over the wings into which petrol bowsers were loading fuel for the sweep, and checking the ailerons and flaps. Soon vans full of aircrew drew up at the briefing room and their occupants drifted inside as the clock came round to four p.m.

At the briefing the Wing Commander plotted a familiar course to Cherbourg. We were to be close escort to the bombers – good old 504 – right in the thick of it! Our other two Ibsley Squadrons would give medium and top cover into the target area which was defined as shipping in the main dock and we were to expect heavy flak and twenty plus Focke Wulf 190's and Messerschmitt 109's – "if we were lucky", said the C.O. The two visiting Spitfire squadrons would meet us on the way out to clear our tails.

Back to the flight then, and a dash to collect our escape kit, empty our pockets and check over our kites. I put my parachute ready on the seat just as a roar of engines across the aerodrome signified that the bombers were warming up and starting to taxi one by one to their take off positions. That was our signal and we climbed into the cockpit, zeroed our watches with the control tower and watched as the last of the Venturas heaved itself off the ground. Called out 'All O.K.' to my ground crew, who had just finished checking that I was safely lock in, I shouted 'Contact'. pressed the starter button and with a cloud of blue smoke, the engine roared into life in concert with the other Spits around me. One of the other squadrons of fighters was already airborne and had formed up behind the bombers which were flying at about a couple of hundred feet in a formation of four vics of three in a gentle right hand turn towards the coast, just above us, as we took off. Taking our own formation around the bombers, there were four of us behind and just above them, while the other two sections of four took up station on either flank. Up above us, another squadron had positioned itself and glancing around I could see in every direction yet more Spitfires

## 1943

skimming just over the top of the tree-covered hillside which housed our billets as we set course out over Bournemouth. It was a stirring sight – the bulky bombers, swift and deadly, surrounded by swarms of fighters roaring over the beaches in the direction of France. Switching on my long-range tank, I held the plane nose down until I was less than thirty feet over the sea, so that, for the first half of the way across the Channel there was a glorious sensation of speed and urgency. There was little time to concern ourselves with what might be, for the second half of the trip turned into a fierce climb once the bombers started to pull up from sea level into the sky. We switched on our oxygen and throttled back a little to stay with them, now near enough to France to occasion a goodly watch around the skies.

A sudden piercing whistle in my earphones told me that the German radar had picked us up and there would be no surprise about our intentions. Climbing rapidly, I could see the French coast quite clearly with Alderney and Jersey over to the right, a quick reminder that some of our own countrymen were maybe watching our arrival from down below us, and we wondered just what they were feeling about us. Cherbourg harbour, some ten thousand feet below stood out clearly, the twin docks projecting out from the town with a patchwork of fields and hills surrounding it and disappearing into the hazy distance beyond. It looked very like those sections of the English coast I knew so well, peaceful and beautiful with the sun shining hotly down on a millpond sea – nature at her best. Yet to us, now at twelve thousand feet, the brilliance of the sun held no comfort, only the threat of enemy fighters roaring down on us; the cool, green fields would soon be spurting destruction around our heads.

The Wing Commanders' voice broke into our ears, "change gear ... watch the sun," and almost as he spoke there appeared just below me a jet black ball which had, for a fraction of a second, a brilliant orange centre and then blossomed out into a dirty grey flower. Within seconds there were many more around, above and below – the new ones hard looking and deadly, the old ones grey and filmy like mist. "Keep with the bombers", "stay with them" ... the Wing Commander again as the flak piled up like a cloud all around the bombers which had gone into a diving turn and were heading vertically down towards the target. "Stick with them" called our leader as we stuck our noses down and turned over into a vertical dive round the bombers which were just visible below us in the ever thickening black burst which, despite our 400 m.p.h., buffeted us and threw the plane from side to side. Vicious orange flashes from the town below, reflected in the water, showed that the ack-ack guns were still firing and continued to bracket the bombers as they dived out and I was not surprised to see a straggling bomber pulling out with thick black smoke pouring from his port engine.

It was hard work hauling the stick back and pulling several G's as the sea rushed towards me but we managed to pull out with a couple of hundred feet to spare and our section formed up around the damaged plane as it headed back out to sea. The black smoke, happily, slowly petered out and the bomber pilot was able to pull away and catch up with his own section who were by now approaching half way home.

The buffeting of my plane from the ack-ack subsided and, looking behind, I saw no new bursts in the sky. All our Spits were clear of the barrage and all unharmed, as far as I could see.

There was a great tendency to relax on the way back from a sweep but experience taught us that this was a time of considerable danger as the enemy often stationed some FW 190's in mid-Channel to catch out a returning group. We therefore were keeping a weaving pattern so that we could keep a good rear view against a last minute attack as we gradually regained and closed our formation. Soon the cliffs of the South coast appeared through the distant haze – a welcome sight to all. Ten minutes later, the bombers having left us for their home bases with a word of thanks, we crossed over the cliffs of home in tight squadron formation – such a sight was supposed to boost morale on the home front – though keeping twelve planes wing-tip to wing-tip all the way back to base after an enemy barrage of the kind Cherbourg had provided, was, we felt, somewhat less of a morale booster for us! Still, we gather, on our days off, that people seemed to like it so it probably did some good for their morale; perhaps less for ours! However, on this occasion, we were soon pancaking at base, we mounted the waiting van for debriefing and then off for a refreshing cup of tea in the mess.

The rest of April was pretty busy, the occasional Cherbourg prang with a variety of light and medium bombers, Bostons, Venturas again, and even Whirlibombers, and the almost daily 'morning one-and-six-penny round the islands', i.e. the Channel Islands. There were a few attacks on Carenton fighter aerodrome.

## 1943

Monday 3rd May. "We all flew over to Coltishall on the East coast for a major attack on the power station at Amsterdam by a dozen Venturas and a diversionary raid on oil installations at Ijmuiden down the Dutch coast. In the event I was lucky to be detailed for aerodrome defence (in case of any retaliatory attack on the aerodrome, before the raid returned). Things went badly wrong; the attack was intercepted by numerous FW 190's while climbing up towards the target. Most of the bombers were shot down before reaching Amsterdam and a number of the Spits were lost or damaged. The Coltishall Wing Leader, Wing Commander Howard P. Blatchford, D.F.C., was killed in action, after being shot up by a FW 190 of JG1 he ditched in the North Sea. Gerry Gough collected a least two bullets, as he found out when he got back to Ibsley. One had smashed around inside his tail unit so that it's a wonder it didn't fall off, the other hit his cannon shell magazine in the right wing which could have been very nasty if they had gone up. As it was, he now has a souvenir cannon shell casing with a nice dent about one eighth of an inch above the percussion cap! Myself and a few other actually flew across to Ludham a few miles away to take part in a follow up raid which was part of the plan, but for obvious reasons we were recalled and flew home to Ibsley."

Several Ibsley personnel were called to assist at an incident in Ringwood. A Junkers 88 had crashed in a field near The Bickerley, not far from the town centre and quite close to the Brockenhurst – Bournemouth railway line, at 23.10 hours on Friday 7th May. Tony Harrocks is researching the mysteries of this crash, and says that according to an eye witness the town air raid siren in Ringwood sounded and machine gun fire was heard overhead. The cloud over the moon had cleared temporarily and a twin engine aircraft was seen flying at about 500 feet. The machine gun fire continued by which time the aircraft was well alight. A second aircraft was heard, believed from its engine noise to be a Beaufighter. This aircraft closed to within 300 feet of the first aircraft and then veered away. Sight of both was then lost, to be followed by the sound of the crash.

Leading Aircraftsman Maurice Annison was stationed at Ibsley at the time and recalls how the duty sergeant instructed him to take a three ton lorry with two other servicemen and drive down to Ringwood to guard the site of the crash.

Tony Harrocks says that eye-witness accounts of the last terrible seconds of the Junkers 88 do not entirely agree as to the direction

## So Much Sadness, So Much Fun

that the bomber took as it flew, completely ablaze, over the rooftops of Ringwood. Had it crashed in the town centre then probably its entire bomb load would have exploded with great loss of life. At least one of the bombs detonated and all four crew members were killed instantly.

The three R.A.F. personnel from Ibsley were released from the crash scene at 0500 hours. Despite the dim illumination (blackout regulations) what they could have seen would have been horrific.

Maurice Annison resumed duty at the crash site at 1700 hours on the Saturday afternoon and was horrified to see the number of unexploded bombs, by then taped off. Railway wagons were shunted on to the line opposite the crash site, in order to absorb some of the blast, were any of these bombs to explode. It took three days for combined R.A.F. and Army Bomb Disposal teams to defuse the bombs, remove them and clear up the crash site.

The badly mutilated bodies of the four crew members were removed in a hearse owned by Mr. Charles Bailey. There is mystery here too, because Mr. Bailey's son recalled how, whenever he talked about the crash his father would be upset by the fact that one of the blanket wrapped bodies appeared to be that of a child, about 14, because the hands were so small and delicate. His father also said that he took five bodies to the public mortuary in Ringwood, and yet only four were buried in Ellingham Churchyard on 12th May, 1943. The presence of a fifth body seems to have been common knowledge in Ringwood and Maurice Annison was told by other members of the R.A.F. recovery team that five bodies had been recovered.

The four crew members of the Junkers 88 were Hauptmann Dietrich Von Buttlar, pilot; Oberfeldwel Karl Pflitch, the co-pilot; Unteroffizier Johannes Weiser, the radio operator; and Feldwebel Josef Sturm, the air gunner. In 1963 their bodies were exhumed from Ellingham Churchyard and re-interred side by side, with an unknown German soldier in the adjacent grave, in the large German War Cemetery on Cannock Chase in Staffordshire.

Ellingham Church still holds an Imperial War Graves Commission wooden cross from the grave of an Unknown German Soldier, bearing the date 7th May, 1943. Could this possibly be the fifth victim mentioned earlier? A mystery yet to be solved.

Brian Eyre said "The most exciting trip was on the 16th May. It was an armed shipping recce with four Whirlibombers. Just West of

*1943*

Cherbourg we were jumped by a few FW 190's who dived on us out of the sun and had a few squirts. We were only a few feet over the waves but went into a very sharp break right and as I started to black out one of the attackers hurtled past so close to me that my Spitfire bounced, his slipstream caused my engine to splutter and I thought it had stopped. Fortunately, all that training paid off. I pulled up from the waves, grabbed the correct buttons and levers and hauled myself into a quick climb away by which time the enemy had disappeared, though we had quickly reformed a defensive circle around the bombers. The 190's did not return after that and we brought the bombers safely home."

George Pyle was a pilot with No. 129 (Mysore) Squadron, and a magazine article prompted his memory of an operation from Ibsley on 17th May, 1943. George says many people, both air minded and otherwise, will have seen the movie 'Memphis Belle' which tells the story of the first Fortress crew to complete a tour of twenty five missions over Europe. The temptation, says George, is to believe the harrowing experiences of the crew on that trip with one severely injured gunner about to be thrown overboard (with parachute I must add) in order to save his life. But we should always beware the cinematographic licence taken by film producers and this was no exception. I had always thought that the near rebellious flight took place over Germany....until, that is, I read the account of the flight in the September 2000 copy of Aeroplane Monthly. Far from returning with injured crewmen on board, there is a photograph of all ten of them running jubilantly from the aircraft after landing. Nor was the target Germany but in fact Lorient in Brittany.

Suddenly the date of the raid – 17th May, 1943 – seemed to ring a bell, which made me look up my pilot's log book. There it was, 17 May 1943, Spitfire V, DV-J – Cover to Fortresses, duration 1 hour 55 minutes. The personal side comments read '100 plus Fortresses – saw Lorient from Guernsey – 5 parachutes in the sea – landed at Harrowbeer short of gas.'. (Though not mentioned in these notes, one Fortress was seen on a slow descent to the sea.)

In fact this was only my second offensive operation with No. 129 (Mysore) Squadron at Ibsley. On the previous afternoon the squadron had flown to Perranporth in Cornwall, and the log book entry adds 'My first Squadron formation'. We stayed there overnight and the following morning we proceeded to Portreath where the fuel tanks were topped right up for the long operation which followed. After landing at Harrowbeer where we once more refuelled, we then flew back to Ibsley.

George concludes: This little bit of history may mean little to anyone else, but the link with the now famous Memphis Belle, and the fact it was an Ibsley based Wing, Nos. 129, 504 and 616 Squadrons, which participated is just a small part of the Ibsley story.

Tuesday, 18th May, and Brian Eyre's diary records, "The Wing flew to West Malling, Kent, for an escort to a dozen Bostons in an attack on the aerodrome at Abbeville, on a beautifully clear afternoon."

"Much to our surprise we encountered no opposition from this notorious hot-spot; the bombing was good and all returned safely."

Wednesday, 19th May. "An armed shipping reconnaissance in the early morning. We attacked what might have been a couple of flak ships. Unusual defensive fire from them, rather like a volley of rockets fired simultaneously the whole length of the ship's side, perhaps carrying up a line of cables supported by parachutes. Haven't see this before. Better not fly over such ships".

"Here I went on another few days leave and my diary comes to an end. After my return, things went on rather as before, with high patrols over the Channel, more Ventura escorts once again, generally to Cherbourg and around the Channel Islands, and occasional trips West to Exeter.

While taking part in an early morning shipping reconnaissance off Guernsey on Sunday 23rd May, Sub Lieutenant P. G. Mercer, RN (Air), of No. 129 (Mysore) Squadron, had engine trouble with his Spitfire VB, EP710, and had to ditch in the sea, near Herm. He was safe but became a Prisoner of War.

Operationally it was more of the same in May for No. 616 Squadron, with two more Focke Wulf 190's claimed damaged/ probable by Pilot Officer Jacques Joubert and Sergeant Croquet, to add to the squadron total. Also on 23rd the squadron was tasked to act as anti-flak escort to a Whirlwind shipping strike near the Channel Islands. In the event the convoy was found just as it was about to enter St. Peter Port. The Spitfires of 616 went in first and blazed away with cannon and machine gun at ships and harbour installations. They were faced with a veritable barrage of ground fire as this was one of the most heavily defended of ports. The aircraft of

## 1943

Flight Lieutenant Leslie Watts was hit in the fuselage, by flak, smashing the rudder controls. Fortunately he was able to keep the aircraft under control and by just using the rudder trim managed to get back to Ibsley! The same day brought one of the few productive (almost) scrambles when 'A' Flight went after a raid inbound for Bournemouth. They saw an enemy formation of some seventeen plus and tried to close to engage. However, the best they could achieve was a very frustrating 1200 yards – so near and yet so far.

Ron Brooke served with the R.A.F. Regiment and was stationed at Hurn (about nine miles from Ibsley) during 1943-44.

He recalls that they were a mixed infantry squadron, but by May 1943 were changing over to anti-aircraft with Bofors and twin Brownings. He clearly remembers being told by the Sergeant. "You lot are going to Ibsley for two weeks with the Army on the Bofors Gun sites. Pack up your kit and throw your kit bags in the Bedford truck.". Someone remarked "How are we going?". "You are marching there in full kit, large and small packs, water bottles filled.". We said "He's joking", but he wasn't.

Some of Ron Brooke's other memories of Ibsley are of the accommodation huts up on the hillside amongst the trees. The pleasant walks to the dining hall, where on a certain day of the week they could help themselves to certain things, and the station band played. Not exactly 'Palm Court' stuff, as a matter of fact, they played so fast they gave them indigestion!!

Bicycles were provided to get them to and from the gun site at Ibsley. "Anybody who cannot ride one, stick him in the middle". "If he falls, we all fall", was the Sergeant's remark said Ron.

The summer months saw no change in the fortunes of No. 616 at Ibsley, and life was as busy as ever with eight major operations in June, the same again in July and ten in August. As usual these were only a small part of the overall flying effort but were always considered to be the highlights of the squadron's activities. Anti-shipping sorties, or rather escort, to anti-shipping Whirlwinds and Hurricanes, took an ever increasing amount of flying effort with a 'trip around the Channel Islands' being the usual option. Most were notable only for their boredom, although continuing problems with the Spitfire VI's engine kept pilots on their toes – and ditching was a well practised art.

Brian Eyre recalled that the same pattern of operation for No. 504 squadron continued into June:. "On one shipping reconnaissance the flak ships were encountered again, and I believe we lost a Spitfire from one of the other squadrons of the Ibsley wing, and one of the Whirlibombers, which may have been brought down by flak ship fire. We even did a little practice night flying locally but the Spit was not very suited to this, the propeller arc and the long nose in particular made landing very tricky."

On 5th June No. 504 Squadron lost Sergeant Pilot Gerald Locke, while flying on a shipping reconnaissance over the Channel. His section had encountered fog and turned back for base, but Gerald Locke's aircraft failed to emerge from the fog bank. The aircraft he had been flying was Spitfire, EN953, a Presentation Spitfire from the people of Holsworthy (Devon).

No. 129 Squadron were involved in escorting Venturas bombing St. Brieuc on 13th June. Sergeant Wilfred Brookes experienced engine trouble with his Spitfire after combat with FW 190's, causing him to ditch in the sea some forty miles off Start Point, Devon, and he was never found.

Towards the end of the month, recalled Brian Eyre, it was rumoured that No. 504 Squadron might be going to Malta, especially when the outlines of a carrier deck were painted on the Ibsley runway. In the following week, with the aid of a navy 'batman', at least one hundred practice landings, each with varied results, were carried out – but nothing came of it and shortly after the Squadron learnt they were to be moved away from Ibsley for a rest in the West Country, to Church Stanton, Somerset.

On 22nd June a detachment from No. 124 Squadron flew in to Ibsley, on detachment from North Weald, their Spitfire VI's bearing the code letters ON. Then on 28th June, No. 453 Squadron, Royal Australian Air Force arrived, led by Squadron Leader K. M. Barclay, from Hornchurch, with Spitfire Mk Vb's, code letters FU.

The following day, 30th June, No. 165 (Ceylon) Squadron arrived from Peterhead, Scotland, also with Spitfire Mk Vb's, their code letters being SK, while No. 504 Squadron left Ibsley bound for Church Stanton.

Bruce and Douglas Warren were identical twin pilots at Ibsley with No. 165 Squadron. They were known as Duke I and Duke II, Bruce being number I, having joined the Squadron first.

*1943*

Although No. 165 Squadrons' stay at Ibsley was short, it was busy. Douglas (Duke II) Warren recalls how they flew South to Ibsley via Acklington and Wittering. He says just before coming to Ibsley their Commanding Officer Gin Seghers was posted and Squadron Leader Hugh A. S. Johnston took over. Douglas said he was a great change and vast improvement over Gin, both as a fighter pilot and a person. The twins did not know it at the time, but it was the start of a close friendship which was to last many years after their return to Canada. "Johnny" as he was know was an officer with great leadership qualities, and one who inspired confidence, as opposed to Gin who destroyed it.

The first operation No. 165 Squadron undertook from Ibsley was a shipping reconnaissance off the Channel Islands, by Flight Lieutenant Disney, Chalkie White, and the Warren twins. We reported what shipping we saw, and the Navy HQ would decide if it was worth sending torpedo boats out. At this time 165 Squadron had eight Australians, two New Zealanders, two Free French, two Canadians, and ten Englishmen. The Squadron was equipped with Spitfire Vc aircraft and used 45 gallon long range tanks on some missions. Spitfire Vc's were fitted with four 20 mm canon, and were heavier than a Vb because of that extra weight.

On July 15th No. 124 Squadron left Ibsley for Northolt, but for No. 165 Squadron it was an eventful and tragic day. They were one of several squadrons detailed to escort B-26 Marauders of the 323 Bomber Group to attack coke factories North of Ghent in Belgium. The Squadron flew from Ibsley to Martlesham Heath in Essex for refuelling, but took off again with only nine aircraft instead of twelve, as three planes were unserviceable owing to their Radio Transmission equipment not working. On the way to the target they were intercepted over Holland by Focke Wulf 190's of 1./JG 26 based at Woendrecht, and in the ensuing combat three Spitfires of No. 165 Squadron were shot down in the space of ten minutes. Flight Sergeant William Brown (Australia), EP555, SK-C and Pilot Office Andre Imbert (French) AR609, SK-M, were both killed. They were shot down by one pilot, Hauptmann Karl Borris, Gruppenkomander of 1./JG26. The third Spitfire of No. 165 Squadron to fall was EE603, SK-E, piloted by Flight Sergeant John Curry who was posted missing.

Douglas Warren (Duke II) remembers this day well. He says he was on this operation with John Curry (recently returned escapee) as

*So Much Sadness, So Much Fun*

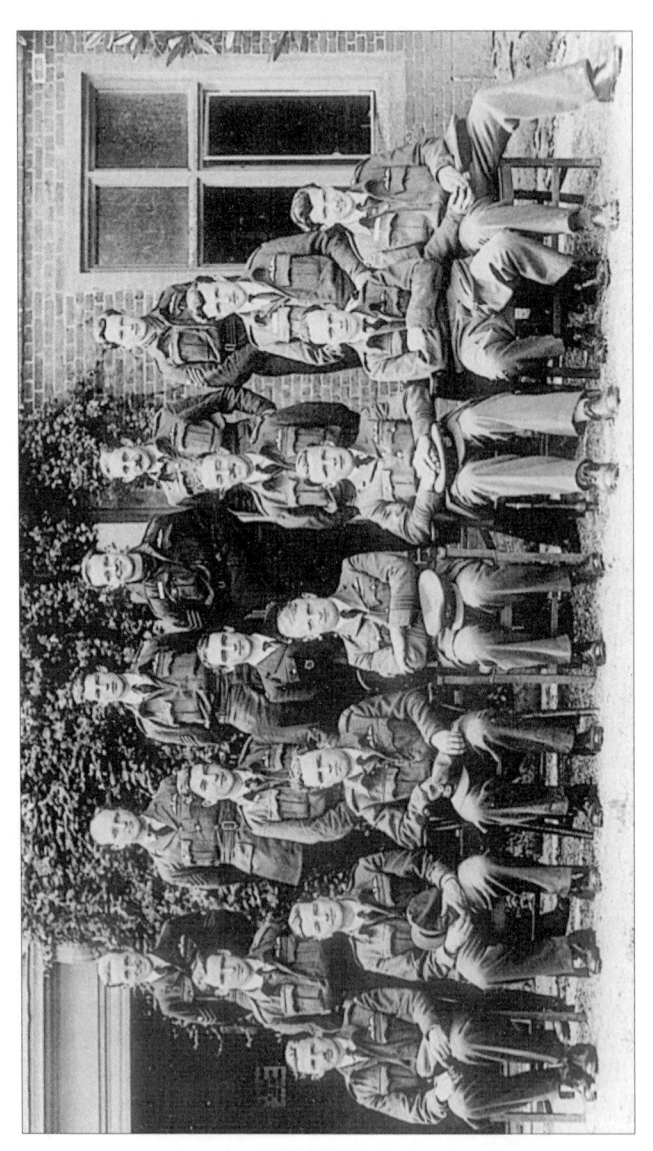

Pilots and Officers of No. 165 Squadron, outside Sattion headquarters, Moyles Court, 1943.
Back Row: ?, Jimmy Quinn, Haslop (Aus.), Lawson (Aus.), Jack Givard, Lewis (Aus.)
Middle Row: Ian Forbes, Eric Shipp, Marcel Le Rand (Free French), Chalkie White (Aus.), Douglas (Duke II) Warren (Canada)
Front Row: Hedley Richardson, Ivan Sinclair Warson, Johnny Johnston (C.O.), W/Cdr. A. H. Donaldson, D.S.O., D.F.C.*, A.F.C. (Station Commander 1943), W/Cdr. T. F. Dalton-Morgan, D.S.O., D.F.C.*, (Wing Leader), Walt Disney, Bruce (Duke I) Warren, (Canada)
Photo: E. Shipp

150

his number two, when the wing was bounced by a large number of Focke Wulf 190's. He remembers how Australian Bill Brown was on his first operational trip, and says this seemed to happen quite often, probably because it takes a bit of experience to realise what is really happening in a big dogfight. For that reason new pilots were put on what it was hoped would be an easy operation, but of course the Luftwaffe did not always co-operate.

Later that day Duke I (Bruce) and two other pilots were sent to replace the losses, and the following day Douglas flew as Duke's number two, escorting Marauders again, but this time there were no engagements for No. 165 Squadron. The Marauder was a sleek two engine bomber with tricycle under carriage. By standards of the time it had a high take-off and landing speed, consequently a number were lost in accidents because of this.

*The Canadian Warren Twins, No. 165 Squadron, Ibsley, 1943.*
*Bruce (Duke I) and Douglas (Duke II).*
Photo: D. Warren, D.F.C.

*So Much Sadness, So Much Fun*

Bob George joined No. 616 Squadron at Ibsley on 20th July, just about the time that Squadron Leader Leslie Watts became Commanding Officer. Bob was put into 'B' Flight and remembers that on 5th August Flight Lieutenant Dennis Barry, Officer Commanding 'A' Flight was sent on urgent matters to Charmy Down, three miles North of Bath. The weather was awful, with cloud base just over the hill tops. Watty wouldn't risk a Spitfire flying, and none of the pilots had flown a Tiger Moth since initial training and Bob himself had never even flown a Tiger. He had just done about 700 hours on Proctors but was "volunteered". Flight Lieutenant Barry said he would show him how to land a Tiger when they got to Charmy Down. His method was to stick the nose down, throttle open, achieve the approach speed of a Spitfire, and then on levelling out they floated the full width of the aerodrome. At the third attempt he stuck the wheels on the grass and they eventually rolled to a stop. On the way back Bob said he was rarely more than fifty feet above the ground until they got to the Avon Valley in which Ibsley lies and he made a perfect landing. Spanners Ellis, their Engineering Officer was having kittens. He had heard an absolute tyro was flying his beloved Tiger, but after seeing Bob's landing he spoke to the C.O. and from then on Bob flew the Tiger almost every time it went anywhere.

News had reached Ibsley that Squadron Leader Peter Lefevre had avoided capture after being shot down on 16th April and, in good 616 Squadron escaping fashion, was on his way back via Gibraltar. He re-joined 616 Squadron on 11th August but was soon posted to command No. 266 Squadron at Exeter on Typhoons. Tragically on 6th February 1944, while leading No. 266 Squadron, flying from their base at Harrowbeer, Devon, to attack guns at Aber-Wrack, Brittany, he was shot down by flak and killed.

On July 29th No. 165 Squadron left Ibsley to go to Exeter. Twins Bruce and Douglas Warren were posted to another Squadron shortly after the move to Exeter. Both served with No. 66 Squadron in 1944 where Bruce was 'A' Flight Commander and Douglas 'B' Flight Commander, something Douglas believes to be unique. Most of the pilots could not tell the twins apart, so both having the nickname Duke, they assumed that whoever was giving them orders knew which flight they were commanding. Both were awarded the D.F.C., and at their Investitures at Buckingham Palace on 23rd March, 1945, the King said, "I don't think I have ever done this

*1943*

before," meaning awarding D.F.C.s to a pair of twins. In 1951 Bruce, who became a test pilot with Avro, was tragically killed in the crash of a prototype CF-100 jet fighter, the accident thought to have been caused by an oxygen system malfunction. Douglas's career with the Royal Canadian Air Force was to last thirty seven years.

The Summer of 1943 had also seen Ibsley airmen participating in Ringwood's "Wings for Victory", and another distinguished visitor to Ibsley at this time was the Right Honourable Sir A. Ramaswami Mudaur of the Indian Government. He had come to address the members of No. 129 (Mysore) Squadron. This was a squadron that was the gift of the Province of Mysore.

General Smart, the Chief of Staff of the Australian Army was another visitor to Ibsley during the Summer of 1943, where he addressed members of No. 453 Squadron of the Royal Australian Air Force.

Mike Cooper recalled how Monday August 16th was a beautiful day, not a cloud in the sky; so naturally a fighter sweep was laid on and No. 616 Squadron were to be 'Free Lance Wing' to some bombers attacking Bernay Airfield near Le Havre. In his book 'One of the Many' Mike said: "I was to lead 'Blue' Flight and climbed into my own kite YQ-S, but found there was an oxygen leak, so hastily strapped myself into 'R' and we took off from Ibsley about 1100 hours.

The visibility was terrific and we could see the French coast long before we had reached mid-Channel. We crossed the coast at 23,000 feet just North of Le Havre. Our Controller told us over the radio telephone that there were no Huns about. As we turned South from Le Havre I could see the bomb bursts on Bernay. I had just opened my throttle to keep in position on the outside of the turn when I felt my engine run rough. I could see no flak about so did not worry. We were about sixty kilometres inland when I noticed the roughness increase. While turning westward, back towards the coast, the roughness became steadily worse. I called up my Squadron Leader and reported the vibration and he sent another flight to cover me. Oil pressure had dropped right off the clock and the glycol temperature was way above the safety level. I called again saying that I had 'had it' and was heading back into France. (All escape lectures stressed the coast area was to be avoided because it was the defended zone). Right from the onset of things I had one thought; to evade capture and return to England.

## So Much Sadness, So Much Fun

As I turned inland the 'boys' wished me well. "Leave the French girls alone", "Good Luck", "See you in the Chez Moi" (a 'dive' in London frequented by squadron members when in the area). The last I heard was "Cut the natter!" from the Commanding Officer and I was on my own heading south-east at 17,000 feet. The engine was very hot but still working. Nonetheless I made up my mind to bale out. I wasn't scared, I'd done it twice before, so why not again. Looking below I saw a town to my left and open country to my right. At this time the engine had become extremely hot and was beginning to smoke. I was afraid of fire and made the immediate decision to bail out. I detached my oxygen tube and wireless plug, undid my straps; the speed 200 mph, height 9,000 feet. Barrel rolling onto my back, bracing myself and pushing the stick hard forward I managed to eject myself from the kite and was falling through the air. Everything was rushing past me. As I turned over and over I pulled the rip cord. Instantly I was jerked upright, all was quiet and still.

I started to take an interest in my surroundings; my kite was doing aerobatics on its own; I was swinging wildly from left to right; there was a large wood about four or five miles to the north of me. I thought of the dance I could lead the Jerries in wooded areas and decided to make that particular wood my objective.

I had to work hard on the parachute cords to stop swinging. I had lost site of my kite by this time and the earth was beginning to rush up towards me. At about one hundred feet I realised I would make a direct hit on a tree below me. I straightened my body, kept my legs together and did indeed hit the tree, dead centre. Crashing through the branches I came to rest ten feet from the ground, apples falling all around me. I noticed, with some amusement, as I hung there bobbing up and down, that it had been a fully loaded apple tree until I hit it.

Not without some difficulty I released my harness and landed, spread-eagled at the foot of the tree. I could just reach the parachute straps and tried to drag the silk canopy from the tree, but soon realised it was an impossible task. Giving up and taking stock of my surroundings I noticed a man in civilian clothes coming towards me. I shouted at him to go away. He stopped in his tracks and I took advantage of that moment to run off downhill. I was in orchard farmland, fairly well wooded with many hedges. Running on I eventually came to a stream bordered on both sides with trees and thick undergrowth. I jumped into mid-stream, took off my helmet and Mae West, flung them into the bushes and headed up stream towards my objective, the wood.

It didn't take me long to realise what a fool I'd been. I should have hidden my helmet and Mae West because they were now a good indication as to which way I had gone and that scared me."

Fortunately Mike Cooper evaded capture and with much help made his way down through France and Spain to Gibraltar before returning to England on an Imperial Airways Dakota on 22$^{nd}$ December, 1943. When Mike returned to No. 616 Squadron he found they were based at Exeter, having left Ibsley on September 17$^{th}$, and had been re-equipped with the special high altitude Spitfire Mk VII's.

No. 453 (Australian) Squadron left Ibsley on 21$^{st}$ August, bound for Exeter.

The 67$^{th}$ Recce Group of the United States Army Air Force arrived at Ibsley on September 5$^{th}$, 1943, in the form of No's 12 and 107 Squadrons. Flying Mustang FB VI's they stayed until September 10$^{th}$.

There was a short period in September 1943 when no units were based at Ibsley, so during this time a decoy unit was moved in and dummy Spitfires were erected around the airfield.

During late September three Czechoslovakian squadrons arrived at Ibsley. The first to arrive was No. 312 Squadron who came from Skeabrae on the 18$^{th}$ with Spitfire Mk Vb's and Mk Vc's, code letters DU. First member of No. 312 to arrive at Ibsley was Flying Officer M. A. 'Tony' Liskutin, D.F.C., A.F.C., who because there was no volunteer to ferry the squadron Tiger Moth, their communication aircraft, took on this task. In his book, 'Challenge in the Air', A Spitfire Pilot Remembers, published by William Kimber, Tony Liskutin tells of how the idea of flying some 600 miles South in a slow machine with open cockpit offered another experience.

The original destination for No. 312 Squadron was given as R.A.F. Hornchurch, Essex, and Tony Liskutin had done all his planning for this London suburb. It was only just before going to the Tiger Moth that he was told orders had been changed, and the squadron would be going to Ibsley. Four days were allowed for the journey in the Tiger Moth, but Liskutin did in fact arrive a few hours before the squadron, which gave him a feeling of great satisfaction.

## So Much Sadness, So Much Fun

At Ibsley No. 312 Squadron went through another of its periods of personnel changes. Squadron Leader Tomas Vybiral was leaving, to be replaced by Squadron Leader Frantisek Vancl, D.F.C., as the new squadron commander for the next period of operations.

The second Czech squadron to arrive was No. 313 who flew in from Hawkinge, Kent, on the 19th, again with Spitfire Mk Vb's and Vc's, code letters RY, and the third arrival was No. 310 Squadron from Castletown, on 22nd, also with Spitfire Vb's and Vc's, code letters NN.

Len Rose was on the Maintenance Staff of No. 313 Squadron. Of his time at Ibsley he says; "I was on duty many times during the Squadron's short stay. In the Control Tower at night, one of my duties was to control aircraft landing schemes, and with Ringwood in the black-out this was not easy, the pilots requiring every assistance at dusk and dawn."

"Radio contacts during the long nights were made from the coastline, Southampton to Weymouth, and the defences were often quite active. Dawn patrols were flown from Ibsley most days, just above the river fog."

The duty pilots slept in Nissen huts to the North of the airfield, so if necessary I would have to cycle from the Control Tower and wake them up, hoping they would follow in their own transport, help warm up the aircraft, take up all the portable landing lights and aids on the runway, and wait by the Church for the Duty Officer of the Watch to send up his rocket to get them airborne."

Len also said "The Spitfire Wing was sometimes joined by a flight of Whirlwind aircraft from R.A.F. Warmwell. Great competition on the part of the pilots to see who could make Weymouth Bay in so many minutes."

"I also remember that I could never convince the Czechoslovakian pilots that the New Forest ponies were not for eating.". Ibsley holds a special place in my heart, and brings back memories of many happy days."

During operations from Ibsley the routine remained very much as before; daily readiness, scrambles against enemy intruders, fighter sweeps over France, bomber escorts and patrols over convoys. One of the bomber escorts on 24th September, 1943, was particularly memorable for Flying Officer Tony Liskutin.

## 1943

The Wing was detailed to act as target support for bombers attacking Brest harbour. Luftwaffe fighters were waiting for their arrival and attacked before the target area was reached. No. 313 Squadron were acting as top cover and immediately engaged a squadron of Me210's. Tony Liskutin said "For all of us who witnessed the encounter it was a most spectacular combat! I have a particularly strong memory of its speed. It was so brief and so dramatic. In only a few seconds three Me210's were falling down in flames. But No. 313 Squadron also lost some aircraft. Pilot Officer John Cochrane, an English volunteer attached to the squadron was one of those who died. Squadron Leader Jaroslav Himr and Flight Lieutenant Vladislav Chocholin were the others."

"My job consisted of looking after the safety of our bombers, but I could not help watching with awe that amazing spectacle. The most memorable sight close by was the three burning Me210's streaking down, towards the sea off Brest harbour, where Cochrane's Spitfire could have fallen. Squadron Leader Himr's and Flight Lieutenant Chocholin's aircraft also went down in the sea, but I did not see them"

"The decisive striking action of No. 313 Squadron succeeded in pre-empting the enemy attack against our bombers. There is no doubt that it prevented heavy losses amongst the Bostons, Mitchells and Marauders. As it turned out, after a few minutes some of the bombers were lost and others damaged by very accurate anti-aircraft fire from Brest. Because No. 312 Squadron was acting as close escort we went with the bombers through this bombing run, as per order. The flashes, the clouds of black smoke, the smell of cordite still remain deeply impressed in my memory. One of the Mitchell MkIIs was about three hundred yards from me when it received a nearly direct hit. I was conscious of being the spectator of a tragedy, forgetting for a moment my own insecure existence", said Tony Liskutin.

To his surprise, the Mitchell remained flying; nobody baled out. It had lost one engine, but kept flying with reduced speed and dropped out of the formation. Tony Liskutin realised that this aircraft and any other stragglers would be finished off by the lurking Me210 and FW190 enemy fighters which kept appearing in the vicinity throughout the operation, waiting for the opportunity to strike.

Without thinking, without any hesitation, Tony Liskutin and Frantisek Mlejnecky moved out of formation in order to protect the

## So Much Sadness, So Much Fun

wounded bird. Moments later the anti-aircraft fire thinned out, as they were getting out of range. This meant the Luftwaffe fighters would be on the scene trying to finish off stragglers at any moment.

The minutes passed slowly, waiting for the attack, but nothing happened, not even after the coast North of Brest was crossed. Very strange! No sign of Luftwaffe. Tony Liskutin started to feel that they were slowly getting out of danger; getting away with it!

Coming close to the Mitchell they were escorting they had a look at the damage, trying to assess its chances of getting home. The starboard engine was burnt out and without propeller. There were many holes visible all over the aircraft. However, the pilot was showing "thumbs up" and the rear gunner looked very much alive. It seemed that all was comparatively well; there was nothing to say or do; just stay on guard with our protégé all the way back until we reached our own airspace.

Tony Liskutin goes on to recall how Franta Mlejnecky took up a position some 300 yards on the left side, while he himself settled at about the same distance on the right. This meant they were flying at a reduced speed of some 180 mph, to remain at the speed adopted by the Mitchell. At the same time they were losing height, as may have been convenient to them. This setting looked peaceful! He was slowly starting to relax after a prolonged period of tension. In spite of their deceptive sense of near security they were still very much on guard. Their decision in assuming that the fighting was not over was fully justified. Indeed, the Luftwaffe had not given up yet.

About twenty miles North of the French coast, suddenly the rear gunner in the Mitchell came to life. He swung his guns from side to side, indicating a warning. Danger is imminent! Indeed it was. Enemy fighters were approaching from a great height in a shallow dive and at a very high overtaking speed. There was no time to think immediate counter action was needed if response was to have any effect.

With full throttle and the propeller pitch in fully fine, Tony Liskutin's Spitfire responded well to his violent movement of controls to face the enemy. Without hesitating he placed his aircraft onto a collision course with the leader of the enemy formation, and was in a steep climbing turn with a heavy 'G' loading when he pressed the firing button. Impossible to aim properly, but for his opponent the message was clear. He had no choice. To him the pilot seemed to be aiming for a deliberate collision and the flashes from the Spitfire's guns told him that he was flying into a hail of bullets. He had to avoid the collision just as he came into the shooting range, without firing one shot. All this took a second or two and the three FW190s found their attack completely foiled.

This harsh manoeuvre, although unplanned, had worked perfectly and broken up their attack. It could not have been better even if there had been time to decide on the right action. The enemy leader and Liskutin had missed each other by inches, and as he pulled up into a steep climbing turn to the left, he passed above Franta Mlejnecky, who was in a near collision with the enemy number three. Meanwhile, Liskutin's violent turning had placed him in the proximity of their number two, who passed over the top. More harsh turning gave a fleeting opportunity, a brief moment, to place the gun sight on to him, just after he had passed. Barely a one second burst from Tony Liskutin's guns was possible before the enemy aircraft's overtaking speed took it out of range.

At this time too a radio call came from Franta Mlejnecky warning that there were more enemy aircraft behind. Breaking off the encounter Tony Liskutin turned again towards France, to face the new threat.... only to see them turning away. At that moment he experienced such an extraordinary sensation of incredulous surprise. In fact he couldn't understand it. Why did the enemy disengage when their numerical superiority was 6:2? However, the fight was over and they could at last relax.

When afterwards Tony Liskutin tried to understand what might have happened during those few moments, it all seemed difficult to reconcile. His reconstruction of the fight, with Franta Mlejnecky's help, led them to conclude that they were very lucky. What might have saved the day for them, believed Tony, was their probable shortage of fuel. The Focke Wulfs were cruising around the battle zone right from the start. However, getting far out over the sea, with inadequate reserves of fuel was bound to decrease any probability of prolonged aggressive action.

One satisfying fact which seemed to have emerged beyond any doubt, recalled Tony Liskutin , was that his own near-collision with the leading FW190 and the near miss with their number two had not only prevented them from firing at the Mitchell, but also had effectively defeated their attack.

To Tony's great disappointment, however, he learned a little later that his cine-gun film was torn on the first frame, leaving him without any evidence to support his combat report. However, there was a consolation in a message from the Dutch bomber squadron, expressing their appreciation for help, and sincere thanks. Apparently the damaged Mitchell landed safely at base and the crew reported that Spitfire DU-V had saved their aircraft from destruction, scattering the three attacking FW 190s. Flight Lieutenant Quincey, No. 312 Squadron Intelligence Officer, seemed to be very impressed with such unsolicited testimonials; and made a point of calling Tony Liskutin 'Sir Galahad' for a long time, after the incident was forgotten.

During the time No. 310 (Czech) Squadron were at Ibsley, Warrant Officer Antonin Kaminek met Elsie Brown, from Sandford near Ringwood, who before the end of the War became his wife.

Warrant Officer Kaminek had a distinguished flying career. He was awarded the Military Cross, George Medal and Czechoslovakia's highest Military honour. On 8th September, 1944, when based at North Weald, Antonin was shot down by heavy flak when attacking shipping. His Spitfire IX, NN-K crash landing in Holland, where the Resistance were first to reach him. He was taken to a safe house owned by a Dutch doctor for medical treatment. He made his escape out of Holland six weeks later and returned to England by boat to resume flying duties with the Royal Air Force. He was mentioned in despatches for his actions during the raid on 8th September. By the end of the war and de-mobilisation, Antonin Kaminek had flown some 1500 hours as a pilot, including 72 operational sorties over enemy territory with successful combat action. Tragically though, when flying for an Airborne Medical Hospital Service, in Bolivia, South America, in November 1946, Antonin was trying to fly through a severe electrical storm when his plane crashed. When rescue teams reached the aircraft three days later they found both him and his doctor passenger were dead.

Two Pilots of No. 616 Squadron, Alan Smith and Eddie Cole, were killed in a tragic accident on Thursday, 21st October. Not long after No. 616 Squadron had been posted to Exeter, one of them realised he had left his Irvin flying jacket at Ibsley. The Squadron Tiger Moth was borrowed and they flew back to collect it. Rumour has it that the Irvin was left behind on purpose, because while the pilot was back at Ibsley he did some low level beat ups of his girl friends

## 1943

home. Tragically this was overdone causing the aircraft to crash in the front garden of a house in Fairlie, at Poulner, on the outskirts of Ringwood.

Czech Independence Day was celebrated at Ibsley on October 27th, 1943, when there were celebration dances and other festivities.

W.A.A.F. Joan Burland (maiden name Cornish) was posted to Ibsley in 1943, from Manchester, where she had been a Balloon Operator. Her posting was a medical one, for she had had rather a nasty accident, losing a finger on the winch. It was then decided Joan should be posted nearer her home in Bournemouth as she was finding it very difficult to use her left hand, the right one not being able to do very much.

Joan says "During my stay at Ibsley I discovered a dog, a small black and white collie, very, very skinny and terribly frightened. I love animals but I just couldn't get her to come to me. I would fetch food from the cookhouse and put it on a plate outside my hut, but it took ages, and a lot of patience on my part, before she eventually allowed me to get close enough to stroke her. After that it was all systems go, from then on she was my dog, called Bobbie, and became a big part of my life. At night she would cuddle down at the bottom of my bed (good job the Commanding Officer didn't find out!), and in the morning she would disappear. I fed her at lunch time, and in the evenings she would get on my bike (one of the boys made a carrier for her) and off we would go to Ringwood. Here she found a friend in Mrs. Green who ran the Y.M.C.A. in the town. She and her husband were a lovely couple, and would let her stay in their private rooms at the back. It enabled me to go to the cinema or a dance."

"Eventually", said Joan, "a decision had to be made because the R.A.F. were moving out, and the Americans were arriving. On of the SP's told me they were having to get rid of a lot of dogs that were running all over the camp. Sadly this was a common event, and one the police hated doing. So, I took Bobbie home to Bournemouth and she became an important part of our family until she died of old age."

Joan also said "that after the departure of the R.A.F., a few of us were left behind to work with the Americans.",

For a short period in December No. 312 Squadron were at Llanbedr; returning to Ibsley on 18th. No. 313 were also away at Ayr

*So Much Sadness, So Much Fun*

for a short while during January 1944, coming back to Ibsley on 21st On December 5th, 1943, No. 263 (Fellowship of the Bellows (Argentina) Squadron arrived from Warmwell, bringing Hawker Typhoons and Westland Whirlwinds, coded HE. Exactly a month later, on 5th January, 1944, they left for Fairwood Common, South Wales.

*1943*

'B' Flight, No. 312 Squadron, 1944
Back: L. to R. Sodek, Keprt, Posta, Hlado, Kopocek, Svetlik, Liskutin, Perina, Kukucka, Angeter
Front: L. to R. Pernica, Mlejnecky, Truhlar, Ocelka, Konvicka, Popelka, Kohout
Photo: M.A. Liskutin, D.F.C., A.F.C., /F. Mlejnecky

# 1944
## Generous Americans at Ibsley

On 13th January the 100th Fighter Wing of the United States 9th Air Force, under Commanding Officer Col. David Lancaster, arrived at Ibsley (US Station No. 347) from Boxted, Essex. The 9th US Air Force was set up in 'England especially to give tactical air support for the invasion of Europe and beyond.

Wing Commander Tom Neil, D.F.C.*., A.F.C., AE, R.A.F. (Ret'd), was at Ibsley for a few months as an R.A.F. Liaison Officer with the U.S.A.A.F. in both England and France, in 1944.

In a feature, 'A Brit Among the Yanks', published in Aeroplane monthly, February 2000, extracts from which he has given permission for us to reproduce, he tells of some of his experiences, how he adapted to American ways – in between flying and testing a bewildering array of aircraft types.

He tells of how he was joined at Ibsley, the U.S.A.A.F.'s 100th Fighter Wing base, by two more R.A.F. officers, a squadron leader intelligence officer and a flight lieutenant equipment officer. Both were excellent at their jobs. The intelligence officer was a pleasant elderly gentleman who remained with the Wing for almost a year, and the equipment officer until the invasion took place in June. Tom Neil wrote: "Although we were three isolated specks of blue in a sea of denim and olive drab, I do not think any one of us at any time felt threatened or resented, which is a tribute to the courtesy of our hosts."

He goes on to tell of the various aircraft he flew and how, in addition, he was called upon now and then to act as a stop-gap test-pilot and fly other aircraft which an R.A.F. Maintenance Unit offshoot at Stoney Cross, a nearby airfield a few miles from Ibsley had scraped up from the surrounding countryside and re-built. Altogether it was a fairly varied and interesting collection which kept him more than busy.

## 1944

"All the time, went on Tom Neil, I was gradually acclimatising myself to everything American, making new friends and forming relationships that were to endure for 50 years and more. Among others, I enjoyed long and happy associations with Colonel Homer L Sanders, Major (later Colonel) Alvin Hill, Captain Robert A. Patterson, the deputy medical officer, who in years to come was to be Surgeon General of the US Air Force, and Colonel Harry French.

He told of unfamiliar meals (such as breakfast pancakes, swimming in butter and maple syrup and topped with bacon and eggs) but which soon became acquired tastes and eventually a part of daily life.

Towards the end of the article on his experiences as a 'Brit Among the Yanks' Tom Neil wrote:. "It was on March 19, I note, that I was asked by Stoney Cross to fly an Armstrong Whitworth Albermarle. I had barely heard of the aircraft and had to make a few enquiries before I learned that it was a fairly big failed bomber with a tricycle undercarriage, that it had been gifted in large numbers to the Russians, and that it was usually employed as a glider tug and was therefore likely to be in great demand during the forthcoming invasion. I was not altogether enthusiastic about flying it; I regarded myself as a simple fighter boy and not a heavy boiler pilot, having had very little experience on twins other than the Oxford. A trifle concerned I asked Robert Patterson, the medic, to accompany me, if only to operate those cockpit controls beyond my reach.

After driving to Stoney Cross and examining the aircraft I was even less enthusiastic. There being no Pilot's Notes available, I insisted that two competent technicians should join us on the flight. To my surprise, as I felt they might well be going to their deaths, two L.A.C.s agreed to do so with smiles and thanks. After a discussion we all climbed aboard through a hole in the cockpit roof (I was not told about the other two entry points).

Once in the cockpit and even more aware of the vastness of the aircraft, I started the two Bristol Hercules engines with the help of the engine fitter. They shook themselves like spaniels emerging from water before settling down to their regular warming rhythm, one of the two massive propellers flicking wickedly within inches of my left ear. I then taxied out with Patterson sitting on my right in frowning concentration.

At the end of the runway in use I went through the usual mnemonics of my fighter-cockpit drill, adding a few letters for good

## So Much Sadness, So Much Fun

measure, before lining up and opening the throttles with more determination than confidence. As the big aircraft gathered speed, the nose-wheel legs flexing and clonking as if about to collapse, I realised when halfway down the runway that I had neglected to set any flap. With the end of the concrete coming up with unseemly speed it was too late to do anything about it. Not a moment too soon, the aircraft tottered into the air, a line of trees snapping at our heels.

After I had raised the wheels, trimmed madly and synchronised the engines the Albermarle climbed away, wallowing like an inebriated whale, with me wondering what was wrong with the brute. Unfamiliar then with the aerodynamics involved, I recognised even so that either the aircraft I was flying, or the type as whole, had a stability problem. But nothing vital had stopped, we were all in one piece, and that was good enough for me. Then after porpoising our way to the South Coast, I let Patterson take the controls and sat back, feeling like a piece of chewed string.

Almost an hour later we returned to Stoney Cross and joined the circuit. I selected "wheels down", whereupon there was a series of blinking red and green lights which finally told me in the plainest of terms that the wheels were not locked down. Oh God! I selected "wheels up" again and all the lights disappeared. Then "down" again. This time a different permutation of lights, but not the three greens I was hoping for. Now what did I do?

Sensing that something was amiss, one of the L.A.C. experts appeared through a hole up front. I selected "wheels down" again for his benefit, and this time only the nose-wheel showed red. My expert deduced that the problem was wrongly adjusted micro-switches, but did not seem too sure. He examined the hydraulic accumulator and pronounced it full. I then asked him what the emergency method of lowering the wheels was, but he insisted that, as the system seemed to be working any emergency action would not work any better. Patterson and I hunted around the cockpit but could not find anything promising to press or pull. Then, after trying the wheels again without success, I headed for Ibsley, saying that if I was going to prang the aircraft I was going to do it on my own doorstep.

At Ibsley I resolved to lower the wheels and bounce the aircraft on the runway; that would probably sort everything out. It did not.

## 1944

With one red light still on and the warning horn blowing like Gideon's trumpet, after the wheels hit I surged into the air again and climbed away, taking stock. By this time the other L.A.C. had stuck his head through a hole behind me and, after a few moments, a further unknown face appeared, to my considerable surprise.

Deciding to land anyway, I told my companions to tie themselves down and brought the aircraft in very gingerly. With red lights galore and the emergency horn blowing lustily, I greased the tarmac, whereupon it ran ahead quite happily, spouting blue smoke, with everyone waiting for the grinding, slithering collapse. Finally, when the collapse did not occur, I drew up with a hiss of brakes, breathed a prayer to the Almighty, then taxied to a hard standing. Five minutes later, almost gibbering with relief, Patterson and I scrambled down, while from another hole in the rear of the aircraft six people emerged, including two W.A.A.F.s, none of whom I had ever seen before. Then, without prompting, they all began to clap.

I feel it necessary to record that I made two more flights in that Albermarle from Ibsley before returning it to Stoney Cross. On each one the undercarriage worked perfectly.

By the end of March I had been with the 100th Fighter Wing almost three months. I had flown many new aircraft, made many new friends, and was even becoming inured to syrup being poured over my morning eggs and bacon.".

Planning for the invasion of Europe was now reaching an advanced stage and in March, 1944, a U.S.A.A.F. servicing group arrived at Ibsley to pave the way for the second American occupation of the base.

This time it was in the shape of the 9th Air Force, 48th Fighter Group, (Nos. 492, 493 and 494 Squadrons) flying P-47D Thunderbolts. By April 1944, almost three thousand Americans were at Ibsley, many of them being housed under canvas.

Col. Jacob L. Cooper, USAF., Ret. in his historical compilation 'The 493rd Fighter Squadron in WWII' recalls that the Squadron flew its first combat mission on April 20th, 1944, when a fighter sweep took place, after only being in the European Theater of Operations a scant twenty-one days. Almost concurrently, the Group Commander was transferred, Col. Dixon M. Allison had led the Group though its most critical period and his expertise was needed at higher headquarters. The new Group Commander was George L.

## So Much Sadness, So Much Fun

Wertenbacker, Jr. who took over at a no less critical time. Change seemed to be the rule of the day as the Group and the three squadron's classification was changed from Fighter-Bombers to Fighter, although there was no change in the types of missions flown.

Included in Col. Jacob Cooper's book are memories contributed by 493rd Squadron personnel who were at Ibsley. These include diary extracts from John Chlopick, – Ibsley, April 19, 1944. Bought me a bike today – an old one. I sure can use it because it is a long way down to the airplane from where we stay. June 6th, 1944. D-Day!! What have we been waiting for, Snoozer's shoes are in my plane over France. Snoozer's shoes – that means my little girls shoes. I call her Snoozer. My little girls shoes are in the well of the gas tank. I put them there every day that my plane goes out on a mission. That was for good luck.

Tony Porter's recollections: I celebrated my twenty sixth birthday on the Queen Mary being chased by German subs. After docking we were soon on a train to our new base at R.A.F. Station, Ibsley. There we were greeted by a field of P-47s, not the P-51s we expected. The "Wheels" had discovered that the P-47 was much better suited for close air support mission and the P-51 for heavy bomber escort duty. There were only enough of the latest model P-47s to equip one of the three squadrons, so the three squadron commanders drew lots to see which squadron would be flying the brand new silver JUGS, as we so affectionately called the P-47. Bill Bryson, the 493rd Commander, drew the lucky number.

Technical Supply Chief Parks Lafferty's recalled how they arrived in Greenock and left late at night by train for Ibsley. He said: "The little old British train was so small that a seat was hardly big enough for one, with full packs, let alone three! So, I can't say I enjoyed the trip one bit, and of course, I was worn out from the lack of sleep when we arrived at Ibsley.

We arrived at Ibsley the afternoon of March 29, 1944. I certainly had a time getting supplies – I had to make frequent trips to depots all over England by plane to get the required supplies to keep our P-47s flying. I really hated making those trips and certainly was happy when I arrived back at our base.

I will never forget the afternoon of June 5th, 1944, as I was returning from a two day trip to northern England in a C-78 airplane. As we approached the field at Ibsley for a landing we were

## 1944

signalled by flares that we didn't have our wheels down. Captain Harold and I began to sweat. After three more approaches things began to look bad for us. The pilot ordered the Captain and me to put on our parachutes. He would fly over the coast, let us bail out, and make a belly landing by himself. We tried on the chutes and they were at least four times too large. We told him that we were not going to bail out and would take a chance with him on the belly. This made him very angry. He said the pilot had complete charge of the passengers and their safety and he ordered us to bail out. Captain Harold told him that he outranked him and we were not bailing out. I asked the pilot if the plane didn't have an emergency release and he said that he didn't know. In fact, he said he had never flown this type of plane before the trip we had just made. I got down on the floor of the plane and looked all over it for the release. After quite a while I finally located it – by this time we were almost out of gas, having flown around the field for over an hour. I cranked and cranked but could never come to a stopping point, so I told the pilot to go ahead and make another approach and the tower would let us know if the wheels were down and locked. We did make the approach and finally landed without any trouble. The Captain and I were scared badly. My stomach was so upset that I couldn't eat a bite for two days. The airplane was checked out and it was found that the pilot didn't turn on the generators before leaving for Ibsley, therefore the battery was too weak to bring the wheels down. The Captain and I went to Headquarters and had the pilot grounded for one month. Was he mad since he couldn't draw flying pay that month!

Bob McLuckie had a sad memory from his time at Ibsley. Clarence May was cleaning the gun and ammo wells on the left wing of his P-47. He slipped and touched off the bolt of a 50 calibre machine gun and accidentally hit the sear with a screw driver as he was attempting to stop himself falling off the wing. The armour-piercing shell in the number four gun blew out his left knee which was dangling over the front of the gun. We heard the report in the Armament shack just across the taxi strip from the revetment where Clarence was working. I ran over, but one of the aircraft mechanics beat me there. He had the presence of mind to cut off a rope from the wheel chock and was applying a tourniquet when I arrived. Clarence never lost consciousness. I lit a cigarette for him and he looked up at me and said, "I guess I really screwed up this time

Mac.". Our first casualty in the 493rd. Clarence lost his leg. His friends contributed thousands of dollars to be sent home to his wife and family. (His mother called me in 1953 to tell me that Clarence, his wife, and two children were killed in an auto accident on their way home for Mother's Day).

The 48th were also joined briefly by Nos, 404, 405 and 406 Squadrons of the 371st Fighter Group, 9th Air Force, due to the condition of their base, the Advanced Landing Ground, at Bisterne (Sandford).

Higher Command of the U.S.A.A.F. had decided to use the Advanced Landing Ground at Bisterne (Sandford) as their 'guinea pig', to test their efficiency under field conditions, something which was certainly justified. Although they adjusted quickly to their living and working conditions, the area was so swampy that the tent floors had to be built up to prevent flooding. Cut trees became coat racks, and bits of wire were twisted into coat hangers.

The operation of the airstrip however, presented a much more difficult problem. The airfield at Bisterne (Sandford) had been, and still was, a cow pasture, overlaid with a wire mesh tracking, which after just one week of heavy pounding under the five ton weight of the Thunderbolts, landing and taking off, reduced the runways to a series of deep ruts and bumps which were extremely hazardous.

Inspectors from the 9th Air Command finally closed the strip for reconstruction and transferred the planes, and enough equipment needed to operate, to the tarmac strip at Ibsley some six miles to the North. Until 1st May, 1944 all missions were run from here.

Allen Anderson was Crew Chief of P47 9Q-D with No. 404 Squadron, 371st Fighter Group of the 9th U.S.A.A.F., at Bisterne and Ibsley in 1944, and recalls the evening when they replaced the right wing of Lieutenant Haney's plane at Ibsley. The electrician S/Sgt Speery asked him to turn on the switch to test the camera, which is synchronised with the machine guns. Anderson said he remembers how he flipped the switch and fired 52 rounds, 13 from each of the machine guns. It was a good thing I hadn't moved my fingers from the switch or I might have fired a heck of a lot more. The rounds went up at an angle because with a tail wheel the plane is pointed up when on the ground. Needless to say the Military Police and a lot of other people came in a hurry. We had a lot of explaining to do. The wiring was wrong and that was the cause of the incident. We were

*1944*

absolved of any blame. We were never told if any damage was caused or if anybody was hit by the bullets. Anderson says he still often thinks of this incident.

Allen Anderson said they had four flights in the 404th (A) with T/Sgt. Powers, (B) with T/Sgt. Alford (C) with T/Sgt. Gus Jennett and (D) with T/Sgt. Onge.

Second Lieutenant Eugene Sanderson of 405 Squadron, 371st Fighter Group was killed in an accident on 12th April, and Allen Anderson, who witnessed the incident said "after he landed he spun out not too far from my revetment. His plane also caught fire and he could not get the sliding canopy open. By the time we got close to the plane it was too late, the flames were so intense, we could do nothing except watch him die. That is something I will never forget, it was horrible.". Sanderson is buried at the Cambridge American Cemetery in England.

Back at Bisterne once more, the Group was inspected by Major General Elwood "Pete" Quesada, and he found the new metal matting unsatisfactory. It had been a headache to many pilots, causing a spate of burst tyres that had narrowly missed causing casualties. Again operations had to be transferred to Ibsley. Pilots and ground crews had to shuttle back and forth the six miles between the two airfields, bombs and belly tanks had to be moved by truck, and portable mess kitchens set up. Around three thousand personnel were at Ibsley at this time, and over one hundred and forty P-47 Thunderbolts were on the airfield itself. Briefings were held in a tent and frequently the 371st and the 48th Group, which also occupied the field, virtually overlapped on taking off.

At Ibsley, on Thursday May 11th, 1944, the 371st Fighter Group of the U.S.A.A.F. was starting on a mission when it became noticeable that one of the Thunderbolts seemed to be circling the field crazily. It was recognised as that of Lieutenant Walling of No. 404 Squadron. Suddenly it veered sharply to the left and in an effort to reach the runway lost altitude too quickly and hit the wooden Ellingham Women's Institute Hut at Rockford, both plane and building bursting into flames.

Captain Willis (Wally) Walling, who was traced by Mr. Geoff Bartlett, in the course of his research into the Advance Landing Ground at Bisterne, visited England in 1994. Geoff was able to show him the site on which the Rockford Women's Institute Hut had once stood. He was also able to introduce him to Peter Smith who had been a pupil at Rockford School at the time of the crash. The pupils of Rockford School frequently used the W.I. Hut for Physical Training on wet days, school plays, dental inspections, etc., but thanks to the Grace of God no one was in it on that fateful day.

Wally's personal account of his crash is as follows:

"Re my English tear up a plane experience. I had taken off and was forming up for a German mission when the cockpit suddenly filled with smoke. We were not far from Ringwood. Major 'Mac' called and asked if I thought I should bail out, but with a full load of gas, etc., I hesitated – before my next thought there was an explosion in the cockpit and things got fuzzy after that. I can remember prior to the explosion turning toward the field considering the possibility of saving everything by landing. I believe my Mayday call was received by the Tower while planes were still taking off. The next thing I remember was seeing a large stone building coming up at me – I hit right rudder – skidded to the right – missed the stone building, had no power and ploughed through a wooden building"

"Went through the roof – came out on edge of field minus wings, engine, and tail (this was told to me). I do remember burning – pushing up on the cockpit sides with arms – legs seemed inoperative – and not being able to see anything fell out the right side of the cockpit. Blank after that until coming to on an X-ray machine."

I was told two British Ack Ack gunners on the field pulled me out of the fire on to the root of the wing. One was injured as a gun went off and caught him in his right thigh or cheek. They pulled me away and released my parachute and the ambulance took me to the Station hospital."

On the second day – now conscious – a Lieutenant Colonel told me aside from face and hand cuts and burns I might have trouble walking again as stomach muscles were badly torn, but that internal bleeding was under control."

"Thirty days later I flew one hour – still using a bad right leg – that put me back on the roster – and then the Commanding Officer gave me two weeks Rest and Rehabilitation to get back in shape. Returned just after D-Day, June 11th, I believe."

*1944*

*Col.Dixon M. Allison (R),
Col. George Wertenbacker (L),
at change of command ceremony,
Ibsley, April 1944*
Photo: Col. J. L. Cooper

*Col. Bingham T. Kleine,
Commanding Officer 371st
Fighter Group, 9th
U.S.A.A.F.,
Ibsley April-May, 1944*
Photo: Major D. Wood

*So Much Sadness, So Much Fun*

Col. Jerome J. McCabe, Commanding Officer, 492 Squadron, 48*th* Fighter Group, U.S.A.A.F. in cockpit of his P47 Thunderbolt 'Paper Doll' at Ibsley, 1944
Photo: Col. J. J. McCabe

1st Lieutenant Carlos J. Ball, 492 Squadron, 48*th* Fighter Group, U.S.A.A.F. Tragically he was killed in an horrific accident at Ibsley on 27*th* May, 1944
Photo: Col. J. J. McCabe

"The walking and rehabilitation I credit to a very strong Swedish therapy nurse for my deliverance. She busted my chops to get up, pass out, get up and pass out and get up again until I got it right. She sure knew her business."

"That's about all I know. The two British boys really save my butt and I'll forever be indebted to them for the chance they took on my behalf."

Peter Smith, a pupil at Rockford School (now the Alice Lisle Inn) at the time, vividly remembered that day, and the terrific crash and flames. He recalled how "Miss White, the Headmistress, grabbed her whistle, ran outside and blew it furiously, after telling the children to sit still. Of course they all rushed to the window to see what was going on". The thing Peter remembered most was the continuous noise as the ammunition exploded.

The aircraft just missed Heather Cottage (the white stone walls Wally mentioned) and had clipped the wooden W.I. Hut setting it on fire. It then hit the Gorley road, went through the barbed wire entanglements inside the hedge and finished up just inside the airfield perimeter.

Crew Chief Allen Anderson, U.S.A.A.F. also witnessed the crash of Lieutenant Willis 'Wally' Wallings aircraft. and said "I was in a position where I could see his plane, just after it hit the building. The engine fell off on a road (the Gorley Road), but the fuselage kept on going and crashed on the airfield. At the time no one knew the pilot had escaped with his life.

The hospital Wally Walling was taken to was at North Gorley, formerly known as the As You Like It Motel, latterly The Open Country, but now closed. Geoff Bartlett was also able to show him, in 1994, the building where he received treatment after his crash.

Wally had always wondered if there were any civilian casualties resulting from the crash and was relived when, fifty years after the incident, Peter Smith was able to re-assure him that there were none.

The wooden W.I. Hut at Rockford was replaced with a more substantial building, and the Ellingham Women's Institute continued until the nineteen eighties, when it was disbanded. The hut was then demolished and a house built on the site.

W.A.A.F., Joan White, (maiden name Stevens) a teleprinter in 46 Group came to Ibsley, in 1944, from Hurn. Whilst serving at Ibsley she met her husband, Malcolm, then an R.A.F. Mechanic. Joan remembers that the Americans were occupying Ibsley at the time and that it was through their generosity that they were able to have a fruit cake for their wedding.

On Saturday, May 27th, 1944, there was a horrific accident on the airfield when a Thunderbolt of No. 492 Squadron, 48th Fighter Group, flown by First Lieutenant Carlos J. Ball of 492 Squadron, burst a tyre on take-off and slithered to a stop near the end of the runway where it burst into flames.

Information received from the Air Force Historical Research Agency, Maxwell Air Force Base, U.S.A., stated the accident occurred on take-off for an operational mission, at 1725 hours. The aircraft was loaded with two external wing fuel tanks and a 1,000 lb bomb. About two thirds of the way down the runway, the left tire blew and First Lieutenant Ball was unable to keep the aircraft on the runway. It ran off to the left, and to prevent the aircraft going through a fence around the airfield, the pilot forced the aircraft into a ground loop to the right. It caught fire immediately and the pilot was burned in escaping the plane. Fire fighters and Medical men, not having seen the pilot run away from the aircraft approached the accident and while they were attempting to put out the flames the bomb load exploded, killing one and injuring eleven.

In a written statement a witness to the accident, Martin J. Mullen, said: "I was at the side of the runway, waiting to cross, as P-47D-20, serial number 42-76571 was taking off on an operational flight. The plane looked as if it was about two-thirds of the way down the runway when the tire blew out, plane skidded on runway and then swerved to the left and burst into flames. When myself and others reached the airplane the pilot had just gotten out, his clothes were on fire, we extinguished his clothes and wrapped him in a blanket and put him in an ambulance, and about that time the bomb exploded."

In 'The 493rd Fighter Squadron in WWII' book by Col. Jacob L. Cooper, Warren Welter recalled this incident. He said "I was driving the ambulance and when the bomb exploded I fell to the ground for a minute. I then got up and helped the Medics put the pilot into the ambulance. I drove to the field dispensary. We carried the pilot into the emergency room where they wrapped him in Vaseline gauze strips. I left when I thought everything was under control."

Sadly First Lieutenant Carlos J. Ball, who had been awarded the Air Medal with Oak Leaf Cluster, died from his injuries on 28th May, and now lies in the Cambridge American Cemetery.

Pvt. Wood Hibberd a bystander was killed when the bomb exploded, three others received major injuries, they were Pfc Fred Botha, Pfc. John Germis, and Pvt. Gordon Greene, while Pvt. George Panagopoulas, Pvt. Edward Tahwa, T/5 Robert Beach, Pvt. Clifton Gibson, T/4 Norman Line, Pvt. Wilfred Devine, Cpl. Frances Costa and Cpl. Frank Mamelite all received minor injuries.

Col. Jerome 'Jerry' J. McCabe, Commanding Officer of 492 Squadron, recalls how he had just taken off on the mission and witnessed the incident in his rear view mirror, but there was nothing he could do to help, he had to continue. The only information Jerome said he can add is, that on the day of the accident Carlos and myself went for a short flight in an R.A.F. twin engine aircraft he had borrowed. He always wanted to give me a ride in an administrative aircraft. We joked and kidded around until I was called in for the special flight to Germany later that day. It was then that Carlos talked me into going on the mission with him.

Carlos came to us from the Royal Canadian Air Force and joined us in England. He proved immediately to be an expert pilot and I awarded him the title of "C" Flight Commander. His "flight" had total confidence in his leadership and professional integrity.

Investigations show that the accident was caused by one hundred per cent material failure, left tire. The cause of the material failure was undetermined because the tire was completely demolished in the accident.

Peter Smith recalled how May 27th was a very hot sunny day and he was sitting in his garden when he heard the large explosion and saw a massive plume of black smoke coming from the airfield. Soon ambulances were racing past his home to the Station Hospital at North Gorley.

A large number of windows in Rockford School (now the Alice Lisle Inn) were blown out, and in view of the dangers to which it was exposed the school was immediately closed down for the remainder of the war, and the children attending were transferred to schools at Harbridge, Hyde, Ringwood and Fordingbridge.

Another crash occurred when a Thunderbolt failed to take off properly using the South-North runway and crashed straight into

Hearns Copse in Mockbeggar Lane. A fortnight to the day later another one did exactly the same thing. Interestingly, a reminder of this is the Hawthorn hedge, now some fifteen feet high, which the War Department planted to replace the old hedge, torn out in the crashes.

However, intensive training using the bombing range just to the East of the airfield quickly brought the 48th Fighter Group up to operational standard and they carried out numerous sweeps before D-Day, attacking marshalling yards, airfields, bridges, coastal batteries and radar stations. D-Day itself was something of an anti-climax for they were confined to convoy and beach cover, but they later reverted to their destructive sweeps. During June the 48th flew 68 missions from Ibsley involving 1,956 individual sorties.

James Harrison was a pilot with 404 Fighter Squadron and recalls that on 6th June, 1944 the 371st Fighter Group was assigned the mission of flying down the French Coast to the Brittany Peninsula, then go in over France and 'prevent any movement of any type over the roads, – tank, automobile, truck, bicycle or horse drawn vehicle'. James recalls how their aircraft, P-47's, were equipped with 165 gallon belly tanks of fuel which were to be dropped before crossing the Coast. I was the 'tail end Charlie' of our Squadron and did not realize my tank failed to drop when we jettisoned them. We dropped to low level for strafing of vehicles and were in quite intense flak for many minutes as we raced back and forth over our assigned area. After completion of the mission we left and were flying back to base. As we left the tip of the Cherbourg Peninsula the Squadron asked for a fuel check. I was aghast when I checked to see my gauge almost on 'Empty'. I knew I could not make it across that part of the Channel and expected to have to ditch in the Channel or maybe turn to France. I reported my status and was told my belly tank had not dropped. I was therefore able to make it back to base and land, with belly tank dropping off as I touched the ground. So, I always remember D-Day and how good our Base looked after my 'almost ditching'.

One way in which the village benefited from their American visitors was by way of the two large dumps on Ibsley Common. The 'Yanks' certainly had plenty of supplies and were quite wasteful (maybe compassionately). Many of the villagers would quite unashamedly (because with wartime rationing everything was so

*1944*

*Aircraft used by U.S.A.A.F. at Ibsley, 1944*
*Top: P47 Thunderbolt*
*Middle: P38J Lightning*
*Bottom: FB-6 Mustang*
*Drawings by D. Williams*

scarce) wait for the lorries to arrive at the dump with clothes, food (such as cans of syrup) and wooden cases. There were frequent minor squabbles over 'finds' on the dump. One, between a farmer from Gorley and a soldier over a pair of socks ended with them having one each!! Peter Smith's family still have a set of draughts (checkers) and board which he found on one of the dumps, as well as several toolboxes and an American serviceman's kit bag bearing the name of Clarence C. Benhoff.

The Americans were in fact very generous to the local children, sweets and chocolate (or candy, as the Yanks called it) were always being handed out, as were other gifts. Peter Smith recalled being given a football and a baseball bat, the latter his family still have. He also remembered his mother and father being given a half hundred weight (35 kilos) of K-ration chocolate, and this was hidden in the roof of his home. Quite often he would take some to school at Harbridge, (where he had been transferred when Rockford was closed). On those occasions he was just about the most popular boy there!!

There is also an amusing but true story of a villager who asked an American serviceman if he could get him a wooden box with which to make a hut for his young son's rabbit. The following day a six wheeled G.M.C. lorry arrived at the villagers house, with not just one box, but full of packing crates, which were all unloaded, and from which the villager not only constructed the required rabbit hutch, but a large garden shed as well.

The village lads were never at a loss for something to do in those days. One of their pranks was to take large lorry tyres from the dump and roll them up on to the top of Ibsley Common. There the lads would wait until the American airmen came with their girl friends to lay in the bracken on the hillside (which they often did). When this happened the lads would set the tyres rolling down at them, and then run off, as fast as their legs would carry them!!!

Use was also made of the damaged drop-tanks from U.S. aircraft, which were found on the dump. The father of one village lad would thoroughly wash them out, then cut a large hole in the tank, big enough to accommodate two boys, and these made excellent canoes for use in the local water filled ditches and streams.

The 48th Fighter Group moved out to the Continent in late June to be followed at Ibsley by 367th Fighter Group, 9th Air Force, Nos. 392,

*1944*

393 and 394 Squadrons, U.S.A.A.F. in early July with P-38J Lightnings. They came from nearby Stoney Cross airfield, which was needed for the U.S. 9th Air Force Bomber Command, on 5th July. With barely a pause in operations, Nos. 393 and 394 Squadrons took off on a mission only a couple of hours after their arrival when Col. Crossen led a dive-bombing attack against enemy troops near Caen.

Many of the pilots and officers of the Group were billeted in Cuckoo Hill, the large house at South Gorley.

Bad weather in early July meant that the aircraft were grounded for several days, thus enabling the ground crews to catch up on some much needed repairs and inspections. With better weather the 367th Fighter Group were soon back in action with armed reconnaissance missions, attacking railways, roadways and strafing convoys of military vehicles.

On July 17th the aircraft of Larry Blumer of 393rd Squadron was badly damaged when on a raid near Caen, but he managed to nurse his crippled Lightning to British lines before baling out. Blumer arrived back at Ibsley a few hours later after hitching a lift on an R.A.F. plane, and declared himself fit to go on missions the following day.

On Wednesday, July 26th there was low cloud when four members of No. 393 Squadron set off on a mission, and almost immediately after take-off two P-38's collided. The aircraft flown by Lieutenant Albert Cooksey crashed so close to the thatched property, Ivy House at Blissford, near Fordingbridge, that it set the cottage on fire. Tragically Lieutenant Cooksey was killed.

The property, which was completely destroyed, was set alight by burning debris from the plane, but Mr. Roy Deacon who was in residence, with his aunt Miss Dora Deacon, at the time, managed to free, and lead his horses from an adjoining wooden stable, which was also ablaze.

The pilot of the other P-38 involved in the mid-air collision, Lieutenant Robert Brandt, baled out, but injured his left foot so severely that it later had to be amputated. His aircraft fell about half a mile away at Chilly Hill, Blissford. Two young boys went to the crash site with a wheelbarrow, and each took a propeller blade from the plane. They pushed them on the said barrow to the home of one of them at North Gorley. Fifty eight years on one blade is still owned by a member of the finders family.

## So Much Sadness, So Much Fun

The following statements on the crash, made at the time, are from the Air Force Historical Research Agency in U.S.A.

By the Commanding Officer: On 26th July, 1944, approximately 1415 hours, Lieutenant Cooksey took off as number three man of a four ship flight, on an operational mission, dive bombing. The weather at base was six tenths cloud cover with the ceiling at one thousand feet and the top at thirty five hundred feet. In climbing through the overcast, Lt. Cooksey and Lt. Brandt collided in mid air.

Cause is undetermined, Lt. Cooksey crashed with his ship and was killed instantly. This statement is true and correct to the best of my knowledge. There were three signatures, Carroll H. Joy, Charles B. Rogers and Grover J. Gardner, all Major, Air Corps, Commanding.

These three also signed the statements concerning Lieutenant Robert Brandt and Second Lieutenant Robert Greene, the first paragraph of each statement reading the same. Brandt's then stated: Lt. Brandt made an emergency jump at approximately one thousand feet. Cause is undetermined. Lt. Brandt lost his left foot by striking the stabilser. Greene's statement said his ship was hit by debris from the collision between Lt. Cooksey and Lt. Brandt's ship. 2nd Lt. Greene's left propeller was completely sheared off and he was forced to make a single engine landing at a nearby base.

2nd. Lt. Robert Greene's own signed statement on the incident read: On 26th July, 1944, the 393rd Fighter Squadron, assigned a dive bombing mission, with one, one thousand pound general purpose bomb and one belly tank. Took off at approximately 1415, Captain R. R. Ray leading the flight. Lt. Brandt, his wing man, Lt. Cooksey, element leader. I was number 4, on Lt. Cooksey's wing. We found our flight below the cloud layer which was approximately 2,000 feet base and 9/10 cover. The flight leader proceeded to climb on instrument through the overcast. We broke through several blue patches at around 3,000 feet and the flight leader proceeded to make a shallow turn to the left, still breaking in and out of very thick cloud tops. At this instant while in tight formation and going through a very thick cloud top, number 2 and 3 men collided, whereupon number 3 man, Lt. Cooksey's ship, burst into flame, followed by an immediate explosion which jarred my ship and tumbled my gyros.

The extent of damage to my ship was as follows: The propeller and housing of the left engine was knocked off. Two minor dents

*1944*

on the onboard side of the left nacelle. I believe the damage was either caused by the explosion or flying debris. I landed single engine with bomb and belly tanks at Stoney Cross at 14.45.

The remaining plane in the flight, flown by Captain Raymond Ray, remained on the mission and joined the rest of the Squadron to attack a railway running from Le Mans to Chateau de Loir. They were attacked by Focke Wulf 190's and in the ensuing dog fight two enemy aircraft were shot down and three others damaged. Lieutenant Burnus Hayden was, however, shot down and killed in the skirmish. Captain Ray's aircraft was also shot down, but he baled out safely. Lieutenant Owen Johnson landed his crippled plane at an Advanced Landing Ground and managed to hitch a lift back to Ibsley. No. 393's last operational day at Ibsley was not a happy one.

During their time at Ibsley one of the Americans painted, on the walls of one of the downstairs rooms of the Control Tower, colourful head and shoulders portraits of three women, one blonde, one brunette and one auburn haired. Although now exposed to the elements, traces of the paintings remain to this day.

Preparations had been going on since 19th July for the move of the 367th Fighter Group from Ibsley to France, but it was not completed until the planes flew out on 27th July.

Willis 'Wally' Walling of the 371st Fighter Group, 404 Squadron, 9th U.S.A.A.F., at Ibsley in 1944, before moving into Europe, remembers his journey home to America, in November 1944. He says: "We were back in England, at Shrewsbury, awaiting a Coast Guard ship that was to take us home. It was a choice of flying in three or four weeks or go by ship this week. One of our returnees had purchased a small red cocker spaniel to take to the States. This was a 'No No' of course. He wanted to avoid the six months internment of the dog in England and then another six months in the U.S., to assure no evidence of rabies – all at his cost, naturally.

The pilots name escapes me now but he was from Buffalo, N.Y. He got some sleeping pills for his own "insomnia". When our call came to go to Liverpool to board the Wakefield for home he gave two of the sleeping pills to the dog. Three hours later at the dock we were still waiting to board, 'At ease' on the dock side. The dog was safely wrapped in the sleeve of a raincoat on the Lieutenant's arm when suddenly it started to moan and groan.

*So Much Sadness, So Much Fun*

There were about twenty-five of us that had elected to go by ship. The British Customs were on the job and as they approached us we all started singing to cover the dogs plight and maybe our arrest for smuggling. After about forty-five minutes of singing the inspector loudly acclaimed "He had seen many groups board for home but never one so happy with such prolonged singing without stopping". By this time the dog was howling and the singing was getting louder and worse than ever. We did not dare give the small dog any more pills but, fortunately, we were called to board and did so still singing, all bunched up together. The howling gave a little better sound to our singing and we got by.

Off Greenland we ran into a very strong storm which broke open two holds – nearly sinking our ship. We limped home three days late at five knots and into Boston, instead of our destination of New York City, at 3 o'clock in the morning. The only people there to greet us were the Salvation Army with tea, coffee and doughnuts – God Bless them. With no customs we all walked off the ship – with dog, and whatever contraband each was hoping to get home as memories of our escapades abroad.

I never heard how the owner and dog made out, but I'm reasonably sure they both enjoyed a great life together. When my locker arrived it was still full of sea water, from the broken holds, but my little alarm clock still worked when it was wound up. They don't make them like that any more!"

Ibsley was transferred back to Fighter Command in October, 1944, but the only unit to use Ibsley during the latter part of the year, was a detachment of 'A' Flight, No. 7 Flying Instructors School who came from Upavon on 12th December, 1944. They stayed until 8th January, 1945, and were then replaced by the 'B' Flight, who also stayed for a month. Both Flights were equipped with Oxfords and their courses had been transferred to Ibsley because Upavon was rendered useless by a very heavy fall of snow during December

# 1945
## Dakotas, Gliders, and Victory

Squadron Leader Ron Whyard, D.F.C., A.F.C., came to Ibsley on January 8th from Upavon, where weather problems were still being experienced, with No. 7. Flying Instructors School.

He recalls living in a requisitioned private house at Ibsley. His arrival was after dark and he was given an upstairs bedroom, so it came as a big surprise to him when he awoke about 3 a.m. to hear horses hooves above his head. He thought he had been hallucinating, but when he looked round outside in the morning he found the owner had built a ramp up to the flat roof so that he could park his car there and the forest ponies had used it.

On 19th March, R.A.F. Ibsley was transferred to 46 Group Transport Command, but no operational units arrived. It was then used as a satellite for the transports at Stoney Cross and Holmsley South.

Later in March, the Glider Pick-Up Training Flight arrived from Zeals, where they had been formed in January, 1945, and where the first aircrew had been trained, with 5 Dakotas and 7 U.S.A.A.F. serialled Hadrian Gliders. Tragically, however, all but one were killed when the Dakota returning them to the parent station, R.A.F. Leicester East, crashed. The only survivor was Flight Lieutenant McKay, the pilot, who was flung clear of the wreckage.

The Station Commander when the Glider Pick-Up Unit was at Ibsley was Wing Commander Folkard, who had lost an arm. The Operations Commander was Squadron Leader Philip W. 'Pete' Peters, who was award an A.F.C. in 1945.

Russell Farman, who served as an engine-fitter with the Glider Pick-Up, recalled how this terrible accident at Zeals was witnessed by all of the servicemen on the ground. The aircraft flew into a clump of trees on a low hill near the airfield. Russell said it was especially tragic as many of those killed had, previously, completed hazardous flying missions including those of Bomber Command and supply drops.

In Russell's words, "We were a close unit, small in size, with a great feeling of esprit-de-corps. Because of the tragedy at Zeals we were glad to make our move to Ibsley, which, in itself, was very welcoming, coinciding as it did with the most glorious of early Spring sunshine, beautiful Spring growth and a significant number or red squirrels (no red squirrels now, all grey ones). It seemed so idyllic tucked away in the woods with a welcoming W.V.S. (Women's Voluntary Service) at hand."

"Although we were told very little it was generally understood that we were preparing for operations in the Far East. The idea was to drop gliders loaded with men or supplies in remote areas, including jungle clearings, and then recover the glider by literally snatching it off the ground after it had been emptied and filled again with returning personnel. The tug plane was that great work horse the Dakota which snatched a WACO/Hadrian glider from the ground."

Staff Sergeant Pilot Instructor S. J. "Jock" East has good reason to remember his time at Ibsley. He says "A quick romance, and marriage to the boss, was the only way he could get any transport as Army on a Royal Air Force site. The lady was Deborah Jones – a blonde sergeant in charge of transport.". That's Jock's story anyway! It was a very good marriage and would still be so, but sadly Jock's wife died of cancer a week after their forty fourth wedding anniversary. "Jock" says "they were blessed with four daughters and nine grandchildren".

The Pick-Up Flight were at Ibsley from 21st March to 25th October and operated continuously during that time.

For those who do not know how the gliders were snatched up from the ground, Jock says "from the nose of the WACO/Hadrian glider a nylon rope about twenty yards long, with a loop at the end, was stretched across two goal posts some fifteen feet high and with twelve feet between each post. The Dakota aircraft had a special channel down the port side to guide the pick-up cable with a hook at the end. The cable was wound around the drum of a winch fitted in the Dakota. The winch was electrically operated and fitted with brakes at various pressures. It was very much dependent on the

## 1945

winch operator as to how smooth a snatch was felt in the glider. The Dakota approached the pick-up loop at about one hundred and forty knots and once it had caught the loop the winch would let out a certain amount of the cable, the operator having to judge the stress, etc., by eye, and sometimes by the feel of the aircraft."

"With a full load the Dakota would shudder as it lost speed on the initial snatch and the glider pilot would also have to make sure that he did not climb too rapidly, as this would pull the rear of the Dakota up and cause the nose to go down. When I have been in the Dakota, on the odd occasion, I have seen the Air Speed Indicator drop from one hundred and forty to one hundred and ten knots in three to four seconds, and also when flying, the glider from nought to sixty knots in three to four seconds. The reason for the short take off was to retrieve gliders and pick up wounded from the jungle area. We also had thoughts that it was possible to take off from Aircraft Carriers and take in equipment and men to the many islands in the Pacific."

The only failure I ever had was when giving a demonstration with a reporter alongside me, and the rope broke on the initial snatch. Fortunately we had just started to move when the rope came hurtling backwards and smashed the port wing. No one was hurt, so we collected another glider and the next time was perfect. The reporter heaved a sigh of relief. As this was the only failure in two hundred and forty seven snatches it speaks very well for the equipment, and the training and standard of flying by the R.A.F. pilots."

"A demonstration of snatching was given every month at Old Sarum airfield, Salisbury for various senior officers of the Navy, Army and Air Force, and after the release I used to put the WACO/ Hadrian glider through its paces with a roll, loop and then a side slip down towards the R.A.F. corporal who was standing in the centre of the airfield, opposite the V.I.P.'s waiting for me to stop the glider as near to him as possible. He could then hook my glider up so that he did not have to walk too far with the loop end to put it over the goal posts ready for the Dakota, circling round, to come and do the snatch. It was always an enjoyable day to show the air worthiness of the glider and the skill of the Dakota pilot to snatch the glider on the first approach. I must say, I can never remember a miss on all those demonstrations."

*So Much Sadness, So Much Fun*

Glider snatching at R.A.F. Ibsley, 1945, by No.1 Glider Pick-up Unit. The approach by the C.47 Dakota to snatch the CG4A Waco/Hadrian Glider. (Ibsley Common in background) Photo: A. Waldron

## 1945

*Glider snatching – The Strike.*
Photo: A. Waldron.

## So Much Sadness, So Much Fun

The late George Wyeth was an L.A.C. with the Unit and recalled flying to Ibsley from Zeals as a passenger in one of the Dakotas.

During the journey to Ibsley George was surrounded by various bits of equipment connected with 'Glider Snatching'. He also told of how the Dakota was a bit special, for one thing there was a long pole hinged in the fuselage complete with running cable and a 'catching hook' at the tail end. Inside the fuselage is a winch, on the port side of the front bulkhead, to which the cable is attached, and perhaps, the most surprising thing was the large doors.

The Glider Pick-Up Unit soon settled down at Ibsley and during their stay often saw a small gallery of watchers on the airfield surround, puzzled at first no doubt as to why a Dakota should sweep so very low over the field and snatch a rope suspended on two upright poles. However, as the course progressed and a glider was attached to the nylon rope they admired the skill of the pilots of the Dakotas and gliders, and their courage. An amazing fact is that there were no major accidents during the glider snatching training. There was some minor damage by way of swinging hooks, etc., and to repair this, or to complete a periodic inspection, the aircraft had to be towed out of the main entrance to the airfield (near the Control Tower), and across the Gorley Road to the hangar in the field opposite. As there were only a small number of 'snatch' Dakotas repairs or inspection had to be carried out overnight.

The hangar was shared with the Motor Transport section – and therein hangs a tale! During a gap between glider snatching courses, (which depended largely on the weather and the learning speed of the students), the aircraft were used by Transport Command for trips to various places. George Wyeth remember that one day when one of the Dakotas returned it had a German Despatch Riders motorbike aboard, intact apart from the distributor, which had been removed by the Germans.

"Jock" East also recalled the story of the motor-bike, and how Flight Lieutenant Legge flew into Guernsey, on the day of the German surrender, with supplies for the islanders and brought back a lot of 'loot, including the aforesaid motorcycle, a small German BMW.

The motor-bike was placed in the hangar where it remained hidden until a certain clever fellow fitted a Morris '8' distributor to it and put it in working order. Sometime later it was ridden away in an overnight trip to a destination somewhere in the Midlands. The

## 1945

journey obviously passed without incident because the rider returned to Ibsley when his leave expired. As the saying goes, – no names, no pack drill.

George also recalled that the Flight was full of 'characters', one of whom was 'Benny'. The scene is an R.A.F. hut in a field off Newtown, South Gorley. It was late and a number of airmen were sleeping peacefully. One bed was empty. The sound of a rapidly moving bicycle was heard, the door flew open and a very wet Benny sloshed across the room, leapt into his bed, wet clothes and all. A few seconds later the door opened again and a policeman looked in and said, "Did someone just come in?". The response was a chorus of "No", and a few other things!

Benny had been riding his bicycle with no lights again, and in attempting to evade the Constable had fallen into the flooded Vennards Ford. He was woken next morning by the sound of the tannoy saying, "Would Benny please rise from his bed and join us as we would quite like him to help us in our efforts!"

The Glider Pick-Up Unit held a Flight dance, in September1945, at the "As You Like It" at North Gorley, which had previously been used as an Officers Mess and then Station Hospital. There was a bar and so although George Wyeth and his friend Bill were not into dancing they decided to look in and support the event. They then planned to go into Bournemouth. However, after they had had a drink or two Bill said, "Come on let's go". George said, "Right, but I must go to the Gents first". The toilet was located on the far side of the dance floor. A ladies choice waltz had been announced and a young blonde lady said to George, "May I have this dance". He was hooked, didn't get to the gents or Bournemouth that night, and two years later was married to that young blond, Enid Viney, at Harbridge Church. Sadly George passed away in 1997 but Enid still lives only a mile or so from the old airfield.

Another story, recalled by "Jock" East concerned the Sergeant's Mess which had the Witches Club (a small broom stick in the lapel, presented to members who were seen in a pub with the ugliest crone by at least two members). Quite a good drinking club until one of the witches found out!

The WACO/Hadrian Gliders were usually kept in the large Bellman hangar off the Gorley Road when not in use. The hangar was surrounded by large coils of barbed-wire entanglements, which provided a challenge to village lads Peter Smith and Gerald Thompkins who wanted a closer inspection of the said gliders.

They belly crawled from Ibsley Common through the heather and bracken and down to the entanglements. Being of smallish stature they were able to wriggle their way through these and up to the hangar. Luckily, the very large doors were left slightly ajar and they were able to enter. Fortunately, too, there was no-one around so that they were able to get a close look at both the outside and inside of the gliders. Having seen enough of the gliders they then turned their attention to some of the large Bedford lorries, which were also parked in the hangar.

All went well until, having climbed into the cab of one lorry, Gerald inadvertently pressed the horn. You can imagine the deafening noise this made inside the hangar. The speed with which they left the building, and negotiated the barbed wire entanglement was unbelievable, but all the time, said Peter, they were expecting to receive a shot up the backsides, but luckily nothing was encountered and they survived to tell the tale.

Gerald was not so lucky when he and Peter were being a bit cheeky to the airman on duty at the Guardroom at Cross Lanes one day. The guard said to them "right, which one of you is coming in here" and promptly got hold of Gerald, who was smaller and younger than Peter, and took him inside. Needless to say Peter ran to his nearby home as fast as his legs would carry him, leaving Gerald behind.

On Wednesday, 15th August, 1945, a memorable Victory Dance was held at Ibsley. There was dancing and other celebrations including the firing of many coloured Verey lights from the Control Tower.

During the latter part of the Glider Pick-Up Units stay at Ibsley, Russell Farman remembers how they were inundated with personnel being kitted out for 'Tiger Force' the code-name for Far East Operations. However, the War ended before they could be used operationally, and on 25th October, 1945, the Unit left Ibsley and moved to Ramsbury, Wiltshire.

With the departure of the Gliders in October, 1945, the end of regular flying at Ibsley was in sight. Very few of the hastily built wartime airfields were to feature in the post-war requirements of the Royal Air Force. The re-fuelling facilities and fire-tenders were the first to go and the use of the airfield was restricted to emergencies only.

*1945*

*R.A.F. Ibsley, Station Headquarters, No. 6. Site, South Gorley, 1946-1952.*
*Photo: P. Lobley*

*Cpl. Terry St. George, Signals Section, Ibsley 1948, outside Moyles Court House, Station Headquarters 1941-1946*

Despite this there were still one or two aircraft movements in November, 1945, including a Lancaster bomber that landed before continuing to Colerne.

Base personnel, which had peaked at three thousand when the American servicemen were at Ibsley, was now down to a mere 350, but the Station diarist recorded that "Christmas arrangements were most satisfactory, and that it was a happy day in traditional R.A.F. fashion".

Prior to the War the Gorley Village football pitch was situated on "Bunny Ground", so called because of the large number of rabbits which inhabited it. This was near Cross Lanes Chapel. With the outbreak of war, all such local sport was curtailed, and the football pitch became part of the airfield, never to return there.

In 1945, however, the Royal Air Force laid out a very good football ground at Rockford, near the School. With the end of the War, this pitch was used by the Station football team for several years, and some of the players who represented the station went on to play in semi-professional and professional football.

In 1949-1950 season R.A.F. Ibsley, competing in Division 2 of the Salisbury and District League, won the League Championship and also the League Cup. The team was Doug Barrington (Captain), "Jock" Calder, George Cramer, Eddie Eliott, "Jock" Filshie, George Green, Bill Hanley, Alan Hill, Roy Kent, Jack Milligan and George Parsons.

Gorley Football Club on its re-forming in 1946 under Hon. Secretary Gordon Shutler, and playing in the Bournemouth Saturday League, shared the pitch with R.A.F. Ibsley until 1950 when it moved to a new ground at Shorthedge, North Gorley, on land which was part of Jones Farm, behind "The Open Country". Sadly, Gorley Football Club ceased to exist in 1988, when the six Youth teams which were being run, in the Bournemouth Youth League, were taken over by Ringwood Town Football Club.

# 1946 – 1952
## End of an Era

On February 22$^{nd}$, 1946, Moyles Court was de-requisitioned as Station Headquarters and all that was left to do was to preside over the winding down of the airfield which had seen many types of aircraft during its operational years. The largest ever to visit Ibsley was a Liberator, witnessed by several villagers, parked just off the perimeter track adjacent to the A338 road. What it was doing there will probably never be known.

Directly the War was over, and the airfield no longer in use, the domestic sites and huts around the airfield itself were used to house families (who were unkindly called squatters) because of the housing shortage at that time. It is estimated that some one hundred and fifty families were housed in these huts until enough housing was built, sometime in the mid-fifties. The No. 2 Communal site (which was re-named No. 6 site) at South Gorley was, however, used as a domestic site to feed and sleep staff for R.A.F. Sopley until August 1952.

Robin "Jock" Campbell was an M.T. Driver stationed at Ibsley from 1946-1948 and recalls being involved in a strange experience. It concerned the appearance of a gentleman with a club foot outside the station's P.B.X., (telephone exchange) along the Gorley Road, not far from Moyles Court. The said gentleman was believed to be the ghost reputed to hang out in and around Moyles Court. At the time of this particular incident there were two chaps in the P.B.X. and they were quite upset by this apparition. A thorough search of the area by a crowd of R.A.F. personnel failed to reveal the culprit.

Another strange event recalled by Robin Campbell during his service at Ibsley involved a small aircraft landing on the airfield in daylight. The Duty Officer, and Campbell as duty driver, rushed to the airfield and prevented it from taking off. Two men had left the plane, run across the airfield and crossed through the hedge on to

Mockbeggar Lane. It was said at the time that a waiting car took them away. Shortly afterwards civilian police arrived and we left them to deal with the pilot.

For a time the runways remained serviceable, but the rest of the airfield was handed back to Lord Normanton's tenant farmers, Harold Bennett, William Sampson and James Sampson, and then ploughed up.

In March, 1946, the airfield officially closed down with the dispersal of most of the staff to Holmsley South, Stoney Cross and Netheravon.

Some of the hangars were used by a detachment of 49 Maintenance Unit for storage, but Ibsley became an inactive site in 1947 and was soon de-requisitioned. All that remained then was a handful of staff in a Care and Maintenance role until about 1948, and as previously stated, No. 2 Communal site was used as the domestic quarters for personnel at R.A.F. Sopley.

John Lennard joined the R.A.F. in July 1946, and after training was posted in late September of that year, to Ibsley as an assistant radar operator. He recalls arriving at Salisbury station and being driven to the airfield, which by this time was closed, in a 5 ton truck, and then to the No. 6 site where the personnel for R.A.F. Sopley were billeted. He says "one of the first jobs I was given was to go round all the wartime sites at Ibsley and collect as many fire extinguishers as I could find and bring them back to No. 6 site, empty them and prepare them for transporting to R.A.F. Middle Wallop. If memory serves me right, it was a glorious 'Indian Summer' and I thoroughly enjoyed wandering through the trees with my little hand cart."

He went on to say "The lovely late summer was followed by a bitter winter, and in January, 1947, we were sent home for three weeks as we were unable to get any coal supplies for our pot-bellied stoves in the Nissen huts. All our supplies were collected from Middle Wallop and food rations were collected daily."

John Lennard also remembers an amusing incident which happened the day after a new acting Station Warrant Officer, a sergeant, was posted in. He says "the normal routine of the day started with reveille at 0630 hours. Up to that time we were left to our own devices, as long as we were ready to catch the transport that left at 0800 hours to take us to Sopley. On this particular day

## 1946-1952

the new Station Warrant Officer went round at 0631 and charged all the airmen who were still in bed. He caught one hundred per cent. The C.O. was not amused as he had to take all the charges before we could go on duty down the 'hole' at Sopley. It was at least two hours later before Sopley was on the air"

"I had a very enjoyable time during my short stay at Ibsley, and was introduced to the real Air Force, which stood me in good stead for the rest of my career," said John. John Lennard served in the Royal Air Force from 1946 to 1983 as a Master Navigator.

Aircraftman John Fry was posted to Ibsley in September 1946 and stayed until August, 1948, as a Clerk (General Duties). He recalls that on his arrival at Ibsley, which had recently ceased to be operational, the "ghostly" atmosphere of the station, for it appeared that all personnel had left leaving everything but their own personal possessions behind. He particularly remembers a card index register giving names, home addresses, etc., of airmen and airwomen, a large number of whom were from the Empire and foreign countries.

He went on to say there was no Medical Officer and each morning there was a sick parade with personnel being transported to R.A.F. Stoney Cross. They did have a Station Sick Quarters, however, with two medical orderlies. There was no Accounts Section and all accounting was done by R.A.F. Middle Wallop.

Roy Mitchell arrived at Ibsley in late Summer, 1947, and remembers the Commanding Officer at the time was Squadron Leader Selsdon, the Acting Station Warrant Officer, Sergeant 'Jock' Murray, and the Signals Warrant Officer, Paddy Carney. Roy's billet was the Picket Post in the top corner of the Cuckoo Hill site.

Roy came to Ibsley from Middle Wallop, where he used to organise dances in the N.A.A.F.I. It was not long before he was doing the same at Ibsley, in the station gymnasium. Music was provided by the band from R.A.F. Old Sarum (although sometimes 78 r.p.m. records were used) and apart from the locals, girls from Bournemouth Telephone Exchange and nurses from Salisbury Hospital were brought in by coach to provide the "interest"!

Another incident recalled by Roy Mitchell was the time the Signals van was "used" as transport to the cinema at Fordingbridge. On the way back to camp the van became ditched in a hedge but was undamaged, soon pulled out and returned to camp where it was parked on the M.T. square. The next morning the M.T. Corporal

## So Much Sadness, So Much Fun

suggested that the branches and twigs should be removed from the roof of the van before the Commanding Officer came on duty.

Ken Gill was at Ibsley as an AC1 Clerk Special Duties, from 1947-1949. He recalled how the Russians set up the Berlin Blockade, and when the Airlift was instituted he was posted with five others from Ibsley to become involved. Ken, and A.C.s J. Smith, Ken Manners, Tony Coomber, Ken Avery and Dunford were sent to Lubeck to set up an Operations Room. We were there nine months, said Ken, nine months of concentrated work, but that is a story not connected with Ibsley. Towards the end of our term in Germany one of our team was killed in a road accident, AC1 Ken Avery, a very popular and likeable lad.

Shortly after this accident we were posted back to Ibsley. The five of us arrived at the Guardroom late at night and were shown to an empty Nissen hut as temporary quarters. We thought a lie in next morning was called for, Sergeant Murray not being about when we arrived. 6.30 a.m. and the door of the hut burst open and in strode Sergeant Murray brandishing a large stick, slamming it down on the foot of each bed, not a glint of humour showing on his steely face. We rocketed out of bed thinking the Russians had arrived, but only had to report on parade, feeling disgruntled. We never did find out who told Sergeant Murray of our return. Guess the culprit was too scared to admit.

Early in 1948 Derek Hayton and his pals, Greg Denbigh and Ken Ladd arrived at Ringwood Station, after becoming fully qualified Fighter Plotters, or, as they were classified "Clerks Special Duties", on posting to R.A.F. Sopley.

Derek recalls how they phoned R.A.F. Sopley to come and pick them up, which they duly did, only to find that they were actually billeted at Ibsley.

Eventually they were taken to Ibsley, by which time it was dark and the scratch meal which had been drummed up in the cook house did little to cheer them up. There was just one un-shaded bulb to light the whole room, which hadn't even been cleaned up from the evening meal. First impressions were not very encouraging and the whole place resembled episodes from the one time radio programme "Much Binding in the Marsh".

"However", Derek says "we soon settled into the daily routine of travelling back and forth to Sopley". Sopley was a Ground Control

## 1946-1952

Station at that time as well as the control centre for about six airfields of Fighter Command, including Tangmere, Middle Wallop, and Odiham.

Derek went on to recall, "that life at Ibsley was great. They were about 240 strong, all male, and mostly in their late teens. Rationing was still on, so meals were pretty basic (one egg a week), and plenty of brawn, which was served up in various disguises.

There was no N.A.A.F.I. on camp but a small shop was run by a volunteer who sold cigarettes, toothpaste, boot polish and bottles of lemonade. One day volunteers were called for as decorators. It was planned to close down the M.T. Section and in due time to open up a properly run N.A.A.F.I. The M.T. Section was shaped like the letter 'H', one half was to be for the N.A.A.F.I. staff living quarters, the centre section was the shop and cooking area, and the other was to be the food and recreation room."

"The grand opening called for a dance, so invitations were sent to local telephone exchanges to get as many girls to come as possible. As we were an all male station it was necessary to find a place where the girls could hang their coats and visit the small room. One building, which had always been locked while I was there, was opened up for the purpose. This little building was a revelation to us all," says Derek, "as the graffiti on the walls was all American. I think most of us at that time were totally unaware that Yanks had formerly been at Ibsley. However, the evening went off well."

"Another improvement to our life at Ibsley was the conversion of one of the huts into a cinema."

A quarter of the hut was turned into a projector room, while some other genius made a very professional looking screen and curtains. We had to take our own chairs and site round the stove in the centre of the room, but it was great. We managed to get films from the Arts Council of Great Britain in London, some of which were really ancient, recalled Derek. He remembers seeing King Kong and the Hunchback of Notre Dame in the silent versions. There was sound equipment because when Derek was collecting entrance fees one week he saw the film Hollywood Canteen about a dozen times. Derek also founded the Music Club which met once a fortnight, and here again they were able to request records to be sent to them from the Arts Council.

National Serviceman, Aircraftman 2$^{nd}$ Class, Jim Chadwick recalled how he was posted, after driving instruction at Weeton, in the North of the country, to a command centre somewhere in England. Apparently a fully trained MT driver who knew the meaning of fear, was very hesitant, but knew the Highway Code backwards, was urgently needed for some top level operation at a disused airfield in the heart of Hampshire. And so, this "erk" was secretly dropped at Ringwood Station on a cold, moonless night in November, 1948, then had to board a bus with orders to ask for Sopley.

Eventually an unsympathetic bus conductor stopped the bus in the middle of nowhere and pointed vaguely into the inky blackness. "It's down there" he leered and quickly signalled the bus driver to get away quickly.

Somewhere in the blackness there must be a road. Once out of the ditch "erk" Chadwick groped painfully down the mysterious lane into the unknown dragging a heavy kitbag, backpack, sidepack and all the other packs that high command deemed essential to fight a modern war. At last the hedges gave way to a chain link fence. There, in the murkiness was a thin shaft of light, which came from what appeared to be a shed.

From what turned out to be a Guard House came the doubtful singing of "Guilty" by a decidedly Welsh voice. Inside was a man in an air force shirt but no trousers. These were being lovingly pressed with an iron powered by a piece of flex hanging from a light socket!

"Er, is this Sopley" in wondrous disbelief from someone just released from one of the Country's leading "Bull Centres".

"That's right Boyo, but you shouldn't be here". It was then "erk" Chadwick saw the jacket with corporals stripes. Even worse, lying in the corner was the telltale white belt.

He had never spoken to an SP without being ordered to stand to attention and now he was being told he shouldn't be here, and he'd caught a corporal with his trousers down, so to speak. The situation had all the makings of a "charge". What a start to joining a new camp.

"They're always sending bods like you here. I'll get someone to take you to Ibsley", complained the corporal. By now this "erk" was beginning to suspect that Ibsley was some kind of detention centre, but this was soon dispelled after a screeching of brakes outside, the door burst open and the Corporal was greeted with "Hi Taff". The Aircraftman Driver who had just arrived was a typical role model for

## 1946-1952

a cartoon MT Driver. Sleeveless leather jerkin, gauntlet gloves, stained uniform and a grubby, flattened forage cap that would have earned at least fourteen days at Padgate. By the time we arrived at Ibsley the whole place was asleep and this "erk" was bedded down in the nearest Nissen hut.

Next morning all the Hut inhabitants slouched off into parade leaving "erk" Chadwick all alone, when in strode a fierce looking Sergeant. This was more like the real thing that one expected. "You. Get this mess cleaned up". After issuing this command, the Sergeant stamped out to search for another victim. Not belonging in the Hut, or anywhere else for that matter, the Sergeant had obviously mistaken this "erk" for one of the Hut's regular members. That was the assumption anyway because how could the Sergeant possibly know that here was the latest product of the R.A.F. Motor Transport academy.

After the parade, when it seemed safe to venture outside, I reported to the Station Warrant Officer's office. A vicious growl answered the timid knock on the door inviting me to enter. There, glowering behind a desk was the Sergeant from the Hut. "Oh, it's you" he acknowledged. "Well, did you get that billet cleaned up?". "Well, er, no Sergeant. You see ...". At that time there was still capital punishment and following the Sergeant's outburst at this confession, the firing squad seemed a distinct possibility.

"Didn't they teach you to obey orders where you came from" he thundered.

"Well...er..yes Sergeant....but I thought that maybe you thought that I belonged in that Hut".

"I know where you belong boy and you'll soon be going there.". The Sergeant threatened menacingly.

Then followed a session of probing questions that appeared to amuse the Inquisitor. Relief finally came with the Sergeant's mug of tea and Eccles cake which was the signal for this "erk" to withdraw discreetly. Now to report to the MT section.

The Flight Sergeant in charge of MT was called "Chiefy" by everyone and he seemed genuinely interested in his latest addition. A glance at the paybook informed him that this "erk" claimed to have been a commercial artist in civvy street. "Ah, just what we've been waiting for" beamed Chiefy.

## So Much Sadness, So Much Fun

Thinking that he was about to be allocated a Humber Saloon to patrol the country lanes in, "erk" momentarily took to Chiefy until he said "Go to the stores, get yourself some denims, a pot of white paint, and paint all the number plates for a start"

Chad had arrived at Ibsley.

Although more than fifty years ago since Owen 'Don' Blissett, a Clerk Special Duties served at R.A.F. Ibsley some things remain indelible in his memory and will never be erased.

In recalling his first twenty four hours at Ibsley he said "we had travelled all day from R.A.F. Bawdsey (Suffolk) where we had completed our training as Clerk S/D's later to become Fighter Plotters."

"We arrived at the Guard Room very tired and fed up after a long train journey and what seemed an even longer journey down Sandy Lane (now known as Ibsley Drove), to be greeted with "who are you?" and "where have you come from?"

"Our billet, after a tortuous walk through the dark turned out to be a Nissen Hut which was the farthest from the main gate, with no lights, no fire, and a complete lack of any refinements. It would appear that the wooden huts that we had lived in since our 'Call Up' were four star hotels compared with this 'home from home' to which we were introduced. The walls ran with water and the bedding was so damp it was a wonder that we did not all catch pneumonia sleeping in it. That night we had no meal and went to bed cold and starving."

"The following day, a Saturday, the whole billet overslept. However, we eventually found our way to Station Headquarters just in time to see the morning parade being dismissed. A voice roared "Who the hell are you?", this was our introduction to "Jock" Morrison the acting Station Warrant Officer, a gentleman who was well respected by all and sundry."

"Our first parade at Ibsley, recalled Owen Blissett, was in the confines of his office. When we told "Jock" Morrison of our lack of facilities, in the way of heating, lighting and food, the Orderly Corporal for the previous day was summoned. I'll never forget him, very tall, with thick black moustache, who always seemed to wear his "best blue" with a serge beret instead of the usual forage cap. His name was Davidson. It would appear that he had been detailed to

## 1946-1952

arrange the commissioning of our billet, instead, as he "lived out" he had gone home to a nice warm fire, and not bothered about our accommodation. After "Jock" Morrison had finished with him, in front of us all, I do not think he would ever dare to pull that trick again."

" "Jock" then wanted to know what we all did in "civvy street". All went well until he got to me. My reply being a "clerk, sergeant". This was not a sufficient answer for him and I was further asked what sort of clerk and where I worked. After explaining that I was a clerk in a Mental Hospital, which obviously brought forth guffaws of laughter, his reply was "bloody hell, last week it was a !*@11*11 ballet dancer", which was perfectly true, his name was Smith.

" "Jock" then gave us a pep talk on the station and how we would travel to Sopley each day, and that we would be working shifts, etc. We were then left to sort ourselves out until working parade on Monday morning."

"The washing facilities that we had were minimal to say the least, "hot water" was drawn from coal fired boilers, into galvanised bowls, which were then placed onto concrete troughs for the purpose of washing."

"Regrettably there was a snag in the system, in that someone had to light and stoke the boilers, which were likened to the old wash boilers that were used in our grandparents time. The stokers name whilst I was there was a chap called McKenzie, a Scotsman, no, a real Cockney barrow boy, who liked his bed so much that hot water seldom existed in the ablutions. However, it was surprising how much one could wash, with boiling water from a mess tin, which we heated in the billet on our meagre ration of coal."

On another occasion Owen remembers waking one morning to find that their camp had been split into two. A stream which ran through it was crossed by a plank bridge, but during the night there had been torrential rain, and the stream had overflowed. This brought its diversion however, for apart from having to get out to the main road and back into camp via the main gate, which was a change, a salmon appeared in the deep water under the bridge, and it eventually went the way of all good salmon, via the application of a large brick.

January 1$^{st}$, 1949 was a day which ended in tragedy. Transport to and from Sopley was by 3 ton Trooper lorries with canvas tilts (no such thing as buses). Tragically a collision occurred between one of he Troopers and a lorry loaded with meat, at Bisterne, which resulted in the deaths of three and injuries to others.

Sergeant Jimmy Moir recalls how they had assembled at the Ibsley guardroom with a full crew for night flying at Sopley, to control duty aircraft. He said "the weather deteriorated from the time we arrived at Sopley and no aircraft were able to take off. After some considerable delay Group H.Q., decided to cancel all operations and we were stood down. All to the transport to return us to Ibsley – still raining torrents. The first vehicle was driven by Corporal Darkie Hamshere, a very experienced and reliable driver. As we were approaching the Farm Bend at Bisterne a large transport (meat lorry) was travelling in the opposite direction with full lights blazing and the rain lashing down on the road. Both drivers found it difficult to negotiate the bend, which resulted in an horrific collision in which three airman including Sergeant Les Grant (a Jamaican cricketer) were killed. Also killed was a Radar Operator Aircraftman Walker, and a Clerk, Special Duties, Aircraftman Lou Laurati.

My driver Darkie was thrown into the steering wheel and dashboard and received severe leg injuries. I was sitting beside him in the cab and was catapulted through the windscreen, and simply remember an airman saying, "here Sarge, have my hanky" for which I was most grateful, to help stem the blood flow from my head and facial injuries. Having regained my senses we then all mucked in to take the injured and others to the nearby Farm House which had very kindly been offered as a Casualty Clearing Place.

Ambulances arrived promptly and the injured were taken to Boscombe Hospital, Bournemouth and checked over. "Cheese" Hay suffered a fractured skull. Those who could were returned to Ibsley to recover from the ordeal, and Johnny Scott who was also on the lorry was seen later in the evening, looking very shocked and with his overcoat torn from his shoulder to the hem, but he was unmarked.

After considerable negotiations a trial was arranged at Winchester Assizes for six months later. I was given a posting to Germany, but Group H.Q. said no, I was to stay as witness number one for the trial, Meat Company v The Crown.

A testing examination in the "Box" terminated with the verdict being an "Equal Contest", 'Accident' no claims, no damages. Not a happy New Year.

*1946-1952*

Very often when all the seats on the trooper were filled there was standing room only at the front. It is believed that on this occasion Sergeant Grant, who was wearing his overcoat swapped places with a Corporal from Trinidad who was without his and was stood in the draught. It was as a result of this good turn that Sergeant Les Grant met his death. He is buried in Sopley Cemetery, near Christchurch. Sergeant Jimmy Moir acted as one of the pall bearers at the funeral and recalls that Les Grant's wife came from Jamaica to attend.

January 2nd dawned a depressing day as the result of the previous night's tragedy, and a Bedford 'Utility' bus, with wooden seats, was brought in to replace the "written off" trooper.

This tragic accident also had a profound effect on the lads of the village, particularly Peter Smith, Dave Farrant and Gerald Thompkins. Les Grant was a West Indian and a fine cricketer. During his time at the Station the cricket team were playing their matches on the sports ground which had been laid out in a field belonging to Evans Farm (now Hucklesbrook Farm), adjacent to the No. 2 Communal (No. 6) site, where there were also football and rugby pitches. It was here that Les would give some excellent coaching sessions for the lads, and Peter Smith said, "we learnt a lot about the game from him, not only the technical side of it, but the true meaning of sportsmanship. He always had time for us lads, and was such a great loss".

The route from Ibsley to Sopley, recalled Owen Blissett, was through the main street of Ringwood, and as we left the outskirts of the town bound for the evening shift at Sopley, the newly delivered bus was in collision with a car containing a honeymoon couple, who drove out of the forecourt of the 'Nags Head' pub (demolished in 1998 to make way for housing) just as we were passing. Fortunately there were no serious injuries, only a minor one to Flight Lieutenant Symington who hit his knee on the gear lever, and hobbled about for a short time afterwards.

In February, 1949, the first number of the Ibsley Review was produced, it cost 3d. This was a ten page publication printed with an 'Apology' which read: 'We must ask to be forgiven for the poor quality of printing in this magazine, but it is not altogether our fault. The duplicator we are using is in very bad shape and until we get one of our own the printing won't be any better. It is not known how many Ibsley Review's were published, but the following are a few 'snippets' from the first, with the headings they were given.

## THE STAFF OF THE IBSLEY REVIEW

Executive Editor: Gordon E. Avery.
Sub Editor: Derek R. Bate.
News Editor: John Willgoose.
Sports Editor: Charles Douglas.
Art Editor: James Chadwick.
Secretary: Ronald E. Fox.

## THE FIRST NUMBER OF THE IBSLEY REVIEW

Nearly every R.A.F. Station in the British Isles, and overseas, possess their own Station Magazine. But quite obviously Ibsley is without. Perhaps we should say "Ibsley was without" because here is the first edition of your new Station Magazine.

It is with great enthusiasm that we start this magazine but it will be impossible to make it a success unless we have your co-operation. What we want from you are your criticisms, jokes, cartoons, and suggestions. Also articles of general interest to everyone. With your co-operation, this magazine will be a success. As we get more settled, we will be able to offer prizes of money for the best jokes, and articles etc., but let us get started first.

ళ∞ఁ

## ON BECOMING JUST ANOTHER IBSLEYITE
### by Michael Garrard.

It was a miserably wet night in late November, when I arrived at Ringwood Station. I dumped my kitbag and small pack heavily on the platform peered again at my route form which bore the simple legend, S.S.O.C. SOPLEY. After making enquiries, and having elected the information that "Sopley be a good stretch from 'ere", I walked hopefully from the station into the road.

My luck was in. I got a lift to Sopley. A white gate loomed up out of the rapidly clearing fog, and a light streamed from a small nissen hut. I knocked, and walked in. Inside was like a furnace, one guard lay stretched out full length on a bed and I could hear his deep sencrous snores, the other slumped in a chair, wearily lifted his head, gave me a menacing glare and demanded, in most aggressive tones "Well, what do you want?" I told him.

Four hours later I was hugging my seat for dear life in a small van which was being driven at a terrific speed by a Mr. S. towards Ibsley. I never thought I'd see the next bend, let alone Ibsley!

Still when I got out at Ibsley, I was still in one piece, for which I thank Divine Providence!!

I ate, I slept, and next morning I awoke with a start, and looking through the open door of my hut, met the doleful gaze of a cow! I could almost feel it's moist breath down my neck.

I was up, and dressed and running the rounds with my arrival chit, when a large individual glared down. at me from above and enquired "Do you play Rugger?" I managed a rather squeaky "No". He stalked off in disgust.

The days rolled on, they ran into weeks, and then into months, Ibsley grew on me. It was certainly a station in a class on it's own. Where will you find horses trotting around the billets and chickens clambering over the wire at other camps? Where, at what other place, could you make a dozen complaints a day about the running of the canteen? The fact is, there is no other place quite like it!

But this dialogue, in a train, crowned it all for me.

The other day I was travelling up to town, when a brotherly bod queries. "Where have you come from mate?" "Ibsley, Hampshire" I replied suavely. "Never 'eard of it," he chimed. A superior smile flitted across my face, after all it is a nice feeling living in a little world apart from the crowd, isn't it?

M.A.H.G.

There was no title to the following story in the Ibsley Review.

The time has cum at last, wen I can rite my ecspoerances since I was conskriptid in the Air force, I shoved my toof Brush and sope and touwel in a bag and went to Padgete. At Padgete there was a lot ov other boys as well. They was all called up to. There was grate big quewes as well for meels. After gettin my Uniform sombody sed to me "we are going to West Kerby for square bashing." I arsked him what was skare bashing but he only larfed at me. Wen I got to West Kerby I soon lerned wot it was. I still fink them Sgts. have no farvers. They just don't seem to make up there mindes wat they want us to do. Their was the time wen the sarjent sed Trael arms.

How was I to no that he didnt want us to trael it on the ground e sed to me "You stoopid !?/&%/@£/! WOTS the matter witch yew. Well i arrsk yer. Wots a chap to do abart it. Anyweys arfter 20 weaks at West Kerby they decided to pest me to a yoonit.

When i got to IBSLEY (arfter being picked up by Six corpurels wif wite hats and an orficer) I was asked for my root form agin. But i adnt got one. They expleind to me wot it was like and i remembered that i yoosed it in the "george" before i reported to IBSLEY. Well i arsk yer. How was I to no wot it was for. Aneway they sed I eas to be cherged for loosin it.

On fursday morning I was takin in front of a adydant an he sed sevin days just like that. Well its ate minits to ten now and I have to go to the gardrum now. Yours until Churchill smokes woodbines.
'arry Ibslee.

NOTE FROM THE EDITOR: This airman has just been posted to Ibsley and has promised us further articles. I have printed it as it was handed to me. 'arry Ibslee is an anonymous name to this airman as he doesn't want all Ibsley to know of his capabilities as an Author! (Ed).

## SPORTS REPORT
Semi Final, Ft. Group Cup.
IBSLEY 2 ODIHAM 7

R.A.F. Odiham turned up at Ibsley on Wednesday 16th Feb, for this match, with quite a few supporters, a red and white striped hat, a Fire bell, two or three rattles, a megaphone, and a few W.A.A.F.S.

Ibsley played in gold and black striped jerseys while Odiham wore maroon and white halves.

Ibsley kicked off but soon lost the ball to Odiham's forwards, the O's attacked strongly but Paddy Moran cleared safely, only for Odiham to attack again and force a corner. Ibsley defenders got the ball away and play went from end to end for about five minutes. But 8 mins., after the game started Crispin scored for Odiham with a low drive which gave our goalkeeper no chance. Within half a minute Jimmy Moir who had closed in from the right wing equalised from close range. Odiham looked likely to draw ahead when Hanley misjudged a header and headed towards his own goal, but the ball

*1946-1952*

R.A.F. Ibsley Soccer Team,
1949-50, Salisbury and District League Division 2 Champions and League Cup Winners
Photo: R. Booth

R.A.F. Ibsley Rifle Team at Bisley Championships, 1950
Photo: J. Moir

was cleared and Ibsley attacked and kept up the pressure until the Odiham forwards got moving on the right wing, the ball passed to one forward in the centre who took a first time shot, but Benson got to it well, but fumbled it and the ball ran parallel along the goal line until Spence ran up and poked it over the line for a goal in the 30th minute. Within two minutes Odiham had scored again through Woods. Ibsley were badly shaken and I think this was the turning point in what was up to this time, a quick and open match. In the 40th minute Woods scored again for Odiham. From this time on Ibsley saw very little of the ball.

## HALF TIME, IBSLEY 1, 4 ODIHAM

Soon after play was resumed Odiham forced a corner but outside left Evershed put it behind for a goal kick to Ibsley. Ten minutes later they forced another but this was safely cleared by Williams. In the 60th minute Odiham scored again. Two of the Ibsley defenders appealed for offside, but the ref. took no notice. Ibsley improved in their play and forced a corner. They kept to the attack until an Odiham breakaway brought goal number 6, after 75 minutes of play. Again Odiham took charge of the game, after a penalty was awarded against Ibsley this opportunity was missed. The Ibsley forwards took charge of the ball and Millward scored after 85 minutes. Odiham were then awarded a free kick just outside the penalty area. A goal from an indirect free kick was disallowed. Just before full time, Hummerton, Odiham's centre half took possession of a loose ball. This was lobbed into the Ibsley goalmouth resulting in a seventh goal being scored. Shortly afterwards the whistle went for full time.

To sum up, although Odiham had brawn they had brain as well, as their passing and shooting won the day for them. I am sure all Ibsley will be with me when I wish them good luck in the final.

## THE IBSLEY SUPPORTERS CLUB!

Those of you who watched the Football match between Ibsley and Odiham on Wednesday afternoon, will remember the way the Ibsley supporters shouted at the team!

The leading man of the club being Sgt. Watts who shouted his head off all through the game! But all the same, I must say that Sgt.

Watts certainly made up for all those that were missing! If only he could have laid his hands on the ref. I'm sure there would have been blood flying everywhere!

There were several comic remarks made, such as Mr. Davies shouting, "Don't worry about the ball, get on with the game!!"

Even Cpl. (Butch) Gumbly nearly shouted his head off but not at the players! No, he was shouting at a W.A.A.F. by the name of 'Alice!' But lets hope his wife doesn't get hold of this Magazine!

Of course, half time brought some budding footballers on the field, but they certainly moved when Sgt. Watts shouted "Get off the field, or else I'll put you all on Salvage to-night!" Next time there's a game going on at Ibsley, what about some real loud voices to help the Sgt. out!.

## RED TAPE

Two teams of workmen, one English and one American, decided to hold a contest to see who could assemble a plane in the quickest time.

Three hours after the start an Englishman went across and asked the Americans how they were getting on.

"Not too bad" was the answer. "Six more bolts and we'll be finished, how are you getting on?'

"Pretty well" said the Englishman, 'Six more papers to get signed and we'll be able to start!"

## THE LAST LAUGH

The A.C. in the R.A.F. had been sent up for an intelligence test. Patiently he endured all the queer things they do on these occasions but he was a little startled when two Psychiatrists bent down and peered into his ears, one at each side.

"That's alright," they told him, "If we could have seen each other we would have recommended you for a commission!".

*So Much Sadness, So Much Fun*

Not long after Owen Blissett came to Ibsley he became what was known as Ops "B", which entailed working in the Ops cabin with the duty Fighter Controller, one Fl/Lt. J. H. 'Ginger' Lacey. Lacey had previously been a Pilot Officer with No. 501 Squadron at Ibsley for a short time in 1941. His main interest first thing in the morning was to read the "Daily Mirror". Yes, you've guessed it, to see whether "Jane" in the cartoon strip was dressed or undressed. "Ginger" left Ibsley, on this occasion, to do a conversion course onto Meteors early in 1949.

When Peter Smith left school, in 1949, at the age of 15, he followed in his fathers footsteps and went to work for Mr. Harold Bennett at Mockbeggar Farm. One day whilst working on what, by this time, was the old airfield, he saw a motor-cycle going at great speed around the perimeter track, and also up and down the runways. The motor-cyclist, it later transpired, was none other than the leading rider of the time, Geoff Duke. He was testing the suitability of the surface of the perimeter track and runways for racing. The result was satisfactory, and the early 1950's saw a number of very successful motor-cycle and motor-car race meetings with crowds in excess of twenty thousand. The initial length of the circuit was given as 1 mile 1,743 yards. The start and finish line was along the North-South runway, and the four corners of the track were named Court Corner (S.E.), Sampsons Curve (S.W.), Church Corner (N.W.) and Paddock Bend (N.E.). Some of the leading makes of racing car were at Ibsley, including Alfa Romeo, Allard, Aston Martin, Ferrari, Maserati and M.G. Drivers included Salvadori, Sopwith, Stewart, Hill and Brabham. A.J.S., Norton, Royal Enfield and Velocette motor cycles also raced at Ibsley. This was the last use to which the Ibsley runways were put before they were bulldozed and ploughed up.

Sgt. Jimmy Moir recalls some of the sporting success achieved by R.A.F. Ibsley in 1950/51, the Rugby team winning both the 11 Group Cup and the Fighter Command Cup, and becoming champions of Fighter Command. A member of the successful team himself, Jimmy remembers their Captain was F/Lt. Horsfall (who played for the England Front Row), and the Vice Captain F/Lt. Alan Symington.

Also in 1950, a team from R.A.F. Ibsley took part in the Rifle Shooting Championships held at Bisley.

Peter Lobley was at Ibsley from 1950-52, as a Radar Operator, and was a member of the Station Band which was formed during this time. Peter himself played bass, and recalls other members of the band were Ken Carpenter (guitar), Don Hardiman (piano), Leonard Setright (clarinet), Arthur Ward (drums) and Cpl. Pat McCullough (vocals).

S.A.C. Edmund "Eddie" Alderson was posted to R.A.F. Sopley/Ibsley in Spring, 1951 as an A.C.1.

He recalls there was no accommodation at Sopley so we were billeted at R.A.F. Ibsley. The billets were old Nissen huts and they had, evidently, been condemned for some years as being unfit to live in, but a brand new camp was to be built close to the radar station, but would not be ready for some time. In the meantime we lived in these Nissen huts, which in fact I did not find too bad. The men I was there with were a great crowd and I got on well with them and soon made friends.

Eddie recalled that during peacetime the radar station was not operational twenty four hours a day. As we had two watches it meant that we would alternate between working mornings and afternoons and usually one night watch per week for each watch. As we worked so few hours we were on what was known as a "cushy number" and most of us were enjoying ourselves. However, some of the national servicemen couldn't wait until their two years were over and tended to make life a misery for themselves, working out how many days they had left to serve and crossing them off on the calendar. Some even worked it out to minutes and in one case to seconds; and there were no calculators in those days!

When we were on afternoon watch we had a "fatigue parade" in the morning, after breakfast, and the Station Warrant Officer did his very best to find us unpleasant tasks. As we were in the New Forest our camp was usually invaded by New Forest ponies who came either under or round the boom at the main gate. The easiest task to be given was to be told to round them up and get them off the station. This didn't take too long and we became quite good at it. The next task allocated was to get buckets and shovels and clean up after these same beasts! The worst job of all was called the s**t run! This entailed going round the married quarters on the back of an open lorry emptying the dustbins and standing, or sitting, on top of it all until we arrived at the rubbish tip in Ringwood. The one consolation here was that the lorry driver knew a café in Ringwood where we could have a full fry up with chips for two shillings and sixpence and this was a treat enjoyed by all of us. It didn't quite make the job worthwhile, but almost! I wonder if the locals in the café could smell all the rubbish on us?

As our new accommodation had been delayed and would still not be complete for several months it had been decided by "the powers that be" that some of us would take over part of the empty hospital at St. Leonards, for a short while. It had previously been occupied by the Americans.

Meanwhile, back at Ibsley we were preparing for our move. The corporal in charge of our billet said that he had been at Ibsley for many years and we couldn't leave without doing something spectacular, so we planned on playing a joke on the occupants of nearby 6 site. The plan entailed that we had to do a little shopping first, and that we duly did. On the last night of our stay at Ibsley the men in our hut went to bed as usual. We were up again about 2.00 a.m. and put our battledress on over our pyjamas and moved quietly along the narrow path up to 6 site. There were about eight Nissen huts and one of us stood outside each hut with our "shopping". This consisted of the largest "banger" fireworks that were on sale and a box of matches each. The man at the hut furthest from our own billets lit his fireworks first, opened the hut door and threw the lighted fireworks inside the hut. As he ran past the next hut our man there did the same and eventually we were all there to throw fireworks into the last hut. By now the chaps weren't just throwing them in the huts but placing them under and on top of the beds. Soon there was a deafening sound of explosions from the first hut plus a lot of shouting and cursing. This got worse as now there was a chain reaction as fireworks in the other huts exploded. As the huts were made of corrugated iron the sound was exaggerated. However, we didn't stick around to admire our handiwork and were running hell for leather back to our own hut. We didn't put a light on and within a couple of minutes to all appearances we were fast asleep. From the time of lighting the first firework to us being back in bed must have taken only a matter of minutes. Next morning at breakfast we thought there might be repercussions but nothing was said. Our officers evidently heard about the escapade but decided that our high spirits should not be investigated. I can imagine that if we did this today there could well be a problem with the health and safety people!

The R.A.F. appeared to be worried that squatters would move into our old camp at Ibsley, so each evening a few men were sent

## 1946-1952

there to guard it. When it became my turn I was lucky as the corporal in charge of the guard had arranged with the police corporal in charge of the guardroom at Sopley to give him a ring if the Orderly Officer left the station. We were supposed to walk around Ibsley all night but instead we put on our pyjamas and went to bed knowing that we had plenty of time to get dressed if we heard that the Orderly Officer was on his way. However, one of us had to operate the antiquated telephone exchange, so we took it in turns. Because this had been the main exchange for the whole camp there were dozens of cables and sockets, although in fact only a few were in use. It was not too easy to operate the system with only a couple of minutes instruction and I remembers that at some stage I had the dubious distinction of cutting the C.O. off.

Walter Spink arrived at Ibsley in the Summer of 1951, as an L.A.C. Radar Mechanic. He recalled how one very dark night, they were in their billet reading letters, books, etc., when the door burst open and an airman flung himself in, slammed, and quickly locked it. He was completely out of breath, and when we asked him what the matter was, he could only gesticulate at the closed door. Then we heard the sound of horses hooves outside. When he got his breath back he said that he had left the bus stop on the main Ringwood-Fordingbridge road, started walking along the pitch black lane, literally feeling his way along the hedges. Then he felt something breathe on the back of his neck, and nuzzle him. He took fright and ran the mile or so back to the billet at top speed.

For a time the station gymnasium, on the No. 1 Communal site was used by the local people as their Village Hall, and became a popular venue for dances. It has been said, many times, that it had one of the best floors for dancing in the area. Ibsley's present Village Hall was built in 1968, on land purchased from the Earl of Normanton, and which had been part of the Communal site. It still has the concrete bases of some of the wartime huts around it, and there are many others together with several blast shelters still visible in the adjoining field. For a time, before demolition, one of the huts was also used as a Village Shop and Post Office, run by Mr. A. G. Hatch.

For several years, in the fifties, the Bellman hangar along the Gorley Road was used by the British Drug Houses from Poole as a chemicals store. About a dozen local people were employed by the Company, including Fred Smith, and on demob from the R.A.F. in

1954, after two years of National Service, Peter Smith. The chemical company's occupation of the hangar was not without incident, however, for on Whit Monday, 1953, a major fire occurred, thought to have been caused by the hot weather at that time. Local residents, many of them tenants of the Ringwood and Fordingbridge Rural District Council, who were inhabiting the former R.A.F. huts, were alerted by a series of explosions, with fragments of glass and chemical cylinders hurtling over the Gorley Road, while flames and dense acrid smoke was coming from the building itself.

When firemen from Ringwood, under Leading Fireman Teddy Hine arrived they found the fire appeared to have started in containers stacked outside the entrance to the hangar, which was closed at the time. The heat from the fire had set light to boxes and cases inside. Reinforccements were needed, and immediately called for, Ringwood Brigade being joined by those of Fordingbridge and Cranborne, but they were unable to approach on account of the acrid fumes. Meanwhile, Sub Officer Gulliver, from Lyndhurst, arrived with a wireless control car and immediately sent a message for breathing apparatus. Bournemouth Fire Service emergency tender with Station Office Collingbourne responded, and after pouring water on to the hot corrugated iron walls of the hangar the firemen were eventually able to open one large door and enter, protected with breathing apparatus.

Damage in the hangar was confined to cases and chemicals at one end, and part of the walls. A short distance from the hangar was a large store of glass carboys containing nitric, sulphuric and other acids. Some of these were broken or leaking through their stoppers, probably because of the heat, and added to the acrid fumes which could be smelt over a mile away from the depot.

Officials from the British Drug Houses came and advised the firemen how to deal with the various chemicals. They also gave assurance that there were no high explosive containers stored on the site.

British Drug Houses moved from Ibsley to new purpose built premises at Broom Road, Parkstone, Dorset, in 1959, after which the Bellman hangar and adjacent huts were demolished.

Throughout World War II Betty Hockey of Bournemouth ran a Concert Party for the Forces, both British and American, in the old

*1946-1952*

*The Whit Monday, 1953, fire at Ibsley's Bellman hangar off Gorley Road, occupied at the time by British Drug Houses.*
Photo: V.Smith

Southern Command Area, which stretched from Portsmouth to Weymouth and North to Salisbury Plain, even out to sea when they were called on to give 'Shows' on board battleships as they came into Poole Bay for shelter. Betty recalls that they clocked up well over a thousand shows prior to "D-Day" and carried on until about 1948 when television began showing it's mark and theatres started to die.

Betty's was a large Concert Party, call the 'Nonstops Troop Show". It consisted of sixteen Artistes, so consequently they had nearly every type of Act available. Shows were performed in Garrison Camps, Units, Ship and Shore bases, but they concentrated mainly upon the small Units, often wallowing in mud in the New Forest on their lead up to "D-Day", as this was where they were sadly lacking in entertainment, to boost their morale. Many times, recalls Betty, there would be no Stage, but most venues managed to rig up some sort of platform. Sometimes the back of a large truck would be used, and these performances would be known as Tailboard Shows.

"I well remember Ibsley", said Betty, the Can-Can Dancer, "who didn't". "It had a wonderful atmosphere and was close to our

## So Much Sadness, So Much Fun

doorstep". It was certainly one of our favourite places to be, and extremely popular with us". "We saw the numerous and varied Squadrons come and go". "Just getting to know them all, when off they would pop at the drop of a hat, many times without warning".

Betty also recalls going across the Green, many a time, to the Officers' Mess where they were wined and dined till early morning. All of the Concert Party had wartime day jobs, but they were young then and could stand the pace. We were also invited to join them on other evenings, at the King's Arm in Christchurch, or the popular St. Leonards Hotel, a great favourite with Air Crews from Ibsley. "The atmosphere then was electric", said Betty. "It was "live for today – tomorrow may never come" attitude". "Both happy and sad days with everybody rallying around each other in times of hardship or sadness".

"Because of rationing, and because the British could not have the generosity of hosting, as that which the U.S. Forces provided, entertaining OUR BOYS, was priority No. 1 for the Concert Party".

During the show 'a volunteer' was always asked for, to dress as a Sheik for the Eastern Dancer so that she could twirl about him. Betty still wonders whether any of these Sheiks are still around to tell the tale.

"Then there was another corny act which required four 'volunteers'. They were required to sit on the laps of four dancers and suck milk from the teat of a boat shaped glass baby's bottle. The first to finish was the winner, duly awarded an enamel baby's potty signed by the entire cast. Have any of these potties survived, perhaps tucked away in someone's attic? Because of the audience participation both of these acts brought the house down, believe it or not, especially if we could lure one of the Officers to take part."

A few years after the War finished, quite by chance, Betty said that she came upon the dear little hut which served as the 'Theatre' at Ibsley, and ventured inside. Long since gone were the doors and windows, but right in the middle of the derelict Dressing Room, stood a wicker skip, simply full of costumes. She couldn't believe here eyes, and hesitated to try and guess WHY it was still there after so long, or why nobody had taken it. It would certainly not have survived today. It was certainly an asset in providing lovely costumes for the Non-Stops shows, especially as rationing of

## 1946-1952

clothing was still in being. "Getting costumes was one of our greatest problems and we had to rely upon Grannie's attics, etc.", said Betty. "but we were always known as the best dressed Concert Party around".

"Yes, IBSLEY brings back so many, many memories for me and I still hold lots and lots of Forces Signatures taken over the years. May Ibsley always remain in peoples' memories and continue to keep alive the part it played in World War II. I know it will for me" – Betty Hockey, The Can Can Dancer.

Ten years after he was stationed at Ibsley/Sopley Owen Blissett recalls how he made a nostalgic pilgrimage back to his old haunts, and tells of what he found. He said "The derelict airfield is still there, as it always was. Pretty chintz curtains decorate the windows of "comm" site huts and children's laughter echoes round the buildings.

The main camp has all but gone, with Nissen huts no longer to be seen. Two lovely bungalows have been built where the airmen's mess once stood, grass grows in profusion, the doors of the bathhouse swing in the breeze and birds flit to and fro through the broken windows of the guardroom.

S.H.Q. has gone too. And where our parades were once held stands a threshing machine.

Owen then continued his sentimental journey through Ringwood, Kingston, Bisterne and on to the village of Sopley, where a dilapidated signpost pointed forlornly to R.A.F. Sopley.

As I approached, said Owen, there was some sign of life. Four airmen tore past in a jalopy and another on a bicycle.

The radar arrays still turned and outside the main gate stood a very smart coach, a far cry from our draughty trooper of ten years ago. It was filled with airmen in shirt-sleeve order.

Instead of a white-capped S.P. at the guardroom a notice "Police dogs on patrol"sufficed.

My journey over I turned for my home in Basingstoke. Ten years had passed and things were not the same but I had revived memories of "Yorky", "Tim", "Mike", "Cheese", "Johnny" and many more.

We have mentioned, in the pages of this book, several marriages of people who met their partners at R.A.F. Ibsley. These were just a few of the many happy and long lasting marriages of pilots, ground

So Much Sadness, So Much Fun

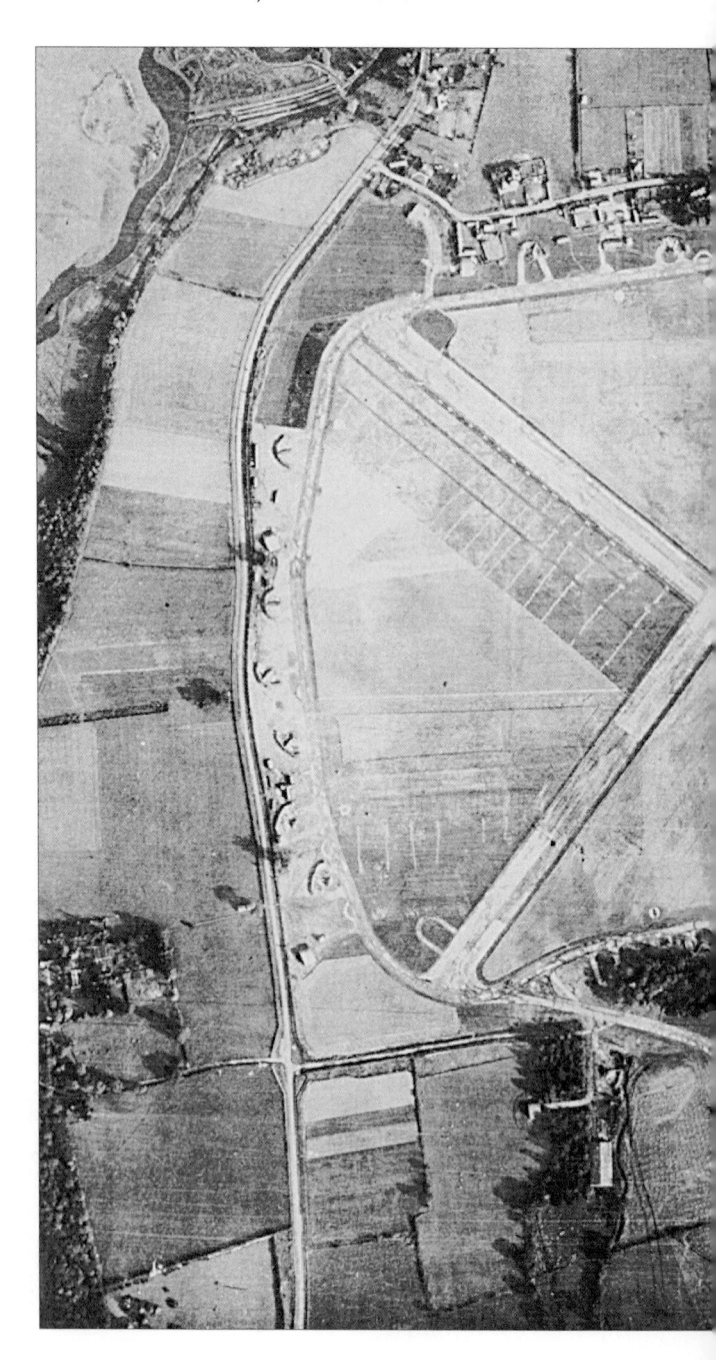

*Aerial View of Ibsley Airfield, after runway extension.*

*1946-1952*

crew, W.A.A.F.'s and N.A.A.F.I. girls, that resulted from service at R.A.F. Ibsley.

Occasionally bits and pieces from those wartime days at are still discovered on some of the old airfield sites. In 1997 a stainless steel American Identity Tag engraved with the name of Lloyd J. Andrews, Jr., was found at South Gorley by a Mr. Cyril Palmer of Ringwood, and donated to the R.A.F. Ibsley Historical Group. A former U.S. Serviceman, Nevin Price, who was known to the Group was contacted, in America, and asked if he could help trace the owner. Nevin kindly obliged, set to work, and eventually made contact with a brother, Bill Andrews, in Arizona.

Lloyd J. Andrews, Jr. was a P.38 Lightning pilot based at Ibsley in July 1944 with No. 392 Squadron, 367th Fighter Group, 9th United States Air Force, before being posted to France.

On 28th October, 1944, Lloyd was involved in a dog-fight with enemy aircraft over Cologne, Germany. After shooting down three of these, he himself was shot down and lost his life, at twenty years of age.

Lloyd J. Andrews Jr., was the holder of the Distinguished Flying Cross, Air Medal and Purple Heart.

S.A.C. Peter Lobley at A338 – Mockbeggar Lane Junction, 1951
Photo: P. Lobley

In 1998 Bill Andrews came to Ibsley where he was presented with the framed Identity Tag of his brother Lloyd J. Andrews, Jr., together with photograph and a Citation, which ended with the words *"One of the many who gave their lives in conflict that we should have freedom"*.

At Ibsley there are a few buildings still standing around some of the old sites, several blast shelters, and concrete bases where huts once stood. On the old airfield itself, now a haven for wildfowl on the large lakes formed by gravel extraction over the last thirty years, the Control Tower still stands proudly, defiant, like the men and women who fought so valiantly in those desperate days against such a ruthless foe. It is, at the present time, the property of the Bournemouth and West Hampshire Water Company, and one of several structures which the R.A.F. Ibsley Historical Group has registered with both the Imperial War Museum's Defence of Britain Project and the Sites and Monuments Register of Hampshire County Council. Also registered are the Battle Headquarters, in Newlands Wood, and the Direction Finding Station Blast wall and twelve remaining compass points on Ibsley Common, a Stanton Shelter, (this is an underground shelter with escape hatch chimney), and a brick built Sleeping Shelter, off Mockbeggar Lane. Long may these structures remain.

R.A.F. Ibsley will not be forgotten, for on 24th April, 2000, two pilots who flew from Ibsley, Wing Commander Christopher Currant, D.S.O., D.F.C., Croix de Guerre, No. 501 Squadron, 1941, then Station Commander, Ibsley, 1942, and Flying Officer Bob George, No. 616 Squadron, 1943, unveiled a fine Commemorative Plaque of R.A.F. Ibsley.

The Plaque, a tablet of polished granite, is engraved with a map of the Airfield complex, 1941-1952, and lists the R.A.F. Squadrons and United States Army Air Force Fighter Groups who were based at Ibsley, the planes they flew, and also makes reference to it being an accommodation base for R.A.F. Sopley. The engraved tablet was very kindly donated by local stonemasons Hoare Banks, and rests on a Purbeck stone plinth within a wrought iron fence both paid for by the R.A.F. Ibsley Historical Group, to protect it from the New Forest ponies, cattle and donkeys which wander freely in the area. By kind permission of Ellingham, Harbridge and Ibsley Parish Council, the landowners, it sits on the existing wartime concrete base of the old

So Much Sadness, So Much Fun

*View from first floor, Control Tower, Ibsley, showing early Watch Office. c. 1957.*
Photo: Courtesy Salisbury Journal Newspapers

*Peter Smith on first floor of Control Tower, Ibsley, 1994, and view of lakes formed by gravel extraction.*
Photo: P.Smith

*1946-1952*

*Recent view of Ibsley Control Tower.
Photo: L. Rose*

## So Much Sadness, So Much Fun

*Lois and Bill Andrews from Arizona, U.S.A., outside wartime hut of R.A.F. Ibsley Exhibition, South Gorley, August 1998, following presentation of Lloyd J. Andrews, Jr's., Identity Tag found at Ibsley in 1997 by Cyril Palmer, pictured right*

*R.A.F. Ibsley Commemorative Plaque, Cross Lanes, Mockbeggar. Unveiled 24th April, 2000*

*1946-1952*

Guardroom/Picket Post at Cross Lanes, Mockbeggar, the North East corner of the old airfield.

This Commemorative Plaque will serve as a reminder, not only to this generation, but future generations, of Ibsley's heroic past and the important part it played in World War II.

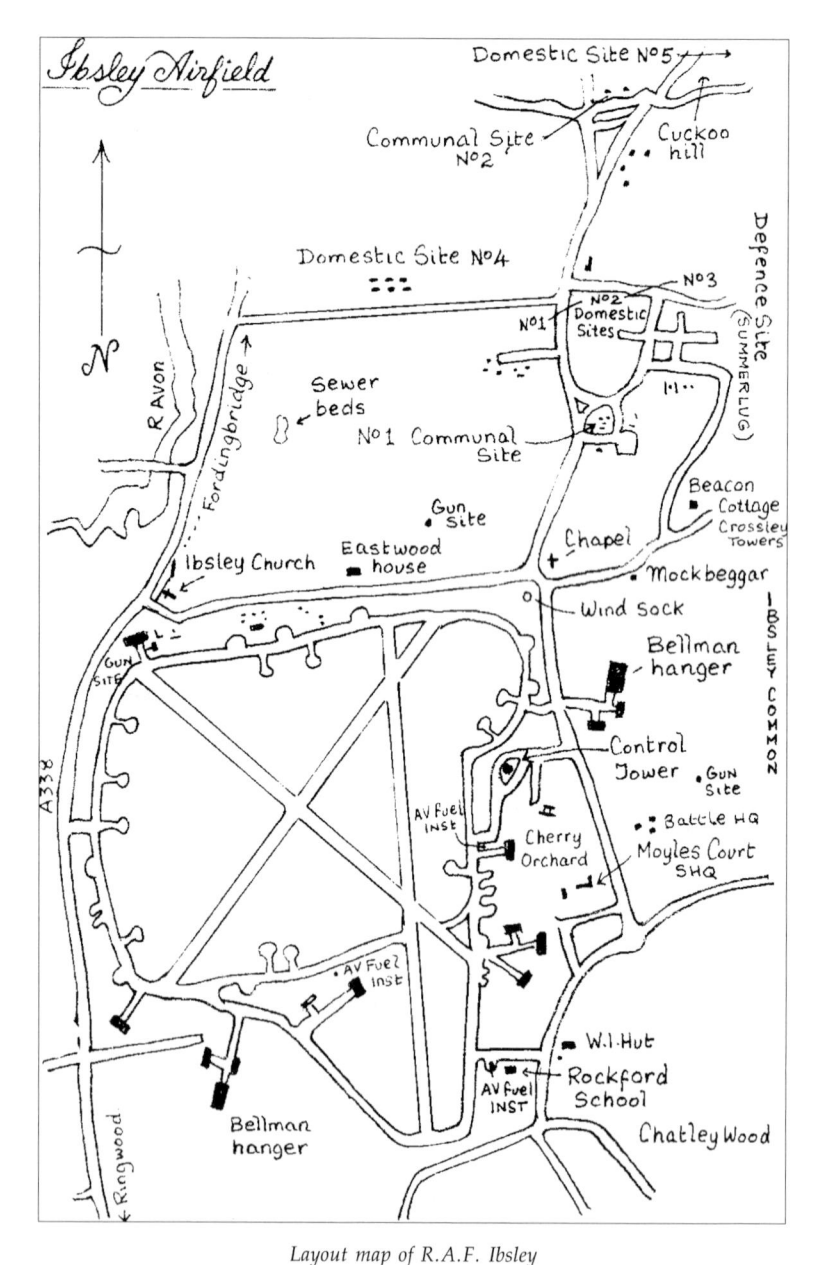

*So Much Sadness, So Much Fun*

*Layout map of R.A.F. Ibsley*
Note: The site numbers shown on this map are as the sites were known at Ibsley, and therefore differ from any Ministry plans of the airfield sites.

The following poems were submitted by Maurice Annison who was stationed at Ibsley, 1941-1943, on Airfield Defence

## *Summer-Lug Gen*

Poems written by
L.A.C. G. J. Prosser, R.A.F. Regiment,
while stationed at Ibsley 1942-43,

### R.A.F. REGIMENT

We have no tradition, we have just made a start,
There's no history at all to our gang,
But on things of the square, we have mastered the art,
Though at mornings we all have a pang,
When we are marched to the Square by our own N.C.O.
And get bashed on the concrete together.
We keep up our spirits and let ourselves go,
Paying no need at all to the weather.
We have no need to grumble – we haven't the right,
And we haven't the room for a moaner:
But here's to the lads, the pride of the flight,
Jim Hemsley, George Gunson and Jonah!

ಙ

### MATTER OF FORM

O simple form that makes one glad to be alive,
O simple form for which we fellows scheme and strive –
Upon its surface we who write,
With pulses beating all their might,
Put down in script so bold and neat
The words that make our leave complete,
And gaining it, see how we dive –
To utilize our "Two Nine Five".

ಙ

## THE BROKEN HEARTED SQUADRON

There's a broken hearted Squadron,
To the north of Ibsley Plain,
Where the boys who work through daytime –
Go to bed at night again.

Where old Lamprey in his slumber
Talks aloud at night in bed,
And we often pause to wonder
What this A.C. plonk hath said.

Then there's Clayton with his antics
Quite a perky little chap,
Using elbow grease and polish
From his toe nails to his cap.

And again there's Sergeant Harding
Fellows call him Uncle Ben,
Running up and down the Hillside
Clinging firmly to his "Sten".

For to see this browned off Squadron
Is enough to make one cry,
When they are doubled up the mountain
By an N.C.O. named Fry.

It's a "proper institution"
This here mountain home they dug,
And for "better information"
They have called it "Summer-Lug".

Let us get this Blitzkreig over –
That is all that we beseech
Then we'll travel to our homesteads
On a mountain pony each.

❧

## CALL OUT THE FLIGHT

We are ordered out, can't use the lights,
Up above are Jerry Kites.
Chaps are rushing for their kit,
Jerry's dropping lumps of Grit.
Jones has ripped his only vest,

## Summer-Lug Gen

Says his trousers have gone west.
Looking for "tin hat" on bed
Puts the wash bowl on instead.
Lamprey too is in a fix
Puts on Benson's P.T. nicks.

Fisher running in a panic
Wished he was a Flight Mechanic.
Peacock does not care two hoots
Shouts to Clayton – "Where's my boots?"

Bags of action, more alerts
Chaps are mixing up their shirts.
Perspiration drops about
From outside we hear a shout
"Come on chaps, no time to ponder,
Parachutists dropping yonder".

Brophy looking for his gaiters
Trips on Walsh's respirator.
Kites are passing by in batches,
Stevens shouts "who's pinched my matches?"
Someone faints, Smith runs for brandy,
Bumps into naked Sandy.
Prosser chilled up to the marrow
Finds his bow but not his arrow
Then a cry from far away –
Jennings shouts "it's Delahay".

And his patience sure is ebbing
Says he cannot find his webbing.
Fellows all got dressed at last
Hurry on parade quite fast.

Then they are told it's much too late –
Jerry's been and dropped a crate,
And what's more its come to rain –
Lets get back to bed again.

"Two Flight" looking very sad,
Thinks of the time they might have had
And dreaming of nursery slopes and slants
Littleboy in his denim pants – faints.

❧

## IMPOSSIBLE TOAST

To the day when Dodson cleans his brass.
And Lancaster with boots like glass
And rifle sloped comes on the square,
Two hours before the rest are there.

The day when B.H.Q. will not be manned
And Butler takes the full command
While 'Littleboy' with means to end
In leaps and bounds, begins to spend.

And to the day when void of fuss
They do away with syllabus,
And Peacock bursting his long last blister
Turns his thoughts to Clayton's sister.

B.H.Q. = Battle Headquarters

## "STANDING ORDERS"

We don't like 'standing too' at all
At dusk or at the dawn,
We do not like to see that parting
Light, or hail the breaking morn.

We stand about with many a pout,
And many an ugly frown,
There's only one thing that we like
And that is 'standing down'

## BLACK LOOKS

And when the hours of marching we had done,
And the lads were faint, and cold and wet –
We saw at last the goal we'd won,
It was something that we won't forget.
Far in the distance we would see
Standing outlined in front of the sky,
The forms and movement of the enemy,
Exposed as if they wished to die.
But then alas, we saw them stoop –
No longer did their form show out

And our leader out to make a "coup"
Decided he would send a scout –
So the Scout went out in leaps and bounds,
Full willing to pay the price.
But he soon came back to say he'd found
Five Negroes playing with a dice.

ॐ

## THE ROAD TO SANDY BALL

There's a road that leads across yon hill,
Where the moors rise and fall
And its not the road to Burma !
Its the road to Sandy Ball.

And we felt so proud and happy,
As across yon ferns we went,
There was not a browned off fellow
In this new formed regiment.

Corporal Fry was full of tactics,
As he jumped from tree to tree,
But he mixed up information
With the word topography.

And he caused the flight to panic
With an ill formed exclamation –
When he shouted out to follow him
In "arrowroot" formation.

Now the lads got sort of cheesy,
And they called it all a ramp,
But they soon got bright and breezy
When they reached the Nudist Camp.

But they marched right through
And they took no heed,
For they knew the nudes were gone,
And their blistered feet began to bleed,
But the Regiment struggled on.

And they will struggle on till things are square,
For the "Nazi Might" must fall,
And Lamprey will rest in his old arm chair
On the road to "Sandy Ball".

ॐ

## LOST OBJECTIVE

There's a little place called Furze Hill
On the Ibsley Moors set,
  "Is it there today?
  Well I can't say,"
'Cos we haven't found it yet.

There's a burnt out cottage near by
At the bottom of the Hill,
  "Is it there today?
  Well I can't say,"
'Cos we are looking for it still.

❧

## EXTRACT

Extract from modern version
Of Shakespeare's Henry the VIII.
Final Scene – Lancaster addressing
The Regiment after the battle of
'Newlands Plantation'. –

Brothers, Brothers! hold thy remorse,
For Littleboy cometh on his horse,
There is no need to have the blues,
Me thinks he bringeth goodly news,
For down yon path he comes with noble stride,
He bringeth hope, and yea, the gen book too beside,
And wouldest not thou by our section leader stand,
And giveth all they bow, thy arrow and thine hand.
Butler replies in dramatic fashion
This is no time to ponder, laugh or scoff,
'Tis I who leads since Dodson is bumped off.
There is no time for jealousy and strife,
When the smoke, and noise of battle still holds rife.
Epilogue –
But the Regimentarians danced with joy
And shouted out for "Littleboy".

❧

## CURTAIN

*Summer-Lug Gen*

## PROSSER'S 'POST WAR PLANS'

Now what could there be firma
Than a holiday in Burma
At Monywa, or even at Rangoon,
Or to rent a little villa
On the outskirts of Meiktila;
There to rest and spend your second honeymoon ?
Or what could there be brighter
Than to hire a fighter
And to fly away your troubles in the blue;
Or to pride yourself with valour
When you're passing Agartarla,
On a flip that's going to land you at Toungoo.
What could there be sweeter
Than to ride in your two seater
Along the Chindwin River, at your ease,
And to linger with your bundle
In that old proverbial Jungle
Where you used to feel so shaky at the knees.
Now there's heaps more I could mention,
But to live beside convention
I must leave you in the Jungle in the dark,
For myself I'd feel much merrier
In a place, free from malaria –
Such as (Ilkley Moor ba Tat) or Regents Park.

❧

The following poem describing the 31st Works Flight's short stay at Ibsley was submitted by G. Allott. It was written by a colleague (name not recalled).

'Twas in the winter's evening sun,
When Butcher and his 31,
The men who shook the British nation,
Set off in vans from Ringwood station.

As they sped through Ringwood Town,
Making all the locals frown,
By shouting out to each old bag,
And singing loud the red flag.

At length they got to Ibsley 'drome,
Which was to be their future home,

## So Much Sadness, So Much Fun

And when to billets they'd been taken,
They said, "This camp wants to be shaken".
So went the Works Flight one and all,
Down the road to the dining hall,
They made it known with ribald shout,
That there wasn't any grub about.
The cooks went red with this burst of jeers,
And the WAAFs laughed till they were in tears,
Then the sergeant knowing what it was all about,
Said, "Give 'em some grub and send them out",
But the officer said, "All this must cease",
Emerging from the cookhouse to say his piece,
But seeing that there was a chance of a fight,
He made a retreat shaking with fright,
And ordered the cooks up off their knees,
To dish the Works Flight out with teas,
Then for a fortnight all went well,
Till the camp C.O. said, "I'll play hell,
I'll make the Works Flight wash and shave;
If the effort drives me to the grave,
I'll make them bullshit night and day,
Or by Christ they'll have to pay".
So up to four site he did go,
And chewed the balls of the W.O.,
And then to prove that he was nuts,
He moved the lads to different huts.
The Butcher boys cried out, "Shame,
This C.O. will not play the game,
He makes us live on pies and frogs,
And sausages made of dogs".
And now he's made his dire mistake,
Of sending cocoa for our break,
So if he does not mend his way,
We'll lie out in the sun all day,
And spend our time flat on our backs,
Instead of laying Somerfleld Tracks,
Then the C.O will end the tale,
By doing time in Dartmoor jail.

# Bits and Pieces

FROM 'THE IBSLEY REVIEW' of February, 1949, under the heading:

## 'CLEAN but FUNNY

### NASTY LITTLE AIRMAN

The disgruntled airman pointed to the sign over the stores counter, which read:

**"WE AIM TO PLEASE".**

"Why dont you close your stores for a couple of days and get some target practice in!" he barked at the innocent looking storebasher.

൞

### ANOTHER CASE OF 252!

An airman came out of the station barbers shop and met the adjutant who requested him to take his golf clubs back to the Mess for him.

On reaching the mess he met the C.O. who exclaimed, "Have you been playing golf, airman?"

NO Sir", he replied, "Getting my hair cut"...... and he got 14 days C.C.

൞

### NO. 95

"Have you any complaints to make?" asked the prison govemor.

"Yes", replied the prisoner, "The prison walls are not built to scale."

൞

They were sitting on a park bench and the girl friend was very bored.

"Would you like to go for a long walk?" she finally asked him "I'd love to." "Then don't let me detain you!!"

❧

## MIXED UP!

C.O. "I'm afraid I don't understand, who told you we were going to have sports?"

Radar Op: "The Sergeant Sir. He said I was to see you, as I was in for the High Jump!"

❧

## A MODERN TRAGEDY.

Arriving home at one a.m.
I gasped for breath to find
the glamorous creature opposite
had failed to draw the blind.
She soon removed her dainty dress,
As carefree as you please,
revealing lots of shapely curves,
And pretty dimpled knees.
Her shoes came next,
then other things,
My head began to whirl,
as it became more obvious,
How lovely was this girl.
One garment left, its slipping down,
Oh, fascinating witch!
Alas there came a power cut,
and all went black as pitch!

❧

Two Editors were discussing their respective newspapers.

"I don't know what the public would do without my newspaper" said one.

"Probably they would buy toilet rolls!" replied the other.

❧

Little Jimmy came downstairs crying loudly.

"What's the matter now?" asked his mother.

"Father was hanging pictures and he hit his thumb with the hammer" said Jimmy. "That not serious" soothed his mother. "A big man like you shouldn't cry at a little thing like that. Why didn't you just laugh?"

"I did" sobbed Jimmy.

ೞ

## REMINISCENCES OF HIS AIR FORCE CHUM PILOT OFFICER JOHN MAGEE, JR. WHO WROTE 'HIGH FLIGHT'

by Milton Jowsey, R.C.A.F. pilot with No. 234 Squadron, Ibsley, 1941/42.

At Manning Depot, Toronto, John Magee and myself, Milton Jowsey, new R.C.A.F. recruits, met and became friends in October, 1940, during our first air force days. We always lined up alphabetically, the J's and M's were close and we were two eighteen year olds in a strange environment. I was three weeks older than John. We were together for about four months and then went off to different Elementary Flying Schools.

John had the gift of the gab, and I always felt he talked me into various escapades, but I learned that if I stayed quiet he would get us both out of the many jams. Looking back on our boring security guard months at Trenton I wonder how we stayed out of jail. John's background, as he told it, was colourful and at the time one wondered how much was added. In later years, when reading his obituary, I found there was very little if any added. His father was an American Episcopal (Anglican) missionary Bishop in China and he claimed his mother was a family member of the then UK ambassador in Washington which endowed him with considerable drag. One felt that his mother's status was suspect but he certainly got away with outrageous conduct in his flying training school in England and U.S.A.

Magee wrote verse every day to my knowledge. He was always writing on every scrap of paper. There were verses by the hundred stuck up on every wall and corner at Trenton R.C.A.F. station, they

239

were satirical and/or humorous with the Corporal, Sergeant and more often the Sergeant-Major being the butt of the verse. He became the hero of our class and if anyone wanted the poems they were welcome to take them or they went out as rubbish. Of course we did not know he had won the school poetry prize while attending Rugby in England. I have no idea whether he kept any serious verse separately.

Somehow John Magee got about a month ahead of me, of course I was on a slow convoy and spent three weeks in Iceland on route. We both attended 53 O.T.U., on Spitfires, at Llandow, Wales. One of the course requirements was a high flight, that is you flew as high as the MkI Spitfire would go, and I got up to 32,000 feet.

Mike Le Bas, an Argentinian pilot with No. 234 Squadron at Ibsley, was in the same 53 O.T.U. class as John Magee. He reported that after Magee came down from his high flight, at Llandow, he wrote his High Flight sonnet on the back of an envelope. John let Mike have it later. I certainly accepted this version as I had seen him do this scores of times. Mike claimed he took the sonnet to London and showed it to his cousin, the Poet Laureate of England (??? that's what he said), and it was published quite quickly, which seemed to bear out the route Mike reported.

In discussions with Mike Le Bas I pretty well accepted the story as it fitted with my past experience of Johnny Magee writing verse (he was Johnny not John to us). The sonnet fits like a glove for anyone that has flown by themselves in a Spitfire, everything and every feeling fits. It was a great loss that the poet was dead three months later. This sonnet was on the wall of every R.C.A.F. station from mid war to this day.

President Regan quoted 'High Flight' when the 'Challenger' space ship blew up on launch in Florida.

*Bits and Pieces*

# HIGH FLIGHT
## by Pilot Officer John G. Magee, Jr.

Oh! I have slipped the surly bonds of earth
And danced the skies on laughter-silvered wings,
Sunward I've climbed, and joined the tumbling mirth
Of sun-split clouds....and done a hundred things
You have not dreamed of....wheeled and soared and swung
High in the sunlit silence. Hov'ring there
I've chased the shouting wind along, and flung
My eager craft through footless halls of air.

Up, up the long delirious, burning blue
I've topped the wind-swept heights with eager grace
Where never lark, nor even eagle flew-
And, while with silent lifting mind I've trod
The high untrespassed sanctity of space
Put out my hand and touched the Face of God.

Pilot Officer John Gillespie Magee of 412 R.C.A.F. Falcon Squadron, was killed on Thursday 11th December, 1941, when his Spitfire, aircraft number AD291 collided with an Oxford aircraft and crashed at Ruskington Hall, Ruskington, Lincolnshire. Pilot Officer Magee was born in Shanghai, China and was educated at Rugby, England, and Avon, Connecticut, U.S.A. The original manuscript of his poem High Flight resides in the United States Library of Congress. Pilot Officer John Magee is buried in the Scopwick Church Burial Ground, Scopwick, Lincolnshire, England.

Contributed by Milton Jowsey, No. 234 Squadron, Ibsley, 1941/42.

The following has been copied from an original contributed by F/O Desmond Smith, pilot with No. 501 Squadron at Ibsley

## Hints for Fighter Pilots

The hints contained in these notes are elementary knowledge to all experienced fighters. Every one of them must be obeyed if you are to take your place in a squadron quickly and become a useful member of the team with the minimum of delay.

1. **Before take-off on organised operation or on coming to readiness.**
   Make certain guns are cocked. Close hood and make certain it is scrupulously clean. Set reflector sight at 40 feet span 250 yards brilliance then switch off. Make sure correct code card is in holder. Have a sector map in the holder or tucked in your boot. When strapped in take care in adjusting R/T and oxygen connections so that you can turn your hand freely without anything catching (usually on harness split pin). Find out the letter of the Section Leader's A/C to avoid confusion when getting into position for take off.

2. **On Take-off.**
   Develop habit of starting clock when you get into position for take-off. Never raise undercart to below 50 feet. Spitfire has only to sink 6 inches in flying position for airscrew to hit ground. Continue to look forward when closing hood or otherwise you "porpoise".

3. **Climbing to patrol.**
   From 15,000 feet upwards pay particular care not to straggle as speed range decreases rapidly. Avoid clouds whenever possible. Watch your glycol temperature and keep it above 80 to ensure guns are warm enough to function.

## Hints for Fighter Pilots

4. **At height.**
   Over 30,000 feet flow meter does not register increase in flow so do not get excited and turn oxygen on fully, keep it at 30,000 indicated with minimum flow possible. If perspex starts to ice up (condensation of breath freezing) open hood very slightly. It will tend to close but you can keep a small bit of rubber or wood on end of string attached to cockpit light and slip this into position. Squeeze hose piece of mask to tight fit on face to avoid shortage of oxygen. Test oxygen flow occasionally by squeezing tube and watching flow meter. Ice can form in tube but can be broken by squeezing tube. Breathe slowly and deeply and keep an eye on the flow meter.

5. **On approaching area of possible combat.**
   Switch over guns to "fire". Switch reflector sight on. Check glycol temp. to ensure guns are not frozen. Check air pressure to ensure guns will function.

6. **On sighting enemy A/C when combat appears probable.**
   Make certain you are not a straggler. Increase revs. to 2,600 – 2,850. DON'T fire a short burst to warm or test guns.

7. **On free for all battle developing.**
   Be coarse on controls. Never fly straight or follow aircraft more than a few seconds. Keep your ammunition for use at short range only. Always try to turn towards air attack, maintaining height. Remember that a long steep dive will cause inside of windscreen to ice up. Short or shallow when diving. Try to avoid reversing bank.

8. **If separated from your formation.**
   Never fly straight for more than a few seconds. Climb into the sun. It is usually best to go down to 000 feet and make for home flat out. If you find cloud never fly just below it, never pop up through it. When passing flak area pop in and out of cloud, do not remain on steady course in the cloud. To avoid flak take avoiding action by changing both height and direction.

9. **If in great difficulty against superior numbers (or one superior pilot).**
   Go into steep diving spiral but watch your altimeter.

10. **If wounded.**
    Turn on oxygen fully.

11. **R/T**
Correct use of R/T consists in silence, except when you have something of vital importance to say. Always say who you are and to whom you are calling and give the message clearly, don't shout. Always use clock code when reporting aircraft. Fix a piece of elastic to the switch so that you cannot leave it on transmit.

12. **Returning home after flight.**
Although you cannot see any damage your machine may be badly hit so don't throw it about. Resist temptation to victory roll. Land carefully, a tyre may be punctured. Keep an eye on your glycol and oil temperatures. Guns to "safe" when landing. Remember your duty is to land quickly and get refuelled.

13. **If engine is damaged by hits in oil or glycol radiators**
Make for nearest aerodrome at maximum speed; don't nurse the engine, it doesn't pay.

14. **Forced Landings.**
Jettison hood by pulling rubber ball and pressing elbows outwards on perspex. Lower seat and tighten straps fully. Lower flaps, leave undercarriage in UP position always.

15. **Shooting.**
Deflection shooting is a matter of experience but the tendency is to keep on firing for too long. Try to allow too much deflection and let the enemy aircraft fly through the burst.

16. **Attacks.**
Keep speed for a beam attack. Throttle, back for a head-on aiming to open fire at 800-1,000 yards breaking upwards.

17. **Weaving.**
If you are a weaver remember that it is not your duty to search below, your responsibility is to detect aircraft behind and above.

18. **Patrolling.**
Climb into or across sun, never down sun. At sunset you will be easily seen against the sun but if you keep low you will be almost impossible to see against the shadows.

19. **Convoy patrols.**
Sailors prefer to shoot first -, and ask afterwards so don't approach low down or out of the sun. Don't cross over convoy as many ships carry balloons or kites. The Commodore's ship is

## Hints for Fighter Pilots

the one leading the left hand line so try and fly near enough to that ship and parallel to the convoy to be recognised. Your duty is to chase away any enemy A/C approaching the convoy before he has a chance to bomb so don't be clever and wait to attack him until he is in a bad tactical position right over the convoy. Don't follow too close on your leader, if you do he will know you cannot be looking out for enemy aircraft. If you have to land in the sea, land well ahead of a ship or destroyer – at least half a mile.

20. **Attacking enemy aircraft.**
    Me. 109 Any deflection shot at pilot or from below at radiators.
    Me. 110 Aim for just below pilot. Any shot except head-on.
    He. 111 Head-on or beam. The majority are brought down through strikes in the engine.
    Do. 17 If from astern from slightly below, aim for starboard engine.
    JU. 87 Any deflection. Tanks are at wing roots.
    JU. 88 As for He. 111.

# The Formation of an R.A.F. Fighter Squadron

The basic R.A.F. Flying Unit was the Squadron. It was a self-contained organisation which included all the people necessary to ensure that the aircraft forming the Squadron were able to take to the air as and when needed.

At the time of the Battle of Britain the number of aircraft in a typical fighter squadron was twelve, with approximately twenty pilots to fly them. These figures often fluctuated depending on the availability of both replacement aircraft and pilots.

The Squadron was sub-divided into two Flights with the further division of 'A' Flight into Red and Yellow Sections, and 'B' Flight into Blue and Green or White Sections. Each aircraft in a section was numbered either one, two or three.

Every aircraft required maintenance, either during first line servicing between sorties, or when more comprehensive attention was needed. All squadrons had an allocation of tradesmen to carry out some of the specialist services required.

Air Frame

Engine

Wireless

Armaments

Instruments

Photographic

Refuelling

Intelligence Officers evaluated pilot's reports after every mission and additional support from many other trades was provided by the R.A.F. Station on which perhaps two or three squadrons were based.

## Operational Code Names

| | |
|---|---|
| Circus | Bombers heavily escorted by fighters to bring enemy fighters into combat. |
| Ramrod | Bomber raid escorted by fighters aimed at destruction of a particular target in daylight operation. |
| Rhubarb | Freelance fighter sorties on a small scale against ground targets of opportunity. |
| Roadstead | A low level attack on coastal shipping. |
| Rodeo | Fighter sweep without bombers. |
| Scramble | The general term for fighters being given the order to get airborne quickly. |
| Sweep | An offensive formation of fighters or fighter bombers over enemy territory, designed to draw the enemy. |

## Memories of 501 Squadron, 1941.
by
Wing Commander C. F. 'Bunny' Currant,
D.S.O., D.F.C.and Bar, C. de G.

The days wore on, another year, by this time squadron leader,
Of Spitfire squadron five-o-one with pilots young and eager
To shepherd bombers on their way, to strike at German dump
This was their task as once more asked, a flock of fighters flew
Just on the wave tops dirty grey, the battle to renew.
Pull on the stick and lift her up, to clear the chalk cliffs barrier,
And down again to hug the ground, like predatory harrier.
Before the target was achieved, a wall of fog closed tight,
To clamp him like a spider's web, cocooned and blind with fright.
He found himself in steep left bank, his eyes could not discern
The instruments of climb and dive, of level, bank and turn,
They made no sense to brain so tense that imminence of death
Made all his actions seem quite sane as with a bated breath
He took his feet off rudder bar, his hand off stick as well,
Folded his arms across his chest and waited for the knell.
The end was magic, ne'er forgot, as suddenly he found
Himself in sunshine clear and safe, a few feet off the ground.
He climbed away and headed home, his sweating flesh to dry,
And landed back on English soil. Another day gone by.

# The Ibsley Roll of Honour

21/ 2/41 Sergeant Vaclav Skřivanék (Czech)   No. 32 Squadron
Hurricane crashed at St. Clement's Road, Bournemouth. Buried in Ringwood Cemetery.

9/ 3/41 Sergeant Vladamir Kyselo (Czech)   No. 32 Squadron
Hurricane crashed at Blashford, near Ibsley. Buried in Ringwood Cemetery.

4/ 8/41 Sergeant Pilot Cyril Smith   No. 118 Squadron
Returning from Convoy Patrol plane crashed into hillside at Owermoigne, near Warmwell, Dorset and burst into flames. Buried in Woolwich Cemetery, London.

6/ 8/41 Sergeant Alan Beacham   No. 501 Squadron
Lost over Channel during escort to Whirlwind fighter bombers. Commemorated on Runnymede Memorial.

1/ 9/41 Pilot Officer Peter J. P. Anderson   No. 118 Squadron
Shot down by flak from a destroyer North East of Cherbourg. Commemorated on Runnymede Memorial.

30/ 9/41 Sergeant Pilot Geoffrey Painting   No. 118 Squadron
Plane hit by pom pom fire while attacking shipping, shot down into sea and pilot killed. He was only seventeen years old, but had given his age as eighteen and a half on joining the R.A.F., so was combat flying under age. Commemorated on Runnymede Memorial.

11/11/41 Sergeant Wilfred E. Sapsed   No. 234 Squadron
Failed to return from a Sweep. Buried at Janval Cemetery, France.

15/11/41 Sergeant Harold Alexander   No. 118 Squadron
Shot down by flak. Last seen in water three miles off Marcouf. Buried Cherbourg.

*So Much Sadness, So Much Fun*

15/11/41 **Sergeant Harry A. Newman**      **No. 234 Squadron**
Failed to return from Strike mission. Buried at Ste. Honorine des Pertes, Calvados, France.

17/11/41 **Sergeant Raymond F. C. Dean**      **No. 501 Squadron**
from Kingston Ringwood. Shot down off French coast. Buried at Brevands Churchyard, Manche, France.

5/12/41 **Sergeant John H. Walker**      **No. 234 Squadron**
Failed to return from a Shipping reconnaissance. Commemorated on Runnymede Memorial.

5/12/41 **Pilot Officer Frank R. Clarke**      **No. 234 Squadron**
Failed to return from a Shipping reconnaissance. Buried at Dieppe Canadian War Cemetery, Hautot-Sur-Mer.

16/12/41 **Flight Sergeant Ronald Birtles, D.F.M.**      **No. 118 Squadron**
Crashed from 30,000 feet at Shrewton, Wiltshire. Believed due to lack of oxygen. Buried at Rowington Churchyard, Warwickshire.

10/ 1/42 **Pilot Officer Eric J. Campbell**      **No. 501 Squadron**
Plane broke up in mid-air, crashed at Rockbourne, near Fordingbridge. Buried at Bristol (Canford) Cemetery.

29/ 1/42 **Sergeant Hardy C. Kerr**      **No. 118 Squadron**
**(Royal Australian Air Force).**
Baled out over English Channel returning from mission to Caen. Buried in Ringwood Cemetery.

2/ 2/42 **Pilot Officer Edward J. Ames**      **No. 118 Squadron**
**(Royal Canadian Air Force).**
Shot down off Point de Barfleur by Me109s of III JG2. Commemorated on Runnymede Memorial.

2/ 2/42 **Aircraftman 2nd class Frederick U.C. Jones**   **No. 118 Squadron**
Nurse Orderly, killed in a road accident while walking back to base from Fordingbridge. Buried in Ashton-in-Makerfield Churchyard, Lancs.

11/ 2/42 **Sergeant Keith Buetell**      **No. 118 Squadron**
**(Royal Australian Air Force).**
Mid air collision with Thomas Mathers near Salisbury. Buried in Ringwood Cemetery.

## The Ibsley Roll of Honour

**11/ 2/41** Sergeant Thomas Mathers              No. 118 Squadron
Mid air collision with Keith Buettell near Salisbury. Buried in Ringwood Cemetery.

**12/ 2/42** Pilot Officer Ivan S. Stone           No. 118 Squadron
(Royal New Zealand Air Force).
Lost after combat with Me109 during Operation 'Fuller'. Commemorated on Runnymede Memorial.

**12/ 2/42** Pilot Officer Dennis E. Pike          No. 234 Squadron
Lost in combat with fighters on Operation 'Fuller'. Commemorated on Runnymede Memorial.

**26/ 2/42** Sergeant Jack Redfern                 No. 234 Squadron
Collided on return flight from 'Hurribomber' escort, lost tail and crashed near Ringwood. Buried Middleton St. Gabriel Churchyard, Lancashire.

**9/ 3/42** Pilot Officer Roderick W. P. McKenzie  No. 118 Squadron
Aircraft severely damaged over Channel, pilot wounded, brought aircraft back to England but crashed on Dover to Canterbury road, and was killed. Buried Streatham Park Cemetery, Surrey.

**15/ 3/42** Flight Lieutenant James E. Hogg       No. 234 Squadron
Returning from escorting Hudsons, crashed in poor visibility in Cornwall. Buried in Ringwood Cemetery.

**22/ 3/42** Aircraftman 2nd Class Cecil L. Bowey   No. 234 Squadron
Lost when Spitfire coming in to land, was taken by sudden gust of wind, bounced in the air, came down striking the airman. Son of John and Alice Bowey of Ringwood. Buried in Ringwood Cemetery.

**27/ 3/42** Sergeant Childs                       No. 501 Squadron
Killed when Spitfire AB965 spun into ground, near Burley, New Forest during practice interception.

**4/ 4/42** Flight Sergeant David S. Thomas        No. 501 Squadron
Lost while on Convoy Patrol. Buried Brookwood Military Cemetery, Surrey.

**15/ 4/42** Flight Lieutenant Denys E. Mileham    No. 234 Squadron
Claimed by Me 109s of JG26 off Cherbourg. Commemorated on Runnymede Memorial.

*So Much Sadness, So Much Fun*

15/ 4/42 Pilot Officer Michael L. Simon (U.S.A.) No. 234 Squadron
Claimed by Me 109s of JG26 off Channel Islands. Commemorated on Runnymede Memorial.

16/ 4/42 Pilot Officer George Bland No. 234 Squadron
Lost near Rauville while on Ramrod 20 Commemorated on Runnymede Memorial.

16/ 4/42 Pilot Officer Ralph S. Woolass No. 234 Squadron
Attacked by Me 109 while on an Air Sea Rescue sortie off Cherbourg. Commemorated on Runnymede Memorial.

18/ 4/42 Sergeant Edward A. L. Fairman No. 234 Squadron
Collided, West of Ibsley, with Pilot Officer Cameron, when returning from a Sweep to Cherbourg. Buried St. Annes Churchyard, Stranorlar, Co. Donegal. Cameron baled out safely.

24/ 4/42 Flight Lieutenant Vivian E. Watkins No. 234 Squadron
(U.S.A.)
Shot down by FW 190s of JG 26, during Circus to Ostend. Buried at Bergen-op-Zoom Cemetery, Netherlands.

25/ 4/42 Pilot Officer Donald Y. Claxton No. 118 Squadron
(Royal Canadian Air Force).
Shot down into the Channel during combat with enemy aircraft. Claimed by JG2.

25/ 4/42 Sergeant Landon P. Mooney No. 118 Squadron
Combat with enemy aircraft, went into the sea 20 miles South of Bournemouth. Claimed by JG2. Commemorated on Runnymede Memorial.

25/ 4/42 Flying Officer Robert Wheldon No. 501 Squadron
Lost after engaging with Me 109s near Cherbourg. Commemorated on Runnymede Memorial.

25/ 4/42 Flying Officer
Antony Palmer-Tompkinson No. 501 Squadron
Lost after engaging with Me 109s near Cherbourg. Commemorated on Runnymede Memorial.

25/ 4/42 Sergeant Miroslav Rocovski (Czech) No. 501 Squadron
Engaged with Me 109s near Cherbourg. Baled out but lost when parachute failed. Commemorated on Runnymede Memorial.

## The Ibsley Roll of Honour

25/ 4/42 **Sergeant Karel Vrtis**  No. 501 Squadron
Lost after engaging with Me 109s near Cherbourg. Commemorated on Runnymede Memorial.

26/ 4/42 **Aircraftman 2nd Class Ronald Shepherd**  No. 234 Squadron
Buried in York Cemetery.

30/ 4/42 **Sergeant Gaston Fernand (Free French)**  No. 118 Squadron
Shot down by FW 190s in the Channel, 20 miles South of Bournemouth.

9/ 5/42 **Sergeant Michael B. Green**  No. 118 Squadron
Shot down by JG26 near St. Omer. Commemorated on Runnymede Memorial.

9/ 5/42 **Squadron Leader John H. G. Walker**  No. 118 Squadron
Shot down by JG26 near St. Omer. Buried St. Leonard's Church Cemetery, Woollaton, Notts.

9/ 5/42 **Flight Sergeant Franklin Hough**  No. 118 Squadron
Shot down by JG 26, 10 miles North of St. Omer. Buried Dunkirk Town Cemetery, Nord, France.

9/ 5/42 **Pilot Officer Edward W. Gillespie**  No. 501 Squadron
American pilot with Royal Canadian Air Force. Shot down in the Channel by FW 190. Commemorated on Runnymede Memorial.

4/ 6/42 **Flight Sergeant Bert Strachan**  No. 501 Squadron
**(Royal Canadian Air Force).**
Shot down in the Channel during combat with FW 190 of JG2, near Cap Levy. Commemorated on Runnymede Memorial.

6/ 6/42 **Squadron Leader John C. Carver, D.F.C.**  No. 118 Squadron
Engaged with FW 190s near Cap Levy. Commemorated on Runnymede Memorial.

6/ 6/42 **Sergeant Lloyd H. Jones**  No. 118 Squadron
**(Royal Canadian Air Force).**
Flying as No. 2 to Carver engaged with FW 190s near Cap Levy. Commemorated on Runnymede Memorial.

13/ 6/42 **2nd Lieutenant Dirk Klink (Dutch)**  No. 118 Squadron
Crashed, on his thirtieth birthday, in Alderholt Park near Fordingbridge. Buried in Ellingham Churchyard on the edge

*So Much Sadness, So Much Fun*

of Ibsley airfield, but later exhumed and re-interred in the Dutch War Graves Section of a London Cemetery.

20/ 6/42  Lieutenant Johannes Veen (Dutch)    No. 118 Squadron
Engaged by JG26 and JG2 whilst returning from escorting bombers to Le Havre. Buried at Longuenesse Cemetery, France.

20/ 6/42  Lt. Paul Stenger (Dutch)    No. 118 Squadron
Engaged by JG26and JG2 whilst returning from escorting bombers to Le Havre. Buried at Pihen-les-Guines Cemetery, France.

20/ 6/42  Flight Sergeant Cornelius Van Houten    No. 118 Squadron
(Dutch)
Engaged by JG26 and JG2 whilst returning from escorting bombers to Le Havre. Buried at Longuenesse Cemetery, France.

24/ 7/42  Lieutenant Albert D.V. Morum    No. 66 Squadron
(South African Air Force).
Lost on Rhubarb to gasworks at Bayeaux. Aircraft hit by flak. Commemorated on Runnymede Memorial.

30/ 7/42  Sergeant John E. Beasley    No. 66 Squadron
Convoy Patrol, crashed into the sea, cause unknown. Buried in St. Peter's Churchyard, Leckhampton, Gloucestershire.

5/ 8/42  Sergeant William R. Leitch    No. 501 Squadron
Scramble. Engaged two He59s and four FW190s North of Cherbourg. Last seen with a FW190 on his tail. JG2 action. Commemorated on Runnymede Memorial.

11/ 8/42  Pilot Officer Stewart G. Brannigan    No. 501 Squadron
(Royal New Zealand Air Force)
Early morning shipping recce. Engaged FW 190 of JG2 and crashed into sea. Commemorated on Runnymede Memorial.

19/ 8/42  Sergeant Allan Lee    No. 501 Squadron
Crashed at Billingshurst, returning to Tangmere from Dieppe raid. Buried St. Andrews Churchyard, Tangmere, Sussex.

19/ 8/42  Flight Sergeant Ronald Loyns    No. 66 Squadron
(Royal Canadian Air Force).
Shot down and killed on Dieppe raid. Commemorated on Runnymede Memorial.

## The Ibsley Roll of Honour

**19/ 8/42**   **Lieutenant Victor R. E. Nissen**     **No. 66 Squadron**
Shot down and killed by FW190 10 miles North West of Dieppe. Pilot South African. Commemorated on Runnymede Memorial.

**1/ 9/42**   **Lieutenant William Pennington**     **No. 94 Squadron**
**(U.S.A.A.F.) 8th Air Force, 1st Fighter Group**
Lightning crashed on to Bofors gun pit at Ibsley.

**1/ 9/42**   **Two gunners, names as yet unknown**     **439 Light A. A. Battery**
killed when Lightning hit the Bofors gun pit.

**18/ 2/43**   **Flying Officer Peter J. Blanchard**     **No. 616 Squadron**
Killed whilst attempting to destroy a drifting balloon. City of London Crematorium Cemetery, Essex.

**4/ 4/43**   **Flight Sergeant Alan J. Symonds**     **No. 129 Squadron**
Crashed into the sea. Commemorated on Runnymede Memorial.

**4/ 4/43**   **Squadron Leader Leslie W. Ivey**     **No. 504 Squadron**
Morning Air Sea Rescue sorties looking for No. 129 Squadron pilot. Crashed into sea. Commemorated on Runnymede Memorial.

**5/ 4/43**   **Sergeant John S. Hetherington**     **No. 129 Squadron**
Escorting Venturas to Landunvez, p.m. Engaged by FW 190s of JG2. Commemorated on Runnymede Memorial.

**5/ 4/43**   **Flight Lieutenant Peter B. Wright, D.F.C.**     **No. 616 Squadron**
Engaged with FW 190s on escort to Landunvez. Commemorated on Runnymede Memorial.

**16/ 4/43**   **Flight Lieutenant Gordon B. McLachlan**     **No. 616 Squadron**
Claimed by JG2 near Brest. Buried Plouguerreau Communal Cemetery, France.

**5/ 6/43**   **Sergeant Gerald Locke**     **No. 504 Squadron**
Lost in fog over Channel on shipping reconnaissance, flying Holsworthy, Devon, Presentation Spitfire. Commemorated on Runnymede Memorial.

**13/ 6/43**   **Sergeant Wilfred J. Brookes**     **No. 129 Squadron**
Escort to Venturas bombing St. Brieuc. Engine trouble after combat with FW 190s, ditched 40 miles of Star Point and not found. Commemorated on Runnymede Memorial.

*So Much Sadness, So Much Fun*

15/ 6/43   Flying Officer Robert J. Sim     No. 616 Squadron
(Royal New Zealand Air Force).
Shot down by flak on Shipping reconnaissance North East of Sark. Commemorated on Runnymede Memorial.

25/ 7/43   Flight Sergeant William Brown,     No. 165 Squadron
(Royal Australian Air Force).
Shot down in combat with FW 190s while escorting B-26 Marauders of 323 B.G. to coke factories North of Ghent, Belgium. Buried in Flushing (Vlissiengen) Cemetery, Netherlands.

25/ 7/43   Pilot Officer André Imbert     No. 165 Squadron
Shot down in combat with FW 190s while escorting B-26 Marauders of 323 B.G. to coke factories North of Ghent, Belgium. Pilot Free French. Buried in Flushing (Vlissiengen) Cemetery.

25/ 7/43   Flight Sergeant John H. Curry     No. 165 Squadron
Shot down in combat with FW 190s escort B-26 Marauders of 323 B.G. to coke factories North of Ghent, Belgium. Commemorated on Runnymede Memorial.

15/ 8/43   Flying Officer Frederick T. Thornley     No. 453 (Australian)
(Royal Australian Air Force)     Squadron
Shot down by JG26 on morning mission to Walcheren. Buried Flushing.

31/ 8/43   Flight Sergeant. Ronald McKillop     No. 616 Squadron
Lost on Air Sea Rescue sortie off Ile de Bar. Combat with JG2. Commemorated on Runnymede Memorial.

31/ 8/43   Sergeant Paul W. Shale     No. 616 Squadron
Lost on Air Sea Rescue sortie off Ile de Bar. Combat with JG2. Commemorated on Runnymede Memorial.

24/ 9/43   Flight Lieutenant Vladislav Chocholin     No. 313 (Czech)
    Squadron
Lost in action off Brest. Combat with Me 110s. Commemorated on Runnymede Memorial.

24/ 9/43   Squadron Leader Jaroslav Himr     No. 313 (Czech)
    Squadron
Lost in action off Brest. Combat with Me 110s. Commemorated on Runnymede Memorial.

*The Ibsley Roll of Honour*

27/ 9/43   Flight Sergeant Thomas Zrnik          No. 313 (Czech)
                                                              Squadron
Lost in combat with JG2 over Beauvais. Commemorated on Runnymede Memorial.

25/10/43   Flying Officer Jan Stastny           No. 312 (Czech)
                                                              Squadron
Baled out after being hit by flak over Brest when escorting B 26's. Commemorated on Runnymede Memorial.

12/ 4/44   2$^{nd}$ Lieutenant Eugene E. Sanderson    404 Squadron
371$^{st}$ F.G., 9$^{th}$ U.S.A.A.F.
P47 Thunderbolt spun on landing, caught fire, pilot could not escape, burned to death. Buried Cambridge American Cemetery, Cambridge, England.

27/ 5/44   Pvt. Wood Hibberd                    492 Squadron
48$^{th}$ F.G., 9$^{th}$ U.S.A.A.F.
Bystander killed when P47 Thunderbolt crashed on take off and bomb load exploded.

28/ 5/44   1$^{st}$ Lieutenant Carlos J. Ball         492 Squadron
48$^{th}$ F.G., 9$^{th}$ U.S.A.A.F.
Died from injuries received when his P47 Thunderbolt burst a tyre on take-off and the bomb load exploded. Buried Cambridge American Cemetery, Cambridge, England.

20/ 7/44   Lieutenant William L. Mushrush       394 Squadron
367$^{th}$ F.G., 9$^{th}$ U.S.A.A.F.
Disappeared in bad weather during armed reconnaissance over France.

26/ 7/44   Lieutenant Albert B. Cooksey         393 Squadron
367$^{th}$ F.G., 9$^{th}$ U.S.A.A.F.
Mid air collision with another P38 Lightning over Blissford, near Fordingbridge shortly after taking off on a mission from Ibsley. The other pilot, Robert Brandt baled out safely.

26/ 7/44   Lieutenant Burnus W. Hayden          393 Squadron
367$^{th}$ F.G., 9$^{th}$ U.S.A.A.F.
Shot down and killed on a bombing mission over France.

## POST WAR LOSSES

1/ 1/49   Sergeant Les Grant, West Indian
(buried in Sopley Cemetery)

1/ 1/49   Aircraftman Lou Laurati.

1/ 1/49   Aircraftman Walker.

The above three were all killed when a 3 ton R.A.F. lorry transporting personnel between R.A.F. Sopley and R.A.F. Ibsley was in collision with a lorry, loaded with meat, at Bisterne.

The names on the aforementioned Roll of Honour, with two, as yet, un-named Gunners of 439 AA Battery, are those known to have lost their lives while serving or based at R.A.F. Ibsley, 1941/52, but there could well have been more, and research is ongoing. A number of others, who had served at Ibsley, lost their lives while operating from other R.A.F. Stations, after their Squadrons were posted.

Note:

**June 1942. Sgt. Pilot A. E. "Teddy" Joyce      No. 234 Squadron**
Lost on 30th December, 1941, on Circus operation. Taken Prisoner of War. In attempting to escape from Stalag Luft III was mortally wounded. Buried Poznan (Polish) Military Cemetery.

There were a number of Ibsley pilots, from various squadrons, lost on missions, taken Prisoner and held in various Prisoner of War camps until the end of hostilities.

*View over part of No.1 Communal Site, South Gorley, from Summerlug.*
Photo: P.Smith

# Appendix

## KNOWN ROYAL AIR FORCE STATION COMMANDERS AT IBSLEY

February 1941 – June 1942
W/Cdr. A. N. Benge
June – August, 1942
W/Cdr. C. F. Currant, D.S.O., D.F.C., and Bar
January – September, 1943
W/Cdr. A. Donaldson, D.S.O., D.F.C., A.F.C.
September, 1943 – February, 1944
W/Cdr. D. Blackwood
March – October, 1945
W/Cdr. Folkard
1946 to 1952
Sqdn/Ldr. Lovell, S/Ldr. Selsdon, W/Cdr. Ford.

## ROYAL AIR FORCE SQUADRONS, AIRCRAFT AND SQUADRON LEADERS AT IBSLEY, 1941 – 1945

(Dates shown for Squadron Leaders include periods when a returning Squadron was away from Ibsley)

### No. 32 Squadron – Hurricane Mk. 1.

Squadron code letters GZ
Badge: A hunting horn stringed.
The hunting horn signifies the squadron's ability to hunt the enemy.
Motto: "Adeste comites" ("Rally round comrades")
At Ibsley
17th February to 17th April, 1941

Sqdn/Ldr. M. Crossley, D.S.O. D.F.C.    Feb. '41 – Apr. '41
Sqdn/Ldr. H. A'B. Russell               Apr.'41 – Apr.'41

Appendix

## No. 66 Squadron – Spitfire Mk Vb and Vc
Squadron code letters LZ
Badge: A rattlesnake.
The rattlesnake typifies aggressive spirit and striking power.
Motto: 'Cavete praemonui" ("Beware I have warned")
At Ibsley:
27th April to 2nd July, 1942
7th July to 15th August, 1942
20th August to 23rd August, 1942
23rd December, 1942 to 9th February, 1943

| | |
|---|---|
| Sqdn/Ldr. C. E. Malfroy, D.F.C. | May' 42 – June '42 |
| Sqdn/Ldr. R. D. Yule, D.F.C. | June '42 – Nov. '42 |
| Sqdn/Ldr. H.A.C. Bird-Wilson, D.F.C. | Nov. '42 – Feb. '43 |

## No. 118 Squadron – Spitfire Mk IIa and IIb
Squadron code letters NK
Badge: On the waves of the sea, an ancient ship in full sail in flames.
The badge acknowledges the squadron's prowess in sinking shipping.
Motto: "Occido redoque" ("I kill and return")
At Ibsley:
18th April, 1941 to 22nd February, 1942
7th March to 2nd July, 1942
7th July to 24th August, 1942
23rd December, 1942 to 2nd January, 1943

| | |
|---|---|
| Sqdn/Ldr. F. J. Howell, D.F.C. | Apr. '41 – Oct. '41 |
| Sqdn/Ldr. H. A'B. Russell | Oct. '41 – Jan. '42 |
| Sqdn/Ldr. J. C. Carver, D.F.C. | Jan. '42 – June '42 |
| Sqdn/Ldr. E. W. Wootten, D.F.C. and Bar | June '42 – Jan. '43 |

## No. 124 Squadron – Spitfire VI
Squadron code letters ON
Badge: A mongoose passant.
The mongoose is an inhabitant of India (No. 124 was the Baroda gift squadron) and is known for its agility and ferocity in killing its enemies.
Motto: "Danger is our opportunity'.
At Ibsley:
22nd June to 15th July, 1943

| | |
|---|---|
| Sqdn/Ldr. T. Balmforth, D.F.C. | June '43 – July '43 |

*So Much Sadness, So Much Fun*

### No. 129 (Mysore) Squadron – Spitfire Mk Vb and Vc
Squadron code letters DV
Badge: The Ghunda Berunda of Mysore.
The badge associates No. 129 Squadron with the Province of Mysore; the squadron was the Mysore Gift Squadron.
Motto: 'I will defend the right'.
At Ibsley:
13th February to 27th February, 1943
13th March to 28th June, 1943
Sqdn/Ldr. H. A. C. Gonay           Feb. '43 – June 43

### No. 165 (Ceylon) Squadron – Spitfire Mk Vb and Vc
Squadron code letters SK
Badge: A double-headed dragon affrontee, necks crossed, spouting fire.
A double headed dragon signifies readiness to attack from any quarter.
Motto: 'Infensa virtui invidia' ("Envy to the foe of honour")
At Ibsley:
30th June to 29th July, 1943
Sqdn/Ldr. H. A. S. Johnson        June '43 – July '43

### No. 234 (Madras Presidency) Squadron – Spitfire Vb and Vc
Squadron code letters AZ
Badge: A dragon rampant, flames issuing from the mouth.
The dragon indicates the fighting role and the flames associate with the name Spitfire.
Motto: 'Ignem mortenque despimus' ("We spit fire and death")
At Ibsley
5th November to 23rd December, 1941
31st December, 1941 to 22nd March, 1942
4th April to 26th April, 1942
Sqdn/Ldr. M. V. Blake            Nov. '41 – Jan. '42
Sqdn/Ldr. F. E. W. Birchfield      Feb. '42 – Apr. '42

### No. 257 (Burma) Squadron – Hawker Typhoon 1b
Squadron code letters FM
Badge.. A chinthe sejant.
No. 257 Squadron was the Burma gift squadron in World War II: the chinthe is a Burmese effigy.
Motto: "Thay myay gyee shin shwe hti' ("Death or glory').

*Appendix*

At Ibsley:
26th January to 8th February, 1943.
Sqdn/Ldr. G. A. Brown, D.F.C.   Jan. '43 – Feb. '43

## No. 263 (Fellowship of the Bellows (Argentina)) Squadron Whirlwind and Typhoon

Squadron code letters HE
Badge: A lion rampant, holding in its forepaws a cross.
The lion represents the squadron's association with Scotland, the cross comes from the flag of Norway.
Motto: 'Ex ungue leonem' ("By his claws one knows the lion").
At Ibsley:
5th December, 1943 to 5th January, 1944
Sqdn/Ldr. G. B. Warner, D.S.O., D.F.C.   Dec. '43 – Jan. '44

## No. 302 (Poznan Polish) Squadron – Spitfire Mk IIa

Squadron code letters WX
No authorised badge.
At Ibsley
11th October to 31st October, 1941
Sqdn/Ldr. S. Witorzenc   Oct. '41 - Nov. '41

## No. 310 (Czech) Squadron – Spitfire Mk Vb and Vc

Squadron code letters NN
Badge: In front of a sword erect, a lion rampant queue fourches.
The lion in the badge is taken from the arms of Czechoslovakia whilst the sword represents the fighter role.
Motto: We fight to rebuild.
At Ibsley:
22nd September to 1st December, 1943
15th December, 1943 to 20th February, 1944
Sqdn/Ldr. E. Foit   Sept. '43 – Jan. '44
Sqdn/Ldr. H. Hrbacek   Jan. '44 – Feb. '44

## No. 312 (Czech) Squadron – Spitfire Mk Vb and Vc

Squadron code letters DU
Badge: A stork volant.
The stork in the badge relates to the French 'Escadrille des Cygelines' with whom the original pilots of No. 312 had flown prior to coming to the U.K.
Motto: "Non multi sed multa" ('Not many but much')

*So Much Sadness, So Much Fun*

At Ibsley:
21st September to 1st December, 1943
18th December, 1943 to 20th February, 1944
Sqdn/Ldr. A. Vybiral Sept. '43 – Nov. '43
Sqdn/Ldr. F. Vancl Nov. '43 -Feb. '44

### No. 313 (Czech) Squadron – Spitfire Mk Vb and Vc

Squadron code letters RY
Badge: A hawk volant, wings elevated and addorsed.
Motto: "Jeden jestrub mnoho vran razhdn".
("One hawk chases away many crows")
At Ibsley:
19th September 1943 to 5th January, 1944
20th January to 20th February, 1944
Sqdn/Ldr. J. Himr (killed in action from Ibsley)Sept. '43 – Sept. '43
Sqdn/Ldr. F. Fatjl, D.F.C. Sept. '43 – Feb. '44

### No. 421 (Red Indian Canadian) Squadron Spitfire Mk Vb

Squadron code letters AU
Badge: In front of two tomahawks in saltire, a Red Indian warrior's head with head-dress.
The Canadian Red Indian is notable for his fighting qualities and the tomahawk is his traditional weapon.
Motto: "Bellicum cecinere" ("They have sounded the war trumpet")
At Ibsley:
16th August to 21st August, 1942
Sqdn/Ldr. F. C. Willis Aug. '42

### No. 453 (Australian) – Spitfire Mk Vb and Vc

Squadron code letters FU
Badge: Perched on branch a kookaburra.
A kookaburra is one of the most popular of Australian birds and has a reputation for killing snakes.
Motto: 'Ready to strike'.
At Ibsley:
29th June to 21st August, 1943
Sqdn/Ldr. K. M. Barclay June '43 – Aug. '43

*Appendix*

## No. 501 (County of Gloucester) Auxiliary Squadron Spitfire Mk IIa. Vb and Vc.

Squadron code letters SD
Badge: A boar's head couped
The boar's head is taken from the arms of Gloucester, the animal is also noted for its courage.
Motto: "Nil time".
At Ibsley:
4th August 1941 to 24th January, 1942
7th February to 2nd July, 1942
7th July to 23rd August, 1942

| | |
|---|---|
| Sqdn/Ldr. C. F. Currant, D.F.C., and Bar | Aug. '41 – June '42 |
| Sqdn/Ldr. J. W. Villa, D.F.C. and Bar | June '42 – Aug. '42 |

## No. 504 (County of Nottingham) Squadron Spitfire Mk Vb and Vc.

Squadron code letters TM
Badge: An oak tree fronted and eradicated.
The "Major Oak Tree" is drawn from the armorial bearings of Nottingham County.
Motto: "Vindicat in ventis" ("It avenges in the wind")
At Ibsley:
24th December, 1942 to 30th June, 1943

| | |
|---|---|
| Sqdn/Ldr. R. Lewis | Dec. '42 – Jan. '43 |
| Sqdn/Ldr. J. I. Kilmartin, D.F.C. | Jan. '43 – Mar. '43 |
| Sqdn/Ldr. R. C. Kilian | Mar. '43 – June '43 |

## No. 616 (South Yorkshire) Auxiliary Squadron Spitfire Mk VI.

Squadron code letters YQ
Badge: A Yorkshire Rose.
The badge commemorates the squadron's association with Yorkshire as the South Yorkshire Auxiliary Squadron).
Motto: "Nulla rosa sine spina' ("No rose without a thorn").
At Ibsley:
3rd January to 14th March, 1943
18th March to 17th September, 1943

| | |
|---|---|
| Sqdn/Ldr. C. F. Gray, D.F.C. | Jan. '43 – Jan. '43 |
| Sqdn/Ldr. G. S. K. Haywood | Feb. '43 – Apr. '43 |
| Sqdn/Ldr. P. W. Lefevre, D.F.C. | Apr. '43 – Apr. '43 |
| Sqdn/Ldr. P. B. Lucas, D.F.C. | Apr. '43 – July '43 |
| Sqdn/Ldr. L. W. Watts, D.F.C. | July '43 – Sept. '43 |

*So Much Sadness, So Much Fun*

## UNITS AT IBSLEY

### No. 7 Flying Instructors School – Oxfords
12th December, 1944 to 8th February, 1945

### No. 1 Glider Pick Up Training Flight
Dakotas, and WACO/Hadrian Gliders.
27th March to 28th October, 1945.
Sqdn/Ldr. P. W. Peters                              1945

From time to time other R.A.F. Squadrons would also have been at Ibsley for short periods, on Detachment from other airfields.

## UNITED STATES ARMY AIR FORCE STATION COMMANDERS AT IBSLEY

8th U.S.A.A.F. 1st Fighter Group
27th August to 14th November, 1942
Col. J. N. Stone

9th U.S.A.A.F. 48th Fighter Group
late March to late June, 1944
Col. D. M. Allison                                   April 1944
Col. G. L. Wertenbacker Jnr.        April '44 – late June '44

9th U.S.A.A.F. 367th Fighter Group
6th to 26th July, 1944
Col. C. M. Young

9th U.S.A.A.F. 371st Fighter Group
April to May, 1944
Col. Bingham T. Kleine.

*Appendix*

## U.S.A.A.F. SQUADRONS AND THEIR AIRCRAFT

8th Air Force, 1st Fighter Group, No. 71 Squadron
8th Air Force, 1st Fighter Group, No. 94 Squadron
  P38F Lightnings

9th Air Force, 48th Fighter Group, No. 492 Squadron
9th Air Force, 48th Fighter Group, No. 493 Squadron
9th Air Force, 48th Fighter Group, No. 494 Squadron
  P47D Thunderbolts

9th Air Force, 367th Fighter Group, No. 392 Squadron
9th Air Force, 367th Fighter Group, No. 393 Squadron
9th Air Force, 367th Fighter Group, No. 394 Squadron
  P38J Lightnings

9th Air Force, 371st Fighter Group, No. 404 Squadron
9th Air Force, 371st Fighter Group, No. 405 Squadron
9th Air Force, 371st Fighter Group, No. 406 Squadron
  P47D Thunderbolts

9th Air Force, 67th Tactical Recce Unit, No. 12 Squadron
9th Air Force, 67th Tactical Recce Unit, No. 107 Squadron
  Mustang FBVI's

# Acknowledgements

The R.A.F. Ibsley Historical Group acknowledge with very grateful thanks and contribution made over the past ten years, either written or or verbal, by the following ex-Ibsley personnel, a number of whom have since passed on, their relatives, and others, which has enabled us to produce this revised edition of "So Much Sadness, So Much Fun", R.A.F. Ibsley 1941-1952.

* denotes ex-Ibsley personnel

*E. Alderson, *G. Allott, A. Anderson, M. Annison, H. Ashley (d.1997), *Dr. A. Babington, *B. Bailey (nee Allen), *G. Ball, *J. Barmby (nee Watmough), *M. Barrett, *D. Barry, G. Bartlett, *H. Barton, *L. Bazalgette, D. Beedle, *A. Bentley, *L. Berry, *N. Berryman, *D. Best, *C. Beswick, D. Biles, *K. Biles, J. Biles, *L. Bishopp (d.1995), Sqdn.Ldr. I. Blair, D.F.M., *G. Blake-Adams, *O. Blissett, *R. Booth, *B. Bosworth (nee Burton), *G. Bowdidge (d.2000) *K. Bracey, *M. Bracey, *R. Bradley, *W. Breakspear, *H. Brealey, *R. Brooke, A. Brooks, A. Brown, *D. Brown, *F. Brown, *G. Bryant, *R. Bull, *J. Burland (nee Cornish), *A. Byne (d.1997), Brig. Gen. P. D. Caine, *Calvert (nee Baldwin), *R. Campbell, *S. Chambers, E. Chapple (nee Sammers), *C. Charsley, *B. Churchill, *M. Clymo, *Cobb (nee Luther), *P. Coleman, *B. Cook, *B. Cooke, D. Cook, *Col. J. Cooper, R. Coombs, *M. Cooper (d.1998), *J. Cordwell, *F. Corfe, *R. Coward (d.1994), *F. Coward, *J. Cozens, R. Cox, *J. Curd, *W/Cdr. C. Currant, D.S.O., D.F.C., C. de G., *S. Curtis, *J. Dadswell (d.1995), *A. Dart, D. Deacon, S. Deedman, *G. Denbigh, J. Dexter (nee Howell), *A. Deytrikh, S. Dooley (nee Joyce), W. Dow, *E. Durbin, *Major S. East, T.D., *R. Ede, (nee *H. Erney, *B. Eyre, D. Fairgrieve (nee Elliott),*R. Farman, *F. Fisher, *R. Foster (nee Hulland), *F. Fox, N. Franks, *B. Fraser (nee Cox), *F. Fraser (d.1995), *R. Fripp, *K. Fritz, *J. Fry, *K. Fry, *K. Gamble, *R. George, *H. Gibbons, J. Gilbert, K. Gill, *J. Gilpin, *D. Glaser (d.2001), R. Gleed, *M. Gorman (nee Kiely), *R. Gould, *L. Gover (d.1997), *I. Green, *W. Greenaway, *T. Hamer, *G. Hames, T. Handley, R.

*Acknowledgements*

Hansen, *G. Hardyman, *A. Harrington, *M. Harrington (nee Bishop), *J. Harrison, A. Harrocks, *D. Haselwood, *L. Hawkins, *D. Hayton, P. Healey, *A. Hepburn, *A. Herring, *A. Hill, *D. Hill, *J. Hill (nee Kelly), *P. Hill, *B. Hockey, *L. Holmes, *V. Hopkins, *G. Horlock, *W/Cdr. P. Howard-Williams, D.F.C., (d.1993), Mr. P. Howard-Williams, *D. Humphrey, *P. Hussey-Smith (nee Thornton), *J. Ireland, *B. Izzard, *J. Jacobs (nee Scard), *G. Jamieson, *A. Jeffreys, *G. Johnson (d.1994), *H. Johnson, *I. Jones, *S. Jones, D.F.M., *M. Jowsey, *M. Keets (nee Green), *G. Keen, *E. Kelly, *T. Killick, *J. Knott, B. Kuropka, *K. Ladd, P. Larmour (d.1997), *J. Laverie, *H. Lawson, *C. Leat, *M. Leaver, P. LeMesurier (d.1995), M. LeMesurier, *J. Lennard, *H. Liddell, *M. Liskutin,D.F.C., A.F.C., *P. Lobley, *E. Long, Dr. E. van Loo, *A. Lumsden (d.2001), *J. Lundy, Col. *J. McCabe, *F. Malone, P. Marrable (nee Joyce), *G. Mattacks, R. Mawbey, *D. Meadows, E. Micklewright (nee Thomas), *E. Mihall, *C. Miller (nee Payne), *P. Miller, *R. Mitchell, *F. Mlejnecky, *J. Moir, *D. Mold, *E. Moore, *G. Moore (d.2000), *P. Morgan, *D. Myles, *W/Cdr. T. Neil, D.F.C.*, A.F.C., AE, T. Neilsen, W. Newbery, *A. Nichols, *P. Nichols, *B. Noble, *T. Noble (nee Buckingham), *F. Nunan, R. Opie, *D. Packard, *J. Parsons, *R. Pedder, Air Commodore G. Pitchfork, M.B.E., *D. Porter (d.1996), *J. Posta, *G. Powell, C. Palmer, *D. Pratt, N. Price, *W. Price, D. Prince, *A. Pritchard, P. Proost, *G. Pyle, *J. Rankin, *L. Read, *C. Risbridger, M.B.E., *L. Rose, *D. Roberts, *G. Roberts, *A. Row (d.1998), *R. Russell, *R. Rutter, *E. Saint, S-A. Salm (nee Mullington) C. Sampson, T. Sampson (d.2000), *J. Saunders, *R. Sawyer (d.1997), *K. Scott, *K. Scratchley, *V. Sellings (d.1999), *E. Sewell (d.2000), *M. Sewell (nee Windsor), Mrs. Shalless (nee Applebee), *C. Shelcott, *J. Shelley, *E. Shipp, J. Simmonds, *J. Simpson, *H. Sims nee Sheppard), T. Smart (d.2001), *A. Smith (d.2000), *D. Smith, *G. Smith, *K. Smith (nee Heane), *L. Smith (nee Bennett) (d.2001), *M. Smith, *N. Smith (nee Godding), P. Smith (d.2002), *R. Smith, V. Smith, *W. Spink, *T. St. George, R. Stebbings, *V. Stedman (nee Miles), *W. Steele, *H. Stephens, *Maj. W. Stockdale, M.B.E., *S. Stone, *F. Studley, *T. Sturges, *Sullivan, *D. Sykes, *A. Tandy, *P. Taylor, *M. Thompson (d.1993), *A. Tocknell, R. Todd, M.B.E., *E. Tomlinson, *K. Townsend, *R. Tozer (d.1994), *L. Trevellyan, V. Truemper, *F. Turner, *A. Waldron, *P. Walker, *Capt. W. Walling, *B. Walton (nee Fry), *A. Ward, *A. Warner (nee Andrews) (d.1997), *R. Warrell, *W/Cdr. D. Warren,

D.F.C., *G. Watkins, *E. Watson, *S. Watson, D.F.C., (d.2002), *H. Webb, *C. West, *A. White, *J. White (nee Stevens), Sqdn/Ldr. R. Whyard, D.F.C., A.F.C., *K. Wilby, *K. Wilcox, D. Williams, *E. Wilson (nee Heathcote), Sqdn/Ldr. I. Wilson,*R. Wise, D. Witt, Major D. Wood, *T. Woodacre, *Air Commodore E. Wootten, D.F.C., A.F.C., (d.1998), *G. Wyeth (d.1997), also Public Records, U.S. Air Force Historical Research Agency, and with sincere apologies and thanks to anyone whose name has, inadvertently, been omitted.